Small States in EU Policy-Making

Small States in EU Policy-Making analyses how small states try to impact European Union policy-making through a range of strategies.

With the last rounds of enlargement and Brexit, the number and weight of small states in the European Union have steadily increased. At the same time, small states face distinct challenges in different institutions, which may impact their strategies. Nonetheless, the existing literature primarily focuses on the Council of the European Union and the European Council and offers few insights into how small states navigate the other institutions. The contributions to this volume examine how small states can wield influence in different institutions, arguing that they do indeed pursue different strategies depending on institutional context. The policy case studies on the EU's foreign and security policies confirm these findings: small states can have influence in EU policy-making and can create situations where their needs are met. They are most likely to succeed when they build foreign policy coalitions, when they anticipate major economic developments and when they manage to acquire a high level of expertise in a policy area. However, the case studies also show that there is a risk of small states becoming policy-takers in cases where they cannot provide leadership in terms of ideas and expertise and/or fail to build political weight through coalitions.

This book will be of interest to academics and practitioners of European politics and the EU in particular, as well as policy-makers and practitioners working on small states.

Anna-Lena Högenauer is Associate Professor at the Department of Social Sciences at the University of Luxembourg. Her research focuses on questions of multilevel governance, EU politics and parliamentary democracy. She is Associate Editor of PRX and a member of the editorial boards of Politics and Governance and of Small States & Territories.

Matúš Mišík is Associate Professor at the Department of Political Science at Comenius University Bratislava. His research interests include small states and energy security in the EU. He is the author of *External Energy Security in the European Union* (Routledge, 2019), co-author of *Energy Transitions in Central and Eastern Europe* (2024) and has published articles in journals including *Nature Energy, Energy, Energy Policy* and *Geopolitics*.

Small State Studies

Half the world's sovereign states have populations of less than 5.3 million, and over 30 have populations of less than ONE million. Clearly, there is scope to consider the impact that small size and scale (of population, civil service, expertise, talent pools, ambassadorial ranks, service providers, and so on) could have on the nature of governance, politics, international relations, economic development, climate action, transportation, etc.

This interdisciplinary new series closes the gap in political and social science literature by encouraging studies on the challenges facing small states, their characteristics and their strategies, thus galvanizing scholarship in a previously neglected area. It encourages comparative studies among small states and between small states and larger states. It addresses the predicament of small size and scale as these impinge on institutional and political dimensions (such as public administration and diplomacy), and critically considers the issues and tensions arising from small but archipelagic and/or federated states.

Series editors:
Godfrey Baldacchino, University of Malta, Malta – godfrey.baldacchino@um.edu.mt
Anna-Lena Högenauer, University of Luxembourg, Luxembourg – anna-lena.hoegenauer@uni.lu
Nicos Trimikliniotis, University of Nicosia, Cyprus – trimikliniotis.n@unic.ac.cy
Roukaya Kasenally, University of Mauritius, Mauritius – roukaya@uom.ac.mu

Titles in this series include:

The Rotating European Union Council Presidency and Small Member States
Small States, Big Challenge
Ieva Grumbinaitė

Agency, Security and Governance of Small States
A Global Perspective
Edited by Thomas Kolnberger and Harlan Koff

The Constitutional Courts of Small Jurisdictions
Edited by Danny Pieters

Small States in EU Policy-Making
Strategies, Challenges, Opportunities
Edited by Anna-Lena Högenauer and Matúš Mišík

For more information on this series, please visit: https://www.routledge.com/Small-State-Studies/book-series/SMALLSTATES

Small States in EU Policy-Making

Strategies, Challenges, Opportunities

**Edited by Anna-Lena Högenauer
and Matúš Mišík**

Routledge
Taylor & Francis Group

LONDON AND NEW YORK

First published 2024

by Routledge
4 Park Square, Milton Park, Abingdon, Oxon OX14 4RN

and by Routledge
605 Third Avenue, New York, NY 10158

Routledge is an imprint of the Taylor & Francis Group, an informa business

Funded by University of Luxembourg.

British Library Cataloguing-in-Publication Data
A catalogue record for this book is available from the British Library

ISBN: 9781032462233 (hbk)
ISBN: 9781032462271 (pbk)
ISBN: 9781003380641 (ebk)

DOI: 10.4324/9781003380641

Typeset in Times New Roman

by Deanta Global Publishing Services, Chennai, India

A.-L. H. To Hanna, Inge and Horst
M.M. To Nada and Matilda

Contents

List of contributors   *ix*
Acknowledgements   *xi*

1   Introduction: The challenges and opportunities of EU membership
    for small states   1
    ANNA-LENA HÖGENAUER AND MATÚŠ MIŠÍK

SECTION I
Small states in the EU's institutions and policy processes   17

2   Small member states in the European Commission of the 21st century   19
    LUKÁŠ HAMŘÍK

3   Small states in the European Parliament: Does size make a difference?   37
    ANNA-LENA HÖGENAUER

4   Bringing the European Union closer to the member states?
    The impact of the rotating EU Council presidency on small
    member states   53
    IEVA GRUMBINAITĖ

5   Small states coalition building in EU policy-making: The cases of
    the Nordic and Baltic countries   71
    TOBIAS ETZOLD

6   Small-state veto power in the European Union? National interests
    and coalition-building capacity of the member states in Central and
    Eastern Europe   85
    BOYKA STEFANOVA

SECTION II
Small states in foreign, security and trade policy 103

7 The economic diplomacy of Luxembourg within the European
Union framework: Between agility and stability 105
HELEN KAVVADIA

8 Small states, subregional minilateralism and European foreign policy 126
MARION FOSTER AND MICHAEL MOSSER

9 Small state influence in EU security policy-making:
PESCO, Frontex and the integration dilemma 143
BÉRANGER DOMINICI, OLIVIER LEWIS AND SEBASTIAN STEINGASS

10 Challenges and opportunities: Estonia's role in shaping
EU cybersecurity policy 159
XINCHUCHU GAO

11 Conclusion: Size is not everything 174
ANNA-LENA HÖGENAUER AND MATÚŠ MIŠÍK

Index *185*

List of contributors

Béranger Dominici works with the European Prison Litigation Network. He has previously been an academic assistant at the European Interdisciplinary Studies Department, College of Europe in Natolin, and gained experience in migration policies working for EU agencies and the public sector. He contributed in his personal capacity.

Tobias Etzold has a PhD in Political Science and is Senior Research Fellow at the Norwegian Institute of International Affairs (NUPI). Having worked at various universities and think tanks across Europe, his research specializes on EU, foreign and security policies of the Nordic countries and regional cooperation (Nordic, Baltic Sea and the Arctic).

Marion Foster is a PhD candidate in Public Affairs at the University of Texas at Austin. Her research focuses on the national security doctrines and policies of small- and mid-sized European states, EU foreign and security policy and security strategies in the eastern Mediterranean and Black Sea regions.

Xinchuchu Gao is Lecturer in International Relations at the University of Lincoln. She is also a research associate at the London-Asia Pacific Centre for Social Science. Her research interests lie at the intersections between international relations, international political economy and European studies and especially on the twin green & digital transitions of the EU and global cyber governance. She has published in *Defence Studies*, *Asia Europe Journal*, the *European Yearbook of International Economic Law*, *Asia Pacific Journal of EU Studies* and *L'Europe en formation*.

Ieva Grumbinaitė is a researcher at the Institute of International Relations and Political Science at Vilnius University and a research manager at Public Policy and Management Institute (PPMI) in Vilnius, Lithuania. Her research interests include European integration, European Union institutions, specifically the Council of the EU, and higher education policy. She holds a PhD in Political and Social Sciences from the European University Institute.

Lukáš Hamřík is Assistant Professor and Senior Researcher at the Judicial Studies Institute (JUSTIN), Faculty of Law, Masaryk University. His academic interests include personalization of politics at the EU level, EU institutions and governance, political and judicial leadership and informal institutions.

Anna-Lena Högenauer is Associate Professor at the Department of Social Sciences at the University of Luxembourg. Her research focuses on questions of multilevel governance, EU politics and parliamentary democracy. She is Associate Editor of PRX and a member of the editorial boards of Politics and Governance and of Small States & Territories.

Helen Kavvadia is Adjunct Professor at the ESSCA School of Management and researcher in residence at the University of Luxembourg. She was Senior Adviser at the European Investment Bank. Her research and publications focus on political economy and economic diplomacy.

Olivier Lewis is Assistant Professor at Rabdan Academy. Previously, he was Lecturer in Defence Studies at King's College London and Research Fellow at the College of Europe in Natolin. During his studies at the University of St Andrews, Olivier worked as an academic tutor.

Matúš Mišík is Associate Professor at the Department of Political Science at Comenius University in Bratislava. His research interests include small states and energy security in the EU. He is the author of *External Energy Security in the European Union* (Routledge, 2019), co-author of *Energy Transitions in Central and Eastern Europe* (Cambridge University Press, 2024) and has published articles in journals including *Nature Energy*, *Energy*, *Energy Policy* and *Geopolitics*.

Michael Mosser is Associate Professor of Instruction of Government at the University of Texas at Austin. He is Executive Director of the Global Disinformation Lab (GDIL), Assistant Director of the Center for European Studies (CES) and a Distinguished Scholar in the Robert S. Strauss Center for International Security and Law.

Boyka Stefanova is Professor in the Department of Political Science and Geography at the University of Texas, San Antonio. Her areas of specialization are European politics, political conflict and regionalism. Dr Stefanova has published extensively on territoriality in the European Union, comparative regionalism and democracy in Eastern Europe.

Sebastian Steingass is Senior Academic Assistant at the European Interdisciplinary Studies Department, College of Europe in Natolin. His research interests include policy-making and governance in the European Union, EU external relations and international development cooperation.

Acknowledgements

This work was financially supported by the University of Luxembourg and by the Slovak Research and Development Agency under the Contract no. APVV-20-0012. We would like to thank both institutions for their support.

In addition, we would like to thank Godfrey Baldacchino, Nicos Trimikliniotis, Roukaya Kasenally and the publishing team at Routledge for their comments, advice and support during the production of the book.

1 Introduction

The challenges and opportunities of EU membership for small states

Anna-Lena Högenauer and Matúš Mišík

1.1 Introduction

The European Union (EU) has faced numerous crises and policy challenges throughout its existence (Schimmelfennig, 2018). Indeed, the large number of crises and a seemingly never-ending continuation of challenges in different policy areas have inspired observers to even talk about a 'polycrisis' (Zeitlin et al., 2019). These crises have often had an asymmetric impact on member states, resulting in noticeable divisions within the Union.

The evidence of the two recent decades is illustrative. The Eurozone crisis divided the richer northern member states and the poorer southern member states (Verdun, 2015). This division was further exacerbated by the impact of the refugee crisis on Southern Europe, which additionally alienated many Central and Eastern European countries. These were reluctant to accept any larger numbers of refugees (Zaun, 2018) and even came up with an idea of a 'flexible solidarity' to reject the Commission's proposal to help the frontline countries via 'burden sharing' (Visegrad Group, 2016). The recent COVID-19 crisis highlighted differences between member states as it hit Southern Europe particularly hard (Ferrera et al., 2021). In addition, important policy divergences on climate change emerged between the green states (e.g. the Nordic countries) and the not-so-green ones (e.g. Poland, Czechia, the Netherlands) to mention just a few of the dividing lines. Most recently, the Russian invasion of Ukraine united most member states; however, at the same time it highlighted different allegiances on the part of some members (e.g. Hungary), an ambivalent position of others (e.g. Germany) and the specific geopolitical concerns of other member countries (e.g. Greece), for which the Russian Federation is not the main or only security risk. These are just the most visible dividing lines emerging within the EU since the mid-2000s on top of which a whole complex socio-economic system of division exists within the Union, manifesting itself to a certain degree during negotiations and voting in the Council of the EU (Finke, 2017; Hosli et al., 2011; Mattila, 2008; Naurin and Lindahl, 2008).

EU politics in general and the above-mentioned crises in particular have been the focus of a large and diverse literature. However, one of the key traits of the existing literature is that it either deals with institutional (i.e. polity) and policy issues from an overarching perspective (Frieden and Walter, 2017; Harteveld et al., 2018; Kratochvíl and Sychra, 2019) or it zooms in on 'important' cases, i.e., the large

DOI: 10.4324/9781003380641-1

member states, that is, Germany, France, Italy and the UK pre-Brexit (Bulmer, 2014; Fontan and Saurugger, 2019), or 'problematic' cases, such as Greece (and the threat of Grexit), Italy or Ireland for the Eurozone crisis (Bull, 2018; Clements et al., 2014), Hungary for the refugee crisis (Kallius et al., 2016) and Poland for climate policy issues (Marcinkiewicz and Tosun, 2015).

However, other member states are not studied that much and we know relatively little about the preferences, motivations, strategies and struggles of many EU member states, especially the small ones. This is problematic, as the EU has changed in ways that have increased the weight of the non-large states. When the European Coal and Steel Community and later the European Economic Community were founded in the 1950s, large states represented 50 per cent of all member states. However, successive enlargements – especially since the mid-1990s – and the departure of the United Kingdom have drastically changed the composition of the EU (Sedelmeier, 2014; Brusenbauch Meislova, 2019) – at least when viewed through the prism of size of countries operationalized in terms of number of inhabitants.

Today, the EU has 27 member states, but only five of those can be considered large. Among those, the fifth largest state, Poland, is – population wise – only half the size of the largest state, Germany. Then there is a substantial gap, with the sixth and seventh largest states (Romania and the Netherlands) are only one-quarter the size of German population. The eighth largest state, Belgium, is slightly more than one-eighth the size of Germany with a population of 11.5 million. From there, the size of member states gradually decreases down to Malta, with a population of 0.5 million. Thus, the group of small-to-medium-sized states makes up over 80 per cent of the member states, while the five biggest states represent over 60 per cent of the EU's population. Moreover, since the first 'round' of eastern enlargement of the EU of 2004 (Toshkov, 2017) the composition of the European Commission was changed with each member state having its 'own' Commissioner. This means an improved position of small- and medium-sized member states compared to the previous system in which biggest members had two Commissioners. In addition to the enlargements, the Lisbon Treaty significantly changed voting rules in the Council of the EU since 2014 (with a transition period until 2017 when old rules could have been used if requested by member states during the negotiations). This change shifted the voting weight away from negotiation capacity of member states – since until 2014 the number of votes was determined by mutual agreement – to size as number of inhabitants became one of the components of voting weight.

Moreover, the deepening of integration over the years resulted in an increase of the number of areas under qualified majority voting, and the culture of consensus further strengthened the position of small member countries (Hosli et al., 2013; Heisenberg, 2005). Such development brought further changes to the mutual dynamics between the big and small members. As a result, Nasra argued already in 2011 that 'the relevance of small states is set to increase considerably,' especially in areas where consensus needs to be achieved due to the different positions of member states (p. 177). Indeed, the position of small member states in the EU has steadily become more important as the changes in EU's composition and decision-making mechanism as well as development of new policies and reshaping of the existing ones increased their visibility and role.

Despite such developments, Grimaud claims that 'small state governmental influence in the shaping and taking of EU decisions has been overlooked' (2018: 24). Small EU member states have been on the margin of academic research since the 1990s as the liberal intergovernmental approach – the dominant theoretical framework explaining European integration represented especially by the writings of Andrew Moravcsik (1993) – has put the biggest members under the spotlight and basically ignored the other member countries. This has changed thanks to pioneering work by Baldur Thorhallsson (2000), David Arter (2000) and others (Bunse, 2009; Larsen, 2005; Panke, 2010). However, by the 2010s, we have witnessed a decrease of interest in this research agenda in book-length publications. Discussion moved mostly from books to journals (however, see Mišík, 2019, as an exception), with the latter focusing on particular countries, issues or policies in the last decade (e.g. Blockmans, 2017; Nasra, 2011; Panke, 2011; Panke and Gurol, 2018). Thus, the significance of the changing dynamics for small states has not yet been fully explored.

In addition, small states may have specific needs and face different challenges in EU politics. While small- and medium-sized states are in a large majority, individual states from this group may struggle to get their voices heard in an EU of almost 450 million inhabitants, especially in processes where decisions are taken mostly by qualified majority in the Council of the EU (as this is considered to be a part of an ordinary legislative procedure). At the same time, they may be particularly dependent on the EU for support, or so-called 'shelter.' Shelter theory, developed in a volume edited by Baldur Thorhallsson, argues that 'small states need external shelter in order to survive and prosper' (2019: 1). Such shelter can be provided by larger states or regional and international organizations. While this volume examined small states – or precisely Iceland – in the international arena, Baldacchino and Wivel (2021) looked at this issue from a theoretical perspective. They argue that small states are more exposed to external pressure, at a higher risk of losing national independence and more dependent on other actors. In light of small internal markets, they are economically dependent on international trade. Their small armies mean that they have a limited ability to defend themselves, especially in the face of threats from substantially larger states, and therefore they support alliances and defence organizations. Moreover, small states' ability to shape international politics is limited by their size and weight.

In the current context, these risks become increasingly salient and stakes for small states visibly higher. The COVID-19 crisis led to a decrease in multilateralism and disrupted the global economy (cf. Dookeran, 2021; Högenauer et al., 2021). Therefore, small member states supported common solutions to pandemic in different forms as they have been supportive of EU action in the area of health policy in the long term (Brooks et al., 2020). Following the Russian invasion of Ukraine, the tensions between the West on the one hand and the Russian Federation and China on the other are rising. The impact on energy and cybersecurity is severe, and, for the first time in decades, a major war involving multiple states is not inconceivable.

In light of these dynamics, the proposed edited volume aims to analyze – in the first section – the strategies of small states in the main decision-making bodies of the EU. The section is looking for an answer, through a series of comparative chapters, to the first and second research question of this edited volume: How can small states overcome the challenge of size and influence EU decision-making in the context of different EU institutions and their specific composition and procedures? How effective are the strategies that member states employ to overcome these challenges? The role of experience, cooperation and prioritization in building up capacity is at the centre of this analysis. In the second section, this edited volume seeks to explore these dynamics further in specific policy case studies to find answers to the third and fourth research questions: How do small members influence individual policies? How does the EU respond (or fail to respond) to the needs of small states? These case studies focus on foreign and security policy, where small states are often particularly dependent on the shelter function of other states or international organizations. These cases allow us to understand not only the strategies of small states but also their specific interests and motivations in these policy areas and the extent to which these policies meet their expectations. By examining both institutional and policy dynamics of small member states' membership in the European Union, this edited volume aims to develop a complex picture of their membership experience and thus contribute to our knowledge about their place and impact in the European Union.

1.2 'Smallness' in the EU context

One of the main challenges when studying small states is how to define them (Long, 2017). Authors have applied a wide range of conceptual definitions, but some have assumed a different approach: for instance, Björkdahl (2008), Blockmans (2017) and Jakobsen (2009) do not provide any explicit definition of 'smallness' and only list member states they consider to be small. This approach, together with a wide variety of explicit but diverse definitions by other scholars, creates a situation when the concept of the small state is used vaguely within studies of both European integration and international relations (Jazbec, 2001; Pace, 2000). As a consequence, the academic discussion is 'plagued by a lack of cumulative insights' (Thorhallsson and Wivel, 2006: 652) as findings from different studies are difficult to compare since they consider a different set of states to be 'small.' On the other hand, Maass (2009) claims that such a situation provides us with conceptual flexibility enabling the deployment of different research designs; and Long (2017) calls for focusing on empirical examination of individual cases instead of trying to find an ideal (and ever elusive) definition of small states.

In the existing academic literature, there are several types of small state definitions. These can be grouped into three main categories. The first type corresponds to a constructivist logic and sees size as a construct that depends on a perception of smallness rather than some kind of material (i.e. physical) characteristic. Whether a state considers itself small or large thus depends on the self-perception of the state; in turn, its position in the international arena depends on the perception of others

(Tiilikainen, 2006: 73). The advantage of such an approach is that (self) perception may provide a better explanation of how states act and of how other states react to their behaviour than objective criteria. A good example might be the foreign policy ambitions of (smaller) France, which pursues the ideal of a 'grande nation,' compared to (larger) Germany, which has actively avoided casting itself as a major military power following the Second World War. However, this approach neglects the fact that material factors such as the size of the population, economy and territory create objective opportunities and constraints, for example, on the size of the military and the public administration (Wivel and Baldacchino, 2022).

Secondly, some studies have resorted to absolute definitions by defining smallness in terms of a certain quantity of a specific factor. In the EU context, political size, usually operationalized as the number of votes in the Council of the EU, was used before the Lisbon Treaty changed the voting mechanism (Mattila, 2004; Schure and Verdun, 2008). Votes in this system were distributed based on an agreement between member states, thus reflecting member states' ability to negotiate as high number of votes as possible, i.e., their position vis-à-vis other member states. However, this definition is questionable, as it zooms in on a single institution and neglects other major parts of European polity, such as the European Parliament (EP) (that directly co-decides on majority of issues) and the European Commission where decision-making follows a different logic. In addition, after the Lisbon Treaty, voting in the Council of the EU now relies on a double majority of states and of population. Beyond the EU context, studies have used physical size (in terms of a state's territory or its GDP) to provide an absolute definition of smallness (Nasra, 2011; Panke and Gurol, 2018) or the size of population (Grimaud, 2018; Jazbec, 2001; Manners, 2000). The most common cut-off point is 1 million inhabitants. However, these cut-off points are most useful when there is a clear break in the data. In the EU context, for example, it is relatively easy to argue that there are five large and relatively large states, because the fifth member state is twice the size of the sixth. On the other hand, it is difficult to draw a line between medium-sized and small member states, because there are no major gaps (except perhaps between the two largest medium-sized states and the remaining 20 states). Any attempt to draw a line and declare it an authoritative cut-off point will inevitably raise the question of whether the next state above the line is really substantially different and whether the cut-off decision is arbitrary. For that reason, the small- and medium-sized states are frequently treated as one single category, although they may still be differentiated by name (Mišík, 2016). Officials also talk about the small-to-medium-sized states as a group in practice, which shows that they treat all of these states as a group, while acknowledging that – within the group – there is a spectrum.

Thirdly, these definitions based on concrete indicators can be tempered by acknowledging that size is a relative concept. This is particularly important in a security context, where it makes sense to take into account the size of the opponent (Wivel and Baldacchino, 2022). Thus, a country of 20 million inhabitants can be considered large in a conflict with a country of 1 million, but it is small in the context of an opponent with a population of 300 million.

For the purpose of this book, we define country size by population size, as this now influences the weight of a member state in the two main legislative bodies of the EU: the Council of the EU and the European Parliament. Moreover, it is also an appropriate measure from policy perspective: for example, in foreign and security policy population size influences the size of various domestic markets (goods, energy, etc.), administrations and armies. This can be considered a relative definition, which considers the size of the state in this specific context. As noted previously, it is difficult to draw a clear line between small- and medium-sized states in the EU, as there is no substantial gap between any two states that would support such a distinction. Therefore, we focus on member states below 7 million inhabitants, i.e., the smaller half of the member states. This is a relatively conservative definition in comparison to major studies like Panke's (2010), which defined 19 states as small based on the number of votes they held in the Council of the EU. We also acknowledge that there is a need for flexibility as context matters, as the above-mentioned perceptions of vulnerability may be context specific. Especially in the context of Central and Eastern Europe, the proximity to the Russian Federation as a historic (and increasingly current) threat influences perceptions of vulnerability, preferences and policies. Besides, this provides an additional external point of reference that needs to be taken into account in the definition of smallness. In the context of the Russian invasion of Ukraine, it is noticeable that Gazprom (that is, however, intertwined with the Russian government) first cut off the gas supply to several Central and Eastern European (Bulgaria, Lithuania) and small Nordic states before it interrupted its supply to Germany and other Western European states. This may be part of a strategy to divide the EU, but it is also indicative of the specific perception of vulnerability of small member states by the Russian government. Added to this, factors such as the level of energy dependency on Russia and the ability to switch to other sources further influence the political size of the country.

1.3 Navigating EU decision-making: How to compensate for smallness

Small states face structural disadvantages in EU decision-making, in that population size influences the weight of countries in a number of processes. For example, while a majority of member states is necessary to take a decision under ordinary legislative procedure in the Council of the EU, these members must represent also at least 65 per cent of EU's population. This is supposed to protect several countries with relatively large populations from being outvoted by a large number of small- and medium-sized countries. In addition, small states tend to have fewer administrative, specialist and financial resources (Panke, 2010). Overall, this means that small states face a double challenge: the decision-making rules tend to reduce the weight of their voice and they have a limited ability to threaten others with blockages, at least in those policy areas where majority voting is required. Today, this is the case for most EU policies, and – in addition – in the European Parliament majority voting is of course the rule. If a state cannot push other members to support compromises, then the ability to argue effectively and convince others becomes particularly relevant.

However, the size of small member countries' public administrations and resources limits the amount of expertise they can produce, which risks jeopardizing their ability to influence others effectively in negotiations (cf. Soetendorp and Hanf, 1998, on the importance of well-staffed ministries; Laffan, 2006). As a result, small member states 'are likely to face disadvantages in uploading national policies to the EU-level since they lack the political power to shape EU directives or regulations in the same manner than their larger counterparts' (Panke, 2010). Thorhallsson and Wivel (2006) also see a dilemma in the fact that, while small states tend to depend more on international organizations (as they see them as an appropriate arena to increase their visibility and present their cases), they have limited influence due to their size. If a state is relegated too often to the role of policy-taker and feels that its own priorities and preferences are neglected, then it may feel the loss of independence stemming from membership in an international organization more strongly and the perceived advantages of membership may be reduced.

In light of these structural disadvantages of small countries, authors like Thorhallsson and Wivel (2006), Björkdahl (2008), Haughton (2010) or Panke (2010, 2011) have taken an interest in these states' strategies to overcome these hurdles. However, while the literature on how small states navigate EU decision-making is growing, it focuses almost exclusively on the Council of the European Union and on the Council Presidency. Within this context, the literature argues that the limited bargaining capacities can be mitigated through institutionalized regional coordination (e.g. the Benelux, the Baltic States or the Visegrad Group) or through strategic partnerships on a case-by-case basis (Thorhallsson and Wivel, 2006; Panke, 2010). In addition, disadvantages in argumentative power due to limited staff resources can to some extent be compensated through prioritization of a small number of key issues and through good contacts with the European Commission, which might allow the state to obtain more information and at an earlier stage (Thorhallsson and Wivel, 2006; Panke, 2010). Finally, while limited voting power may reduce small states' ability to carry out threats (e.g. to block a decision), they can build up credibility by other means (Panke, 2010). For example, they can focus on the role of neutral mediator and thus discretely nudge the decision in the right direction. Luxembourg, for example, likes to adopt the role of 'honest broker' (Harmsen and Högenauer, 2021). Overall, Panke (2010) argues that small states can 'punch above their weight' as long as they make active use of these strategies.

Panke (2010) finds that some small states, like Denmark, Luxembourg, Belgium and Ireland, are far more active in deploying 'shaping strategies' than, for example, Cyprus, Estonia, Greece and Bulgaria. She identifies several factors that explain these differences: firstly, a long membership allows member states (including the small ones) to learn how to act, which facilitates the use of shaping strategies. Secondly, the Council Presidency plays a crucial role in inducing learning. Haughton (2010) confirms that there was an important domestic 'Presidency effect' in the case of the first Presidencies of Czechia (2009) and Slovenia (2008), in that the preparations were taken very seriously, the profile of EU politics was raised, institutional change led to a reinforcement of the EU-related capacity of the state and some mildly Eurosceptic politicians embraced more positive positions. Moreover, the preparation of presidencies is usually done in collaboration with other member states (what was formally established as 'troika' presidency in the Lisbon Treaty; Batory and Puetter, 2013) which then had further impact in terms of learning especially on those member states that hold their first presidency. Besides, it has been argued that a presidency opens up special opportunities to push through the interests of small member states especially when these align with the interests of other actors (Svetličič and Cerjak, 2015).

Thirdly, states that have highly motivated bureaucrats with a sense of ownership are better at developing effective and sufficiently precise positions on policy at an early stage, where it is still possible to influence the direction of policies. The level of experience of individual staff members is indeed highly relevant, in that Panke (2011) shows that small member states can be as active in Council negotiations as larger states, provided that they have sufficient experience.

The Council Presidency itself is seen not just as a catalyst that helps states acquire expertise and experience in EU politics but also as a rare chance for small states to set the agenda (e.g. Björkdahl, 2008). On the other hand, the limited resources of small states also impact on the massive task of the Council Presidency, which requires the member state to chair the Council meetings and thus to be on top of a wide range of issues. Bengtsson (2002) questions the ability of small states to use the Presidency to shape the agenda, as most of the agenda is predetermined by ongoing business. Of course the same can be said for large states: part of the agenda will always be occupied by major events, such as the COVID-19 crisis, the refugee crisis, Brexit or the Russian invasion of Ukraine. Thus, the preferences of the state holding the Presidency will only ever make up part of the agenda. Panke and Gurol's (2018) study of the Maltese and Estonian Presidencies not only confirms Björkdahl's findings but also underlines certain limitations: small states can use the Presidency to pursue national interests, but they are most likely to be successful if they prioritize and focus on a smaller number of key issues. For example, the Estonian strategy of making digitalization the main priority of the Presidency and of incorporating it even into other priorities worked particularly well.

1.4 Content of the book

Considering the above-mentioned findings of the existing literature, this edited volume presents a twofold aim. The first, being examined in the first section of this book, is to deepen the existing knowledge on the extent to which small member states can compensate for the disadvantage of size in EU policy-making and to analyze the strategies that they employ in the current institutional context. The academic literature examining these issues is mostly dated – as shown in previous sections – and thus cannot fully cover the position of small member states in EU policy characterized by fast development. The first section is guided by the overarching research questions as to (1) how small member states try to overcome the challenge of size in the context of different institutions and (2) how effective these different strategies are. The chapters focus on the role of experience, cooperation and (where applicable) prioritization as three factors that have been deemed particularly relevant by the literature. In addition, the section goes beyond the existing literature, moving beyond the Council of the EU and the Council Presidency, and also covers the other major legislative institutions, namely the European Commission, which plays a crucial role in the drafting of policies, and the European Parliament, which is after all a co-legislator in the EU's decision-making process. This allows us to better understand to what extent the strategies that were identified in the context of the Council can usefully be applied in other institutional contexts.

Thus, in the second chapter, Hamřík focuses on the European Commission, an institution that has been almost entirely neglected by the literature on small states. The reason for this gap in the literature might be that the potential challenges to small states are less obvious in this case: nowadays every state has one Commissioner, which suggests that all states are equal. In addition, the Commissioners are formally neutral, i.e., they are not supposed to represent a state. However, the acrimonious negotiations over the size of the Commission during past Treaty negotiations and the refusal of many states to move towards a system of rotation where not every state would have a Commissioner at all times show that, in practice, states attach great importance to their representation in this European body. Hamřík therefore analyzes first the vision of the Commission that different states hold, in order to then dissect their nomination strategies and finally compare the importance of their portfolios to those of larger states. This allows us to understand to what extent a clear prioritization of target portfolios, coalition building and the selection of an experienced candidate can impact the success of the member state.

In the third chapter, Högenauer studies the position of small states in the European Parliament (EP) through the cases of Luxembourg and Malta. This institution is also relatively under-researched in the literature on small states, despite the fact that the majoritarian logic of this assembly makes the structural disadvantage of small states particularly visible. Indeed, many member states have fewer members of European Parliament (MEPs) than the EP has committees. Högenauer analyzes to what extent this structural disadvantage requires the prioritization of a small range of policy areas and whether they can be compensated by experience, which was previously identified by the literature as an important factor in Council negotiations. Experience in the context of the European Parliament can come from having held previous political offices or from serving as an MEP for several terms. In addition, she looks at the cooperation patterns of the MEPs from small states and at whether they are more prone to form cross-party alliances on issues of national interest.

The fourth chapter focuses on the Council as one of the main legislative institutions. Grumbinaite takes a closer look at the role of the six-month rotating Council Presidency through a comparison of six small member states. Since the literature argues that the Presidency is an important opportunity for small states to build capacity and learn, she analyzes through what strategies small states cope with the administrative and organizational challenges of the Presidency and whether this does indeed have a lasting effect on their capacity to engage in EU affairs. She argues that holding the rotating EU Presidency leads to at least a temporary

Europeanization of national administrations and to an improvement of national EU policy coordination practices, mostly from a sociological institutionalist perspective, through changes of attitudes, skill development and networking. She also looks at the ability of small states to use the Presidency to push their preferences onto the agenda, especially in the context of the new Trio Presidencies where three states have to coordinate an 18-month program.

In the fifth and sixth chapters, the authors zoom in on coalitions as a key tool to increase the weight of small states through collective action. Informed by theoretical and conceptual approaches towards small states and coalition building Etzold takes an analytical look at various examples of formal and informal groupings with Nordic and/or Baltic participation, establishing the type of coalition and examining their effectiveness in pursuing Nordic and Baltic interests in EU policy-making. In the process, he analyses which type of coalition is most effective for the pursuit of different types of goals. Stefanova focuses on several small states in Central and Eastern Europe and their attempt to build coalitions that can act as veto players. She analyzes both the strategies themselves and whether they have been successful in achieving their goals. In addition, she looks at whether these strategies have gained wider relevance in terms of creating more autonomy for the EU member states.

The second aim of the book, studied in its second section, is to examine the impact of small EU member states on different common policies. Similarly to the first section of the book, this one also wants to extend our knowledge about the place of small members in the EU and their ability to influence the decision-making process by examining various policies that are being constantly revised in a changing Union. Thus, the contributions of this section are based on the need to learn more about the development of these policies at the EU level – and the contribution of small members to this process. This section is thus looking for answers to the following research questions: How do small members influence individual policies? How does the EU respond (or fail to respond) to the needs of small states? Small member states face challenges especially in policies connected to foreign and security policy, and therefore the second section is looking closely at these policies.

The seventh chapter by Kavvadia examines economic diplomacy of small states using the case of Luxembourg. The chapter argues that small states seek participation in multilateral frameworks and/or cluster around regional unions and asks how do European small states use economic diplomacy within this context. Despite its small size, Luxembourg has developed into the EU's wealthiest country per capita. This has been achieved through an evolving successful economic model, supported through agile and skilled economic diplomacy. Grounded on a long-term strategy that is characterized by vision and policy consistency, Luxembourg has developed effective economic diplomacy to promote its political and economic priorities, especially within the EU governance constellation. Using a structural realist perspective, the chapter posits that Luxembourg has actively and increasingly pursued its economic diplomacy to boost not only its economic perspectives but also its soft power in the European and international contexts.

Focusing on foreign and security policy, Foster and Mosser investigate the effects of minilateralism in Chapter 8. They analyze the EU's 2017 agreement on advancing Permanent Structured Cooperation (PeSCo) as an example of 'embedded concert' and juxtapose it to case studies of minilateral coalitions that have formed around subregional threat perceptions and security concerns. This chapter argues that small member states can use subregional minilateralism to effectively advocate for their security priorities, including for strategies that enhance cooperation and European integration on foreign policy. However, such coalitions may also contribute to tensions over policy priorities. The impact of subregional coalitions on European integration in the field of foreign and security policy is thus indeterminated in its essence and is shaped significantly by pressures from the international security environment and member states' domestic politics.

The following (ninth) chapter by Dominici, Lewis and Steingass continues the security discussion by analyzing the security preferences of several small EU member states in both defence and border control cooperation. The chapter examines how EU small member states pursue their preferences in these areas and evaluates the degree to which these states succeed in their endeavours. By comparing in pairs a group of similar states and controlling for intervening factors (e.g. population, economy, neutrality, geography, threat perception), the chapter focuses on the significance of lobbying, persuasion, compromise and coalitions as determinants of small state influence in EU decision-making. The findings help us to better understand the circumstances under which small states have leverage at the EU level.

The last chapter of the second section by Gao (Chapter 10) investigates cyber-security in relation to small states. The chapter argues that the traditional notion of small states playing a marginal role when shaping the EU's security policy does not apply to non-traditional security issues such as cybersecurity. Using Estonia's significant role in the development of EU cybersecurity strategy as a case study, this chapter argues that non-traditional security issues allow small states to avoid marginalization in the process of EU policy-making. In doing so, it demonstrates empirically that small states exert influence in the field of security. The chapter develops a conceptual framework based on the literature on policy entrepreneur and small state foreign policy. Under this framework, the analysis is conducted based on data derived from secondary academic literature, primary EU documents and interviews.

The book comes to the conclusion that small states face different challenges in different institutions. They are relatively well represented in the European Commission but are in a weaker position in the Council, where they risk being outvoted and where vetoes annoy other states more than they hinder policy-making. And they are in a difficult position in the European Parliament, where the limited number of MEPs does not allow small states to cover every policy area. In addition, it is difficult to obtain certain posts without the backing of a large national delegation.

The strategies thus also diverge across institutions. Whereas prioritization and coalition building are seen to work well in the context of the Council, small-state MEPs tend to be active in a wider range of committees and are thus more generalist than those from large states. Many of them also benefit from previous expertise in politics or with EU affairs. In the case of the Commission, the strategies of small states when nominating Commissioners are similar to those of large states, but their Commissioners are far more gender balanced. This may be an opportunity at a time when the goal is to create a gender balanced Commission.

When it comes to the second section, the chapters in this volume claim that small EU member states are able to exercise influence also in security and foreign policy if they use suitable strategies. These can be utilizing critical junctures to develop domestic expertise that they are able to upload to the EU level (Kavaadia, Gao) or join (or lead) minilateral coalitions that amplify their voice (Foster and Mosser). However, if initiatives are backed by big countries, small members have very limited manoeuvring options. They can only use the development at the EU level to persuade the domestic audience (Foster and Mosser). In practice, small member states are found to be rather active members that are trying to proactively shape the EU and its policies so that their national priorities are as close to EU rules as possible and are not waiting for the EU to respond (or not) to their needs. This section thus confirms the findings of the first section, that small states can navigate the EU's institutions and decision-making processes successfully, even if this may require a little more effort than in the case of large states.

Bibliography

Archer, C., Bailes, A. and Wivel, A. (2017). *Small States and International Security. Europe and Beyond* (Routledge: London).

Arter, D. (2000). Small state influence within the EU: The case of Finland's 'northern dimension initiative'. *Journal of Common Market Studies* 38(5): 677–697.

Baldacchino, G. and Wivel, A. (2021). Small states: Concepts and theories. In: G. Baldacchino and A. Wivel (eds.), *Handbook on the Politics of Small States* (Edward Elgar: Cheltenham), pp. 1–19.

Batory, A. and Puetter, U. (2013). Consistency and diversity? The EU's rotating trio Council Presidency after the Lisbon Treaty. *Journal of European Public Policy* 20(1): 95–112.

Bengtsson, R. (2002). Soft security and the presidency. *Cooperation and Conflict* 372(2): 212–218.

Björkdahl, A. (2008). Norm Advocacy: A small state strategy to influence the EU. *Journal of European Public Policy* 15(1): 135–154.

Blockmans, S. (2017). The Benelux approach to EU integration and external action. *Global Affairs* 3(3): 223–235.

Briguglio, L. (2016). Small states and the European Union. *Economic Perspectives* (Routledge: London).

Brooks, E., De Ruijter, A. and Greer, S.L. (2020). Covid-19 and European Union health policy: From crisis to collective action. In: B. Vanhercke and S. Spasova (eds.), *Social Policy in the European Union: State of Play 2021. Re-Emerging Social Ambitions as the EU Recovers from the Pandemic* (European Trade Union Institute: Brussels), pp. 33–52.

Brusenbauch Meislova, M. (2019). Great expectations or misplaced hopes? The role of the Visegrád Group in the brexit process. *Europe–Asia Studies* 71(8): 1261–1284.

Bull, M.J. (2018). In the eye of the storm: The Italian economy and the Eurozone crisis. *South European Society and Politics* 23(1): 13–28.

Bulmer, S. (2014). Germany and the Eurozone crisis: Between hegemony and domestic politics. *West European Politics* 37(6): 1244–1263.

Bunse, S. (2009). *Small States and EU Governance* (Palgrave: London).

Clements, B., Nanou, K. and Verney, S. (2014). 'We No longer love you, but we don't want to leave you': The eurozone crisis and popular euroscepticism in greece. *Journal of European Integration* 36(3): 247–265.

Dookeran, W. (2021). Book review of G. Baldacchino & A. Wivel (eds.), Handbook on the politics of small states. *Small States & Territories* 4(2): 369–374.

Ferrera, M., Miró, J. and Ronchi, S. (2021). Walking the road together? EU polity maintenance during the COVID-19 crisis. *West European Politics* 44(5–6): 1329–1352.

Finke, D. (2017). Underneath the culture of consensus: Transparency, credible commitments and voting in the Council of Ministers. *European Union Politics* 18(3): 339–361.

Fontan, C. and Saurugger, S. (2019). Between a rock and a hard place: Preference formation in France During the Eurozone crisis. *Political Studies Review* 18(4): 507–524.

Frieden, J. and Walter, S. (2017). Understanding the political economy of the Eurozone crisis. *Annual Review of Political Science* 20(1): 371–390.

Grimaud, M.J. (2018). *Small States and EU Governance. Malta in EU Decision-Making Processes* (Palgrave: London).

Harmsen, R. and Högenauer, A.L. (2021). Luxembourg and the European Union. In: F. Laursen (ed.), *Encyclopedia of European Union Politics* (Oxford University Press: Oxford), pp. 1–21.

Harteveld, E., Schaper, J., De Lange, S.L. and Van Der Brug, W. (2018). Blaming brussels? The impact of (news about) the refugee crisis on attitudes towards the EU and national politics. *Journal of Common Market Studies* 56(1): 157–177.

Haughton, T. (2010). *Vulnerabilities, Accession Hangovers and the Presidency Role: Explaining New EU Member States' Choices for Europe.* Working Paper Series 68 (Center for European Studies Central and Eastern Europe: Leiden).

Heisenberg, D. (2005). The institution of 'consensus' in the European Union: Formal versus informal decision-making in the Council. *European Journal of Political Research* 44(1): 65–90.

Hosli, M.O., Mattila, M. and Uriot, M. (2011). Voting in the council of the European Union after the 2004 enlargement : A comparison of old and new member states. *Journal of Common Market Studies* 49(6): 1249–1270.

Högenauer, A.L., Sarapuu, K. and Trimikliniotis, N. (2021). Guest editorial: Small states and the governance of the Covid-19 pandemic. *Small States & Territories* 4(1): 3–12.

Hosli, M., Kreppel, A., Plechanovová, B. and Verdun, A. (2013). Introduction: Decision-making in the European Union before and after the Lisbon treaty. *West European Politics* 36(6): 1121–1127.

Jakobsen, P.V. (2009). Small states, big influence: The overlooked Nordic influence on the civilian ESDP. *Journal of Common Market Studies* 47(1): 81–102.

Jazbec, M. (2001). *The Diplomacies of New Small States. The Case of Slovenia with Some Comparison from the Baltic* (Ashgate: Aldershot).

Kallius, A., Monterescu, D. and Rajaram, P.K. (2016). Immobilizing mobility: Border ethnography, illiberal democracy, and the politics of the "refugee crisis" in Hungary. *American Ethnology* 43(1): 25–37.

Kratochvíl, P. and Sychra, Z. (2019). The end of democracy in the EU? The Eurozone crisis and the EU's democratic deficit. *Journal of European Integration* 41(2): 169–185.

Laffan, B. (2006). Managing Europe from home in Dublin, Athens and Helsinki: A comparative analysis. *West European Politics* 29(4): 687–708.

Larsen, H. (2005). *Analysing the Foreign Policy of Small States in the EU. The Case of Denmark* (Palgrave: London).

Long, T. (2017). It's not the size, it's the relationship: from 'small states' to asymmetry. *International Politics* 54(2): 144–160.

Maass, M. (2009). The elusive definition of the small state. *International Politics* 46(1): 65–83.

Manners, I. (2000). Small states and the internal balance of the European Union: Institutional issues. In: J. Gower and J. Redmond (eds.), *Enlarging the European Union. The Way Forward* (Ashgate: Aldershot), pp.123–135.

Marcinkiewicz, K. and Tosun, J. (2015). Contesting climate change: Mapping the political debate in Poland. *East European Politics* 31(2): 187–207.

Mattila, M. (2004). Contested decisions: Empirical analysis of voting in the European Union council of ministers. *European Journal of Political Research* 43(1): 29–50.

Mattila, M. (2008). Voting and coalitions in the council after the enlargement. In: D. Naurin and H. Wallace (eds.), *Unveiling the Council of the European Union: Games Governments Play in Brussels* (Palgrave Macmillan: London), pp. 23–35.

Mišík, M. (2016). On the way towards the Energy Union: Position of Austria, the Czech republic and Slovakia towards external energy security integration. *Energy* 111: 68–81.

Mišík, M. (2019). *External Energy Security in the European Union: Small Member States' Perspective* (Routledge: London).

Moravcsik, A. (1993). Preferences and power in the European Community: A liberal intergovernmentalist approach. *Journal of Common Market Studies* 31(4): 473–524.

Nasra, S. (2011). Governance in EU foreign policy: Exploring small state influence. *Journal of European Public Policy* 18(2): 164–180.

Naurin, D. and Lindahl, R. (2008). East-North-South: Coalition-building in the council before and after enlargement. In: D. Naurin and H. Wallace (eds.), *Unveiling the Council of the European Union: Games Governments Play in Brussels* (Palgrave Macmillan: London), pp. 64–78.

Pace, R. (2000). Small states and the internal balance of the European Union: The perspective of small states. In: J. Gower and J. Redmond (eds.), *Enlarging the European Union. The Way Forward* (Ashgate: Aldershot), pp. 107–122.

Panke, D. (2010). *Small States in the European Union. Coping with Structural Disadvantages* (Ashgate: Farnham).

Panke, D. (2011). Small states in EU negotiations: Political dwarfs or power-brokers? *Cooperation and Conflict* 46(2): 123–143.

Panke, D. and Gurol, J. (2018). Small states as agenda-setters? The council presidencies of Malta and Estonia. *Journal of Common Market Studies* 56(S1): 142–151.

Schimmelfennig, F. (2018). European integration (theory) in times of crisis. A comparison of the euro and Schengen crises. *Journal of European Public Policy* 25(7): 969–989.

Schure, P. and Verdun, A. (2008). Legislative bargaining in the European Union: The divide between large and small member states. *European Union Politics* 9(4): 459–486.

Sedelmeier, U. (2014). *Europe after the Eastern Enlargement of the European Union: 2004–2014*, ed. H.B. Stiftung. Working paper (European Union: Brussels).

Steinmetz, R. and Wivel, A. (2010). *Small States in Europe. Challenges and Opportunities* (Routledge: London).

Soetendorp, B. and Hanf, K. (1998). Conclusion: The nature of national adaptation to European integration. In: K. Hanf and B. Soetendorp (eds.), *Adapting to European Integration: Small States and the European Union* (Longman: London), pp. 186–194.

Svetličič, M. and Cerjak, K. (2015). Small countries' EU council presidency and the realisation of their national interests: The case of Slovenia. *Croatian International Relations Review* 21(74): 5–39.

Thorhallsson, B. (2000). *The Role of Small States in the European Union* (Routledge: London).

Thorhallsson, B. (2019). *Small States and Shelter Theory. Iceland's External Affairs* (Routledge: London).

Thorhallsson, B. and Wivel, A. (2006). Small states in the European Union : What do we know and what would we like to know ? *Cambridge Review of International Affairs* 19(4): 651–668.

Tiilikainen, T. (2006). Finland — An EU member with a small state identity. *Journal of European Integration* 28(1): 73–87.

Toshkov, D.D. (2017). The impact of the Eastern enlargement on the decision-making capacity of the European Union. *Journal of European Public Policy* 24(2): 177–196.

Verdun, A. (2015). A historical institutionalist explanation of the EU's responses to the euro area financial crisis. *Journal of European Public Policy* 22(2): 219–237.

Visegrad Group. (2016). *Joint Statement of the Heads of Governments of the V4 Countries* (Visegrad Group: Bratislava).

Wivel, A. and Baldacchino, G. (2022). Studying the politics of small states: A response to Baker, Dookeran and Jugl. *Small States & Territories* 5(1): 195–200.

Zaun, N. (2018). States as gatekeepers in EU asylum politics: Explaining the non-adoption of a refugee quota system. *Journal of Common Market Studies* 56(1): 44–62.

Zeitlin, J., Nicoli, F. and Laffan, B. (2019). Introduction: The European Union beyond the polycrisis? Integration and politicization in an age of shifting cleavages. *Journal of European Public Policy* 26(7): 963–976.

Small states in the EU's institutions and policy processes

2 Small member states in the European Commission of the 21st century

Lukáš Hamřík

2.1 Introduction

The Eastern enlargement of 2004 brought about many challenges for the European Union's (EU's) institutional design. An intended and unprecedented increase in the number of member states mirrored itself in intensified discussions about how an enlarged Union should look. In this regard, especially, the weighting of votes in the Council of the EU, the definition of qualified majority, the number of representatives in the European Parliament and the size of the European Commission (EC) dominated the debates (Gray and Stubb, 2001; Dehousse, 2000; Magnette and Nicolaïdis, 2003). This chapter is devoted to the European Commission, small member states and their involvement in the European Commission's politics. The EC has been for a long time portrayed as the EU institution committed to the EU's general interest while not defending the particular interests of some (large) member states (Nicolaïdis and Bunse, 2012). It can be said that for small EU countries, the EC is their 'best friend' (Wivel, 2010). Such a perception is further amplified by the structural disadvantages the small states face in EU politics as well as the need to rely on the EC's involvement in policy-making at the EU level (Panke, 2016; Thorhallsson, 2000). Therefore, it can be assumed that it is of utmost importance for small states to preserve the Commission's independent and impartial status and actively engage with EC politics, for example, through careful selection of their 'eyes, ears, and voice in Brussels' (Nicolaïdis and Bunse, 2012).

The Chapter seeks to provide answers to three questions: (1) How did the small states perceive the role the EC should play in the EU and their own representation at the level of College? (2) Are there any observable differences between small and larger EU member states when it comes to nomination strategies employed for the posts of Commissioners? (3) How did the organizational reforms introduced by Barosso and his successors affect the small states' access to leadership positions at the level of College?

Based on analysis of small member states' positions presented during the treaty revision process, data on the composition of six Colleges from the mid-1990s and data on profiles and professional backgrounds of the Commissioners, it is concluded that: (1) small states stress the impartiality and independence of the Commission. Due to such perception, the Commission (and small states' representation in it) guarantees that small states' interests are reflected in EU politics;

DOI: 10.4324/9781003380641-3

(2) it is not possible to observe clear differences in nomination strategies of small and large member states. Despite that, some patterns appeared. Both groups of states choose politically experienced persons (mostly from top executive positions) for the office of EC Member. Moreover, small states contribute to a more gender-balanced College, making it no Men's club anymore; and (3) the small states' importance within and influence on EC's politics has grown, especially since the strengthening of leadership positions in the EC and small states' access to them.

The Chapter is structured as follows. The following section summarizes what we already know about small states' positions towards the role, size and composition of EC as observed during the treaty revision process. The nomination strategies employed by the member states when appointing the Members of the EC are discussed as well. Furthermore, this section also highlights some of the internal reforms and developments within the EC as these enhanced the importance of particular positions within the College. Section 2.3 provides information on the data and method used in this study. Section 2.4 then contains an analysis of small member states' positions and perceptions, their appointment strategies and an evaluation of how EC's internal reforms affected access of small states' Commissioners to the leadership positions within the EC. The last section concludes and identifies avenues for future research.

2.2 European Commission and the small EU member states

The European Union is a unique project grounded in cooperation between and integration of European democratic states. Naturally, the positions of member states vary not only in particular policy fields but also in institutional questions. In the history of EU politics, we can identify many situations in which specific cleavages or divides among member states came to the forefront. Typical and well-known examples would include the North-South divide related to the contributors to and receivers from the EU budget (e.g. Nicolaïdis and Bunse, 2012), old versus new member states or the East-West divide. Last but not least, the size of the member states, and especially the distinction between large and small (or more and less populated) member states, played a role on many occasions. In this regard, the most visible instances can be seen in attempts to alter the EU's institutional design during the primary law revision process since the 1990s (Bunse et al., 2005: 14; Nicolaïdis and Bunse, 2012; Piris, 2010: 228–229; Thorhallsson and Wivel, 2006; Geurts, 1998).

2.2.1 Reforming the European Commission

Nowadays, the EU member states are represented in the EC on an equal basis, with each member state having one Commissioner. However, the path to the current status quo was anything but straightforward. Up until the Treaty of Nice, the small-large states divide was explicitly reflected in the composition of the College as large member states had two Commissioners (see e.g. Schmidt and Wonka, 2012). During the Intergovernmental Conference, delegations reached a compromise on whether to preserve an equal representation of member states or to reduce the overall size of the EC. The Treaty of Nice maintained that every state would be represented in the College by one Commissioner. Hence, the large states did not retain their second Commissioner anymore. Nevertheless, the treaty also stipulated that the Commission of the EU composed of 27 member states should have had fewer EC members (Magnette and Nicolaïdis, 2003; Schmidt and Wonka, 2012).

The agreement reached in Nice was, however, questioned during the Convention and the Intergovernmental Conference leading to the Draft Treaty establishing the Constitution for Europe. On that occasion, many small member states opposed the various proposals such as reducing the overall number of Commissioners, adopting a system of equal rotation or creating a two-tier Commission, to name a few (Piris, 2010; Nicolaïdis and Bunse, 2012). The small states argued in favour of the representation of all member states in the Commission while stressing the importance of representation that should be in line with the principle of equality of EU member states (Egeberg, 2006; Böttner, 2018). From small states' point of view, the representation of all states would reduce the risk of the Commission leaning towards the specific interests of some states and would ensure that all perspectives are taken into account, including the small states' specific position (Magnette and Nicolaïdis, 2003; Nicolaïdis and Bunse, 2012). The second most commonly used argument of small states related to the perception of the EC in terms of its legitimacy within the EU. According to this line of argumentation, it is of utmost importance for each member state to have its own Commissioner. The fact that the EC is composed of representatives of all member states would contribute to the trust in as well as credibility and the EU citizens' perceptions of the EC (Böttner, 2018; see also Piris, 2010). On the opposite side of the spectrum, large member states (and some medium-sized ones such as Benelux countries) pointed to the ever-growing College and the eventual negative consequences of the enlargement on the EC's ability to operate effectively and maintain collegially (Thorhallsson and Wivel, 2006; Böttner, 2018; Nicolaïdis and Bunse, 2012).

Despite the unsuccessful ratification of the Constitution, the rotation system materialized itself with the Treaty of Lisbon. The Lisbon Treaty envisaged that the number of EC members would be reduced from one per member state to two-thirds of the overall number of member states, based on a system of equal rotation reflecting geographical and demographic diversity (e.g. Nicolaïdis and Bunse, 2012; Phinnemore, 2013; Piris, 2010). This provision was supposed to enter into force in 2014. However, as a consequence of the Irish referendum where a move to rotation was a crucial point of contention, the European Council seized the possibility to adopt a decision that the EC would continue to be composed of one representative from each member state (Nicolaïdis and Bunse, 2012; Schmidt and Wonka, 2012; Piris, 2010).

2.2.2 Who are the College's members?

The legitimacy and representation arguments for the preservation system of equal representation played a dominant role in debates on institutional reforms in recent decades. Nevertheless, the EC's importance for the small states lies also in more politics-related and pragmatic aspects reflecting the small states' relationship to and perceptions of the EC. First, small states usually have a limited administrative capacity when compared to larger ones. Therefore, they rely on EC's involvement in the policy-making process (Thorhallsson, 2000; Döring, 2007; Panke, 2016; Peterson, 2008). In other words, from the small states' perspective, the position of the EC is seen as a way how to counterbalance the dominance of the large states in the Council of the European Union and influence EU policies (Wivel, 2010).

Second, the EC is perceived as the EU's institution characterized by a collegial nature of decision-making. Moreover, the EC is responsible for promoting the EU's general interest and the members of the EC shall not take instructions from or defend the interests of the governments which nominated them (OJEU, 2012, Arts. 17.1 and 17.3). The mentioned expectations placed on members of the EC suggest that it is difficult to observe a clear dominance of large member states within the EC (Nicolaïdis and Bunse, 2012). Thus, generally speaking, the EC can primarily be seen as the guarantor of the Union's general interests rather than of a particular group of member states (Magnette and Nicolaïdis, 2003). Nevertheless, the recent findings indicate that the overall picture is far more complicated and the reality does not necessarily reflect the formal provisions. At the level of individual Commissioners, recent analysis suggests that Commissioners' personal characteristics (including nationality and partisanship) matter for the bargaining success of their respective states. In other words, Commissioners are in a position to pursue national interests within the EC (Kirpsza, 2024; Thomson and Dumont, 2022). To make it even more complex, besides being the EC members and the member state's representatives, the Commissioners have a commitment to their areas of responsibility. It is especially the commitment to a portfolio that seems to be a crucial element in performing multiple roles (Egeberg, 2006: 11–12). Thus, it is probably correct to talk about the EC as the EU institution that it is 'neither completely independent nor a member state agent' (Deckarm, 2017: 447). Perhaps the most worrying finding from the perspective of small states is that EC's policy positions are not really different to those of many populous member states (Thomson and Dumont, 2022).

Despite the mentioned (formal) requirements tied to the functioning of the EC and its members, and in light of the absence of full independence of the Commissioners, it is not surprising that the governments select their appointees carefully (MacMullen, 1997; Wonka, 2007; Smith, 2003).

In his study (covering the Colleges between 1952 and 1995), MacMullen (1997) analyzed the nomination strategies of member states for the office of Commissioners. A typical profile of a Commissioner is a university-educated male with experience from both national and/or EU-level political office. More specifically, in the period under study, 94 per cent of the Commission members were male, with a university degree, and two-thirds of the Commissioners held office of member of a national or the European Parliament or held ministerial positions within a national government (MacMullen, 1997: 41–46). Two observations are worth stressing. First, there was an ongoing trend of politicization of the College as the member states nominated

Commissioners with evident political experiences. Second, in the course of the European integration process, the member states tended to appoint more often former Ministers of Foreign Affairs or Finance (MacMullen, 1997).

The pattern of appointing candidates with strong political experiences from national legislatures or executives for the post of a Commissioner holds true also when the composition of post-1995 Colleges until the Barroso II Commission is taken into account. In the first Barroso's College, 64 per cent of the members had previous experiences as ministers in national governments (Wonka, 2007: 184–185). As regards the distinction between large and small member states, especially the large states (having two Commissioners) were more willing to nominate also junior ministers, while the small states chose former ministers to office (Döring, 2007). In the Barroso II College, only two EC members have had no previous political experience (Wille, 2012).

2.2.3 Political leadership within the European Commission

The growing number of Commissioners as well as more policy areas transferred to the EU level led to a need of effective political leadership within the EC (Kassim, 2017; Bürgin, 2018). In this regard, two developments affecting the EC's internal functioning should be pointed to. On the one hand, scholars have argued that there is a process of presidentialization or personalization of politics in the EC related to the importance of the EC's Presidency. On the other, besides the powers of Presidents, also role and responsibilities of EC's Vice-Presidents have changed (especially since Juncker's College), making Vice-Presidents more influential.

As a result of an ongoing process of presidentialization (Kassim, 2017) or centralized personalization (Hamřík, 2021) of politics within the EC, the Commission's Presidency has become more important. In the course of the primary law's revisions since the 1990s, the EC's President gained considerable powers allowing her to decide on many aspects of the internal operation of the Commission (Kassim et al., 2017). It is the President's prerogative to decide on the internal operation and structure of the College, the allocation and reallocation of portfolios or the number of Vice-Presidents (Kassim, 2017; Hamřík, 2021).

Perhaps the most important innovation during Juncker's Presidency was the introduction of seven Vice-Presidents (Bürgin, 2018; Kassim, 2017). Obviously, the office of EC's Vice-President is nothing new. What has changed since the Juncker's Commission, however, is the role the Vice-Presidents play and the powers they have. The Vice-Presidents are directly responsible for the work of a group of Commissioners working on specific priority projects (Böttner, 2018; Kassim, 2017; Bürgin, 2018). Moreover, the Vice-Presidents were entrusted with the power to evaluate whether new policy initiatives were in line with the EC President's political guidelines and whether such initiatives could be successfully made by Commissioners within individual project teams. Every such proposal needs the recommendation of the respective Vice-President as well as of the First Vice-President (Böttner, 2018; Hamřík, 2021; Bürgin, 2018). In terms of responsibilities placed on leadership positions, there is no significant difference between Juncker's and von der Leyen's Colleges. Nevertheless, von der Leyen appointed eight Vice-Presidents (including three Executive Vice-Presidents while one of them is at the same time the First Vice-President) (European Commission, 2014, 2019).

Organizational reforms and amendments to the EU primary law and internal Rules of Procedure within the EC gave rise to a 'de facto hierarchy' with a rather small elite group of Commissioners occupying leadership positions (Böttner, 2018; Hamřík, 2021). Thus, in reality, some individuals have a significant influence on the internal operation of the EC and policy outputs. Section 2.4.3 also answers the question of to what extent there is a place for small states' representatives to hold such posts. Before moving to the analytical part of this chapter, the following section presents data employed here as well as information on how the analysis was conducted.

2.3 Data and methods

The analysis presented in the next section covers the period starting with the Santer Commission in 1994 until May 2023. During that period, six different Colleges were appointed (Santer, Prodi, Barroso I, Barroso II, Juncker, von der Leyen) and four major treaties' revision rounds took place (Amsterdam Treaty, Treaty of Nice, Convention on the Future of Europe and subsequent Intergovernmental Conference, Lisbon Treaty). In accordance with the criterion distinguishing small and larger member states as suggested in the introductory chapter of this volume, I identified 13 member states with a population below 7 million inhabitants (based on data from 2020). These include Bulgaria, Croatia, Cyprus, Denmark, Estonia, Finland, Ireland, Latvia, Lithuania, Luxembourg, Malta, Slovakia and Slovenia.

As regards the first research question, small member states' position on two EC-related categories were followed. The first one was dedicated to the institutional reform of the Commission. In this regard, especially the debates on the number of EC members were important. The second category aimed at small states' perceptions of the EC's role within the EU. More specifically, I was interested in the EC's position within the EU's institutional framework as well as the role the Commission should play in particular EU policies. This part of the analysis employs quantitative content analysis, and it was based on the official positions of the (small) member states in the course of the individual revision rounds. The relevant documents were searched primarily by using the DORIE (DOcumentation et Recherche sur les questions Institutionnelles Européennes) database. When using the DORIE, 'Arena' menu was used while specifically looking for documents related to the following fields: IGC/Amsterdam; IGC/Nice; European Convention 2002–2003; IGC/Constitution/2003–2004; and IGC/Lisbon.

The analysis of the composition of the College, nomination strategies and Commissioners' background and previous professional experiences is based on data gathered from the official websites of respective Colleges (accessible via EC's archives website). Table 2.1 provides more details on the distribution of observations (between large and small member states and between individual Colleges).

Table 2.1 Overview of the number of EC members appointed by small and larger member states in the period under study

Commission	Santer	Prodi	Barroso I	Barroso II	Juncker	von der Leyen
EU	15	25	27	28	28	27
Number of small states	4	11	12	13	13	13
Number of larger states	11	14	15	15	15	14
Number of Commissioners (during the whole College's term of office)	20	35	34	32	30	28
Number of small states' Commissioners	4	12	15	15	14	14
Number of larger states' Commissioners	16	23	19	17	16	14

The overall number of Members of the EC in the period under study is 179, out of which 74 were nominated by the small EU member states and 105 by the larger ones. The overall number of observations also includes Commissioners who (1) were replaced during their term of office, (2) their successors and (3) Commissioners without portfolios in Prodi's Commission.

When answering the second and the third research questions, a particular interest lies in who the EC members nominated by the small and larger EU member states are. More specifically, three categories were evaluated: gender, education (do they have a university degree?) and professional background. When looking at the Commissioners' professional background, it was further distinguished between previous experiences. Hence, a Commissioner could have experience as (1) prime minister, (2) minister in a national government, (3) member of parliament or European Parliament, (4) other public service positions (e.g. advisory positions at the ministries) or (5) no previous political experience. I did not count two different previous positions into two categories. Rather, I assigned the Commissioners according to the highest previous position (following the order as presented earlier). Moreover, I also evaluated trends in nominating EC members for more than one term of office (i.e. to what extent do member states nominate incumbents?).

2.4 Analysis

The analytical part of this chapter is divided into three subsections. It begins with the evaluation of small member states' positions presented during the treaty revision rounds. In particular, the following subsection looks at small states' perceptions of the EC's role and their positions with respect to debates about changes in representation within the EC. Then, attention is paid to answering the question of who the EC Members nominated by small states are, with the intention of finding out whether there are observable differences between the nomination strategies of small and large member states. The final part of this section is devoted to the leadership positions within the EC and the role small states play in a more hierarchical Commission.

2.4.1 How do the small states perceive the Commission, its role and their own representation within the College?

According to data on small member states' positions, the Commission should perform three main functions. First, the EC's independent and impartial status within the EU's institutional framework allows the Commission to be responsible for the general interest of the Union. Second, the EC has a monopoly on legislative initiatives. Last, the EC has crucial importance in monitoring how the EU law is implemented in the EU member states. These tasks of the EC were not challenged. Based on the official positions of the small member states, there is no doubt that none of them would be willing to accept any proposal, eventually leading to undermining the mentioned functions. On the contrary, many of them expressed an opinion that there should be more responsibilities and powers assigned to the EC. One of the arguments presented in favour of a stronger EC was the 2004 enlargement (see e.g. Benelux, 2002). Hence, the preservation of impartiality and increase of EC's capacity to move forward decision-making processes in the enlarged EU was seen as essential.

Even though Austria is not considered a small state for the purpose of this study, its position presented during the pre-Nice negotiations illustrates the perceptions of small(er) states vis-à-vis EC's role in the EU. In this regard, Austria considered itself 'as one of the smaller member states' and therefore, it had 'a special interest in seeing the Commission remain a strong and independent institution' (Austrian Permanent Representation, 2000). Some of the small states expressed their perceptions on balancing the interests of small and large member states by the EC in more explicit terms. For example, the Cypriot government stressed the Commission's 'important role in maintaining a balance between larger and smaller states' (Government of Cyprus, 2000).

As regards particular Union policies, it was often suggested by small member states that the Commission should play a greater role in the former so-called second and third pillars. Within the Common Foreign and Security Policy, the EC was supposed to play a more active role (e.g. via a right of initiative or enhanced capacities in representation of the EU). At the interinstitutional level, some small states stressed a need for better coordination between the EC and the Council of the European Union. Also, within the fields of Justice and Home Affairs, small states (e.g. Finland, Luxembourg) have seen the EC as an actor with a joint right of initiative, especially in fields such as asylum, migration or judicial cooperation in civil matters. Apart from these two areas (pillars), it was important for some small member states that the EC should focus on energy, the environment and the fight against unemployment.

Moving to the discussions about the size and composition of the College, in the course of the revision process, there was a broad consensus among the vast majority of small member states on two issues. For the small states, equal representation of member states and equal status of EC's Members were essential prerequisites for the functioning of the EC, its legitimacy and credibility and its ability to promote the EU's common interest. To begin with equal representation, small states argued that all member states should have a Commissioner in the College. Only a few small states were willing to accept a reduction in the number of EC Members and the establishment of the system of equal rotation (Lithuania and Luxembourg).

As far as the equal status of EC Members is concerned, the proposals placed on the agenda of Intergovernmental Conferences related to the possibility of having different classes of Commissioners. If they succeeded, the College would have been composed of, for example, 'junior and senior' Members, or members with and without portfolios and/or full voting rights. Any such proposal leading to a two-tier Commission or hierarchy among its Members was rejected by almost all small member states. The only exception was Bulgarian representation willing to accept a two-tier Commission. Bulgaria proposed that the non-voting members should have had specific portfolios and a right to participate in any discussion (Bulgaria, 2003).

2.4.2 Nomination strategies of the EU member states

Putting aside the occasional willingness of a very few small member states to accept 'unequal representation' in the College, generally speaking, it was always crucial for the small EU member states to be represented in the EC. In what follows, I provide a comparison of the nomination strategies of both small and large member states with the focus placed on the profiles of the appointees, their professional backgrounds and the portfolios they held in the EC.

For many decades, the College was typically composed of male Commissioners. That fact has changed recently. In the period under study, out of all 179 nominated Commissioners, 55 (31 per cent) were female Members. When looking at the overall gender balance of the Colleges' compositions, it is evident there is a clear trend towards more gender-balanced Commission (see Figure 2.1). In this regard,

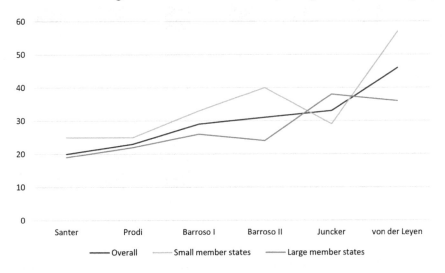

Figure 2.1 Representation of women at the level of College (whole period, in %)

especially the small EU member states contributed the most, as approximately 37 per cent of their Commissioners were women (in comparison to only 19 per cent of Commissioners appointed by large states). It is also important to highlight that while the current College reaches gender balance (both groups, male and female Commissioners, are represented at a level of more than 40 per cent), small states as a group nominated more women than men. When looking at a group of small states only, three observations should be mentioned. First, Bulgaria is the only EU country that has nominated exclusively female Commissioners. On the opposite end, Slovakia appoints all male Commissioners. Second, Luxembourg reached balanced representation in the period under study (three male and three female Commissioners). Last, for the von der Leyen's Commission, Finland and Malta nominated female Members for the very first time.

Even though it is not possible to conclude whether a Commissioner is typically a man or woman anymore, the same does not hold true for their political qualities and experiences. In each College under study, the majority of EC's Members had experiences from executive offices as prime ministers or ministers before joining the Commission (see Figure 2.2). The overall share of Commissioners with experiences from top positions within national governments ranges between 55 (Santer) and 74 (Barroso I) per cent. When also including experiences as members of the national or the European Parliament, it is obvious that the College as such is composed of politically experienced persons. On average, only one-tenth of all Commissioners did not have previous experience with serving as members of a parliament or (prime) ministers within a national government. Thus, it happens only rarely that a member state nominates a person without strong political experience.

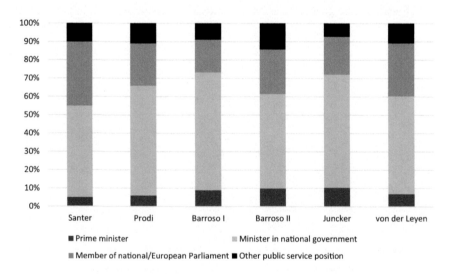

Figure 2.2 Proportion of EC Members according to their previous highest professional experience (whole period, in %)

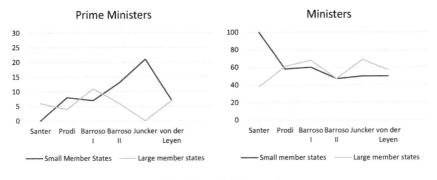

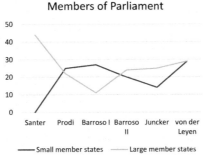

Figure 2.3 Proportion of EC Members nominated by small and large member states, according to their previous highest professional experience: prime ministers, ministers, members of parliaments (whole period, in %)

When looking at differences between small and large member states, it must be concluded that both groups are quite similar in this regard (see Figure 2.3). To begin with prime ministers, an interesting case is Juncker's Commission in which all three former prime ministers nominated as Commissioners came from small states (including EC President). Former ministers in national governments were the most numerous group in each College, followed by former members of parliaments. In both aspects, the nomination strategies of small and large states seem to be quite similar, with no significant differences. It can be, however, pointed out that to the Santer's Commission, small states nominated exclusively politicians with ministerial experience. Nevertheless, the EU was composed of only four small states in comparison to 11 larger ones.

Within the group of small states, Denmark, Malta and Lithuania are consistent in nominating Commissioners who previously served as ministers in their respective countries. In Finland, Latvia, Estonia and Cyprus, all Commissioners nominated for the post had political careers within national executives, legislatures or in the European Parliament. No Commissioner has been appointed from these countries if she held 'lower' positions in public service.

Another analyzed pattern of appointment strategies is whether and, if so, to what extent member states nominate incumbents for a reappointment. Figure 2.4

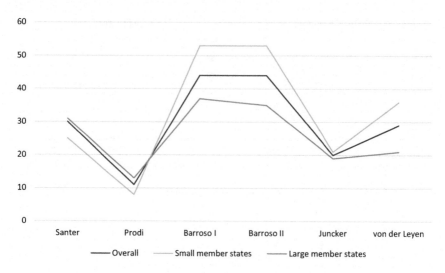

Figure 2.4 Proportion of reappointed incumbents (whole period, in %)

suggests that there is no significant difference between small and large member states. At this point, it must be stressed that an increase in the number of reappointments between Prodi and Barroso I Commission can be explained by the fact that member states that joined the EU in 2004 were represented in the College. However, these Members did not have assigned portfolios. On the other hand, it is evident that the second Barroso's Commission was very experienced, as almost half of the Members were reappointed by the member states. More specifically, 14 Commissioners were reappointed, eight of them by the small member states.

It is also important to note that all small member states had at least once their Commissioner reappointed for another term of office. In this regard, especially Slovakia and Finland tend to reappoint their incumbents most often.

The EC members are usually experienced politicians. Nevertheless, bearing in mind the growing number of policies at the EU level and the number of Commissioners, member states' policy preferences and priorities and administrative capacities (or lack thereof) of small states, it cannot be expected that Commissioners will be responsible for particular policies on equal terms. In other words, for example, it would be counterproductive to assign key portfolios related to the single market to every member state at some point. Moreover, the changing nature of some policy areas and the overlapping responsibilities of more Commissioners operating within project teams make it difficult to identify clear patterns of portfolio allocations. Despite that, some tentative observations can be made.

From a helicopter point of view, there seem to be six policy areas or portfolios which are quite often assigned to the representatives of the small EU states. These include humanitarian aid and crisis management; consumer protection; innovation, education, culture, research and youth; maritime affairs and fisheries; budget and human resources; and, to some extent, agriculture and rural development. On the other hand, there are some instances when small states, as conceptualized in this chapter, were in charge of portfolios directly related to the EU's single market. Such policy areas involve economic and monetary affairs and a single currency (Finland, Latvia, Luxembourg); internal market and services (Ireland); financial stability and capital markets (Latvia, Ireland); trade (Ireland); or competition (Denmark).

For the sake of completeness, as a part of the analysis, I was interested in the education of the Commissioners. In other words, I evaluated whether the Commissioners have a university degree. Except for one member of the EC serving in two Colleges, all others have/had a degree, and therefore, it is not necessary to provide exhaustive discussion or comparison in this respect.

2.4.3 Is there a place for small states' representatives in the EC's leadership positions?

In the last part of this section, attention is given to the political leadership within the Commission. It was demonstrated in Section 2.2.3 that the position of the EC President has become more important. Furthermore, besides the growing powers of EC Presidents, also competences and responsibilities of EC Vice-Presidents have undergone some developments. As a consequence, both Presidents and Vice-Presidents have a significant influence on the Commission's internal functioning and political performance of the Commission. The aim here is to evaluate whether the small member states have access to these leadership positions.

Since 1958, there have been 17 different Colleges. It happened only three times that the EC's Presidency was held by a representative of a small EU state (see also Döring, 2007). On all occasions, the President was a national of Luxembourg (Thorn, Santer, Juncker). In terms of the small-large states divide, more diversity can be seen in assigning roles of Vice-Presidents.

Between 1995 and 2023, the position of a Vice-President at the level of College was held 36 times. This number includes Vice-Presidents, First Vice-President of Juncker's College and three Executive Vice-Presidents in the current Commission. Nevertheless, for the purpose of the analysis as presented in Figure 2.5, I excluded one Vice-President from Barroso II, Juncker and von der Leyen Commissions. More specifically, I do not include positions of High Representative of the Union for Foreign Affairs and Security Policy. The rationale behind this decision is that granting the position of Vice-President of the Commission to a person holding an office of the High Representative does not fall under the EC President's discretion. According to the Lisbon Treaty, the High Representative is automatically one of the EC's Vice-Presidents. The three excluded High Representatives/Vice-Presidents of the EC are representatives of large member states (the United Kingdom, Italy and Spain). Thus, I took into account 33 appointments of Vice-Presidents made by Commission Presidents.

Figure 2.5 reveals that the use of Vice-Presidents became popular since Barroso's first term of office. It is worth repeating that the Vice-Presidents of Juncker's and von der Leyen's Commissions have far more powers. In the context

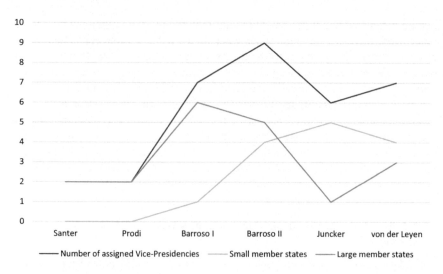

Figure 2.5 Distribution of Vice-Presidencies among small and large member states (whole period, in absolute numbers including replacements)

of the distribution of Vice-Presidencies, three observations can be made. First, in the first Barroso's College, only one Vice-President came from a small state (Estonian Commissioner Siim Kallas). From the Barroso II Commission on, small member states are represented in leadership positions at a level comparable (or even higher) with the large states. Second, the small states' Vice-Presidents dominated Juncker's Commission. Nevertheless, the second most powerful person of the Commission, the First Vice-President, was a national of a large state. The remaining five Vice-Presidents were Commissioners appointed by Bulgaria, Slovakia, Latvia, Estonia and Finland. Third, in the current Commission, President von der Leyen achieved an almost balanced distribution of Vice-Presidencies between small and large member states. Small states are represented by Commissioners coming from Denmark, Croatia, Slovakia and Latvia. What differentiates von der Leyen's Commission from the Colleges of her predecessors is that this time, small member states have a representation in the most powerful posts (i.e. Executive Vice-Presidents). Moreover, small states (Denmark and Latvia) hold two out of three positions.

Although the boundaries between access of small and large member states to leadership positions have narrowed down since 2010, the differences among small member states persist. Four small states (Ireland, Malta, Lithuania and Slovenia) have not had a Vice-President. For the sake of completeness, there also have been five larger states without a Vice-President since the mid-1990s.

This section has indicated that the small states consider it crucial to be part of the EC's politics on a regular basis as full members, and that they approach the nomination process seriously, or at least as seriously as their more populated counterparts. The question remains what lies behind their choices to propose particular candidates? There could be several possible explanations. Of course, assuming that the small states are well aware of the EC's importance, they nominate very experienced politicians for the post. However, there is also a possibility that the small member states' decisions are part of broader calculations or strategies. For example, by sending a politician having previous experiences as a prime minister, there can eventually be a higher propensity to get one of the leadership positions within the Commission. Similarly, knowing that the EC tries to achieve a gender-balanced composition of the College, small states can see a nomination of a female candidate as an opportunity to increase the chances of getting a more important portfolio, or one in line with their own preferences. Nevertheless, for the time being, there are no indications that the EC's President 'rewards' the governments proposing women (Scherpereel, 2023).

2.5 Conclusions and discussion

The analysis presented in this chapter allows us to make three broader conclusions with respect to the small states' perceptions towards the EC's role and their own representation within the EC, patterns of nomination of Commissioners by both small and large member states and developments in leadership within the EC and the influence small states have in the College.

As regards the first area, this chapter's findings go in line with previous work (e.g. Thorhallsson, 2000; Döring, 2007; Panke, 2016; Peterson, 2008; Wivel, 2010). Small states indeed perceive the EC as a promoter of the EU's general interest and especially stress its impartiality and independent position. These could be considered guarantees that the interests of all, but especially small, states are taken into account in EU politics. Moreover, small member states traditionally used to be proponents of the EC's higher involvement in EU politics and they usually were strongly against any proposals leading to the undermining of the EC's powers and position. Such perceptions and considerations naturally led small states 'to fight for their seat in the College' during the negotiations on institutional reforms of the Commission.

Second, even though it is not possible to observe clear differences between the nomination strategies of small and large member states, two remarks could be made. First, the analysis confirmed the ongoing tendency towards the politicization of the College as identified in previous studies (MacMullen, 1997; Wonka, 2007; Wille, 2012). The member states seem to choose their Commissioners carefully, and they usually opt for experienced politicians. An experienced appointee is mainly a person with experience from a top executive position in a national government (a prime minister or a minister). The second most represented group within a College usually is a Member with experience as a member of the European or a national parliament. Second, the EC at the level of College is no longer a 'Men's club' as was the case until the mid-1990s (MacMullen, 1997). The College has become more gender balanced. In this regard, especially the contribution of small states is important as the share of female Commissioners coming from small states is higher when compared to female EC members from large states.

As far as the leadership within the Commission is concerned, three developments affected the small states' influence on policies and politics within the EC. During the second Barroso's College, small member states' Commissioners were appointed as Vice-Presidents to a larger extent. In Juncker's Commission, the small states dominated in holding Vice-Presidencies, this time with way more powers assigned to these leadership positions. In von der Leyen's College, there is no significant difference in the number of Vice-Presidents nominated by small and large member states. Most importantly, small states hold the majority of most influential leadership positions (apart from the EC Presidency).

Despite the mentioned empirical observations, the analysis as presented in this study suffers from some major limitations which are quite typical features of many endeavours to study politics within the EC. Generally speaking, it is very challenging to conduct research on EC members as there are no public data on voting patterns (in occasions when a vote is actually taken) nor presentations of conflicting views of particular members due to the collegiality requirement (Deckarm, 2017; Smith, 2003). For that reason, future research should focus on different data-gathering techniques such as semi-structured interviews in order to find out what role small states truly play in the Commission's politics. Moreover, the rationales behind the selection strategies of small member states would provide us with a better picture of how they really think about the EC's role in the EU, beyond the well-known tasks the EC should perform according to the Treaties.

The role of the EC within the EU and its institutional framework is indispensable. So it is for the interests of the small member states. Recent developments suggest that the small states could influence EC politics well beyond holding a policy portfolio. The composition of the current College demonstrates the fact that even small states can have great responsibilities and powers in EU politics.

Bibliography

Austrian Permanent Representation. (2000). *Basic principles of Austria's position*, 15 February 2000, CONFER 4712/00. Available at https://www.cvce.eu/en/obj/basic _principles_of_austria_s_position_for_the_igc_on_institutional_matters_10_february _2000-en-7fc9caea-a9ec-4b8f-abbb-5bc1cb9579ef.html.

Benelux. (2002). *Memorandum of the Benelux: A balanced Institutional framework for an enlarged, more effective and more transparent Union*, 11 December 2002, CONV 457/02.

Böttner, R. (2018). The size and structure of the European Commission: legal issues surrounding project teams and a (future) reduced College. *European Constitutional Law Review* 14(1): 37–61.

Bulgaria. (2003). *Bulgarian answers concerning the Commission and the Foreign Minister.* CIG6/03.

Bunse, S., Magnette, P. and Nicolaïdis, K. (2005). Is the Commission the Small Member States' Best Friend?. *Sieps: Swedish Institute for European Policy Studies* 2005(9). Available at https://www.sieps.se/en/publications/2005/is-the-commission-the-small -member-states-best-friend-20059/.

Bürgin, A. (2018). Intra- and Inter-Institutional Leadership of the European Commission President: An Assessment of Juncker's Organizational Reforms. *Journal of Common Market Studies* 56(4): 837–853.

Deckarm, R. (2017). The countries they know best: how national principals influence European commissioners and their cabinets. *Journal of European Public Policy* 24(3): 447–466.

Dehousse, F. (2000). The Treaty of Nice? A Watershed in the History of European Integration. *Studia Diplomatica* 53(6): 19–42.

Döring, H. (2007). The Composition of the College of Commissioners: patterns of delegation. *European Union Politics* 8(2): 207–228.

Egeberg, M. (2006). Executive politics as usual: role behaviour and conflict dimensions in the College of European Commissioners. *Journal of European Public Policy* 13(1): 1–15.

European Commission. (2014). *The Working Methods of the European Commission 2014–2019*. C(2014) 9004.

European Commission. (2019). *The Working Methods of the European Commission*. P(2019) 2. Available at https://commission.europa.eu/document/download/325a45ef-a6b1-4e14-bc3c-863e2f53a957_en?filename=working-methods.pdf.

Geurts, C.M. (1998). The European Commission: A Natural Ally of Small States in the EU Institutional Framework? In: L. Goetschel (ed.), *Small States Inside and Outside the European Union* (Springer: New York), pp. 49–64.

Government of Cyprus. (2000). *IGC 2000: Contribution from the Government of Cyprus*, 24 February 2000, CONFER/VAR 3951/00. Available at http://www.proyectos.cchs.csic.es/euroconstitution/library/historic%20documents/Nice/Negotiation/Contribution%20from%20the%20government%20of%20Cyprus.pdf.

Gray, M. and Stubb, A. (2001). The Treaty of Nice – Negotiating a Poisoned Chalice? *Journal of Common Market Studies* 39 (S1): 6–23.

Hamřík, L. (2021). Is there any 'price' for making individual EU politicians more important? The personalisation of politics in the European Commission. *Journal of European Integration* 43(4): 403–420.

Kassim, H. (2017). What´s new? A first appraisal of the Juncker Commission. *European Political Science* 16(1): 14–33.

Kassim, H., Connolly, S., Dehousse, R., Rozenberg, O. and Bendjaballah, S. (2017). Managing the house: the Presidency, agenda control and policy activism in the European Commission. *Journal of European Public Policy* 24(5): 653–674.

Kirpsza, A. (2024). Not so independent? The effect of Commissioners' attributes on EU member states' bargaining success. *West European Politics, Early View* 47(4): 915–941.

MacMullen, A. (1997). European Commissioners 1952–1995: National Routes to a European elite. In: N. Nugent (ed.), *At the Heart of the Union: Studies of the European Commission* (Macmillan Press Ltd: London), pp. 27–48.

Magnette, P. and Nicolaïdis, K. (2003). Large and small member states in the European Union: Reinventing the balance. *Notre Europe: Research and European Issues* 25. Available at https://institutdelors.eu/wp-content/uploads/2018/01/etud25-en.pdf.

Nicolaïdis, K. and Bunse, S. (2012). Large Versus Small States: Anti-Hegemony and the Politics of Shared Leadership. In: E. Jones, A. Menon and S. Weatherill (eds.), *The Oxford Handbook of the European Union* (Oxford University Press: Oxford), pp. 249–266.

OJEU (Official Journal of the European Union). (2012). *Consolidated version of the treaty on European Union*. C 326/13.

Panke, D. (2016). *Small States in the European Union: Coping with Structural Disadvantages* (Routledge: New York).

Peterson, J. (2008). Enlargement, reform and the European Commission. Weathering a perfect storm? *Journal of European Public Policy* 15(5): 761–780.

Phinnemore, D. (2013). *The Treaty of Lisbon: Origins and Negotiation* (Palgrave Macmillan: Basingstoke).

Piris, J.-C. (2010). *The Lisbon Treaty: A Legal and Political Analysis* (Cambridge University Press: Cambridge).

Scherpereel, J.A. (2023). Pursuing 'full gender equality' in the European Commission: the case of a constrained selector. *European Politics and Society* 24(3): 317–335.

Schmidt, S.K. and Wonka, A. (2012). European Commission. In: E. Jones, A. Menon and S. Weatherill (eds.), *The Oxford Handbook of the European Union* (Oxford University Press: Oxford), pp. 336–349.

Smith, A. (2003). Why European Commissioners Matter. *Journal of Common Market Studies* 41(1): 137–155.

Thomson, R. and Dumont, P. (2022). A comparison of two views on the European Commission: engine of integration and conduit of national interests. *Journal of European Public Policy* 29(1): 136–154.

Thorhallsson, B. (2000). *The Role of Small States in the European Union* (Ashgate: Farnham).

Thorhallsson, B. and Wivel, A. (2006). Small States in the European Union: What Do We Know and What Would We Like to Know? *Cambridge Review of International Affairs* 19(4): 651–668.

Wille, A. (2012). The politicization of the EU Commission: democratic control and the dynamics of executive selection. *International Review of Administrative Sciences* 78(3): 383–402.

Wivel, A. (2010). From Small State to Smart State: Devising a Strategy for Influence in the European Union. In: R. Steinmetz and A. Wivel (eds.), *Small States in Europe: Challenges and Opportunities* (Ashgate: Farnham), pp. 15–29.

Wonka, A. (2007). Technocratic and independent? The appointment of European Commissioners and its policy implications. *Journal of European Public Policy* 14(2): 169–189.

3 Small states in the European Parliament

Does size make a difference?

Anna-Lena Högenauer

3.1 Introduction

In the design of the European Parliament (EP), the size of the member states clearly matters. The EP is, and has always been, a body within which the residents of member states are represented according to the principle of degressive proportionality. In other words, larger member states have more seats than smaller member states, though not as many as they would have if proportionality were strictly applied. For example, the three smallest states, Malta, Luxembourg and Cyprus, each have six seats, which represents 0.85 per cent of the total number of seats (705), despite the fact that each of their populations accounts for only 0.1–0.2 per cent of the total population of the EU.

Even though small states are mathematically overrepresented in the European Parliament, one could describe it as the most structurally challenging EU institution for small states: every member state sends a Commissioner to the European Commission. In the Council, some decisions are taken by unanimity, which gives each state veto power – at least in theory. While the literature acknowledges that small states are less likely to make use of the veto in order to maintain the goodwill of larger states, they can nevertheless use the threat of a veto to push for compromises (Mattila, 2004; similarly Slapin, 2011, on how the power to veto allows small states influence on Treaty negotiations). In cases where the Council decides by qualified majority, which requires the majority to represent 65 per cent of EU citizens and 55 per cent of EU states, the smallest of the small states are fairly irrelevant for the first criterion but have equal weight to all other states under the second criterion. In addition, the Council often decides by consensus in cases where it could use a qualified majority, which also gives small states room to negotiate. Thus, all things considered, plenary votes in the European Parliament, where small states hold as little as 0.85 per cent of seats, are the point in the decision-making process where they are at their weakest.

Of course, one of the questions in that regard is who or what MEPs represent: while the European Parliament was originally composed of delegations from national parliaments, MEPs decided almost immediately to organize themselves in political groups rather than by member states. While this gives the European Parliament a *supranational* dimension, the national dimension remains strong: more than 40 years after the introduction of direct elections to the EP in 1979,

DOI: 10.4324/9781003380641-4

European elections remain fragmented and are – in reality – the sum of simultaneously organized national contests. Candidates to EP elections are nominated by *national* parties. Overall, individual MEPs are not elected by 'the European citizens' but primarily by the citizens of the country in which they contest the election and in addition by some EU residents of that country who may also choose to cast their vote there. Even the electoral system varies across countries. As a result, MEPs see themselves sometimes as European representatives and sometimes as representatives of the citizens and residents of their country. This comes through both in the interviews for this chapter, where MEPs speak about the importance of checking the items of the voting lists from the perspective of their country and about key issues where they voted differently from their European party group, and in the wider literature on voting behaviour, which argues that both European party cohesion and national voting play a role (Cicchi, 2011; Finke, 2015). Similarly, Slapin and Proksch (2010) find evidence of dissenting MEPs using plenary debates to explain their national party's stance. The interviews for this chapter show that government MEPs in particular feel that it would be awkward if they voted differently from the national government on issues that are nationally salient.

Beyond the problem of the votes, a low number of Members of the European Parliament (MEPs) raises other questions, such as the question of whether they can cover all policy areas. Fewer MEPs means not only fewer politicians but also fewer assistants. This can be seen as the EP equivalent of the challenge of small administrations and fewer financial resources that the literature has identified in the context of Council negotiations (Panke, 2010a). Fewer people mean a limited ability to produce expertise across a wide range of issues, which in turn jeopardizes the ability of MEPs to argue effectively and persuade others to join their cause (cf. Soetendorp and Hanf, 1998, on the importance of well-staffed ministries in the context of the Council; Laffan, 2006).

Despite these challenges, the small-state literature has barely touched the European Parliament to date, and we know almost nothing about what kind of challenges MEPs from small states encounter and how they affect their work. Authors like Thorhallsson and Wivel (2006), Björkdahl (2008), Haughton (2010) or Panke (2010a, 2011) have focused almost exclusively on the European Council, the Council of the European Union and the European Commission. In order to close this gap and line with the research questions set out in the introduction to this volume, this chapter thus aims to explore the specific challenges that small-state MEPs encounter and how these challenges affect their work (Högenauer and Mišík, 2024).

As this chapter focuses on the challenges and strategies of small states in the European Parliament, its definition of 'small states' follows the common approach of this volume and uses population size as the main reference point (Högenauer and Mišík, 2024). This measure is particularly relevant as it directly influences the number of MEPs who are sent to the European Parliament by the different states. It explores the question through eight qualitative in-depth interviews with MEPs from Malta and Luxembourg, the two smallest EU member states, which have a population of roughly 540,000 (Malta) and 660,000 (Luxembourg) and thus together account for less than 0.3 per cent of the EU's total population (Eurostat, 2023). Together with Cyprus, the two countries are among the three member states with only six MEPs. However, while they are both small, they represent somewhat different cases, with Luxembourg having been part of European integration since the beginning, while Malta joined in 2004, and with Luxembourg being at the heart of Europe, while Malta is a remote island state. These two factors could potentially influence the length of travel to the EP, the perceived centrality of EU politics for the country and the experience of politicians in navigating EU institutions. Panke (2010a) also found in the context of the Council that some small states, like Denmark, Luxembourg, Belgium and Ireland, are far more active in deploying 'shaping strategies' than, for example, Cyprus, Estonia, Greece, Malta and Bulgaria. This makes the pairing of Luxembourg and Malta also relevant.

In light of the lack of literature, the chapter will only briefly summarize the few studies that touch on the EP and some insights from the literature on the Council that could be relevant also to the EP. It will then discuss the main insights from the interviews with a view to understanding the effects of smallness in the case of the European Parliament. It will conclude with some reflections on the transferability of these insights to other small- and medium-sized states.

3.2 A gap in the literature

Unfortunately, the small-state literature is primarily concerned with the security dilemmas of small states, their foreign policies and intergovernmental negotiation strategies. It thus focuses on their motivations for joining international organizations and – in an EU context – primarily on the Council and European Council as the key foreign and security policy actors. As a result, the dynamics in the European Parliament, which is an equal co-legislator in most policy areas, are usually (almost) completely left out. For instance, the work of Jakobsen (2009) on the Nordic influence on the civilian European Security and Defense Policy (ESDP), Björkdahl (2008) on norm advocacy in the EU in the context of Common Foreign and Security Policy (CFSP) and ESDP, Bailes and Thorhallsson (2013) on the security concerns in the context of the EU, Thorhallsson and Wivel (2006) on small states in the European Union, Panke (2010b) on the structural disadvantage of small states in the EU and Panke and Gurol (2018) on Council Presidencies completely blend out the parliamentary side of EU politics. The strong impact of the international relations and traditional security and defence policy perspective on small state studies in an EU context can also be seen in Wivel (2010), where treaty changes that impact small states are discussed but without any reference to the European Parliament. Scholars who work on what constitutes the bulk of EU policy-making – internal policies – might have reflected on the impact of the empowerment of the EP through various treaty changes, including, for example, the extension of the co-decision procedure, which is now the Ordinary Legislative Procedure, on small state influence. After all, while the Council still heavily relies on consensus and protects small member states to some extent even under qualified majority voting, individual small states have very little weight in the EP. In addition, aside from the fact that many small states pursue important economic priorities in the EU, many of the new and soft security challenges would also fall under the Ordinary Legislative Procedure. Thus, the very narrow focus on the Council becomes increasingly problematic.

An exception is Panke (2010a), where the EP is mentioned in passing in the context of a study that focuses primarily on small states in the Council. Thus, she notes that not all member states lobby the European Parliament equally much, with Denmark, Sweden, Finland and Luxembourg being the most active countries (p. 131). She also finds that states that lobby the European Parliament and/or engage in general arguing and problem-solving are more likely to be successful in nego-tiations. However, the effectiveness of lobbying the EP does not depend on the number of seats a state has but on whether they target the relevant rapporteur and committee chair. The qualitative case studies in the book confirm these findings, but as they focus on how the *government* lobbied, they provide few insights into the work of small-state *MEPs*.

Beyond this, the literature on the Council argues that the limited bargaining capacities can be mitigated through several strategies. One of these is cooperation and coalition building with other states, either in an institutionalized manner like the BENELUX or in a more ad hoc manner (Thorhallsson and Wivel, 2006; Panke, 2010a). Second, small states can set narrower priorities in order to focus their lim-ited resources on key issues. Thorhallsson and Wivel argue, for instance, that small states are more likely to 'emphasize positive influence,' i.e., they focus on obtain-ing key decisions and do not have the resources to block decisions 'that are not directly in their favour' (Thorhallsson and Wivel, 2006: 659; Panke, 2010a). The inability of small states to force through decisions and their tendency to try and obtain compromises through persuasion can be an advantage when it allows them to act as 'honest broker' (Harmsen and Högenauer, 2021).

From the literature, it is unclear whether and to what extent these strategies are relevant in the context of the European Parliament, so the interviews also looked at indications of what a small state strategy in the European Parliament could look like and whether these elements were part of it.

3.3 The effect of state size on MEPs

In the absence of a body of literature on the effect of state size on the work of MEPs, the aim of this chapter is to present an exploratory study. The core of this study consists of eight qualitative in-depth interviews with five out of the six current Luxembourgish MEPs and three out of the six current Maltese MEPs. Originally the aim was to also interview MEPs from the previous term, but all of those either could not be contacted or declined. The Luxembourgish interviewees cover all four Luxembourgish parties that are represented in the EP. The Maltese MEPs are unfortunately all from the Socialist and Democrat (S&D) group, with the two EPP MEPs unavailable due to their busy schedules. However, despite these limitations, it should be noted that the responses of the different interviewees are relatively con-sistent within and across cases and that the final interviews largely confirmed and further illustrated earlier responses. It is thus unlikely that additional interviews would have yielded substantially different responses. The main difference is that MEPs from government parties tend to be more aware of and inclined to represent the position of their government. However, opposition MEPs still consider the views of their national party and its interpretation of the interests of their country.

In addition to the interview data, the empirical analysis relies on data gathered from the official CVs of MEPs and data collection on the official website of the European Parliament. The interviews and data collection took place in the spring and early summer of 2023.

The interviews identified two core challenges for small-state MEPs: first, the difficulty of covering the work of the European Parliament with few people, and the related difficulty of covering all national priorities and of meeting the expectations of constituents with so few people, and second, the role of size in the distribution of post within party groups and the EP.

3.3.1 So many policies, so few people

The first and probably most fundamental impact of the size of the member state on the work of MEPs is felt already right after joining the European Parliament: as the new (or re-elected) MEPs enter parliament, they have to join committees as members and substitutes. At this point, it becomes obvious that the number of committees – currently 20 standing committees and four subcommittees – exceeds the number of MEPs from smaller states. As a result, there is yet another problem that makes the EP more challenging than the Council – member states are represented in all Council formations but not in all parliamentary committees. Of course, the same is even more true for national delegations (e.g. the Luxembourgish MEPs from a specific party), which are even smaller. Thus, one of the first questions is whether this affects how MEPs choose committees, and the second question would be whether they try to coordinate with all MEPs from their country, or at least with those from their own party, in order to ensure a good coverage of a range of topics. A third question is how it affects the work of MEPs once they have chosen their committees.

Both the Luxembourgish and Maltese MEPs indicated that the choice of committees was based on a combination of personal preferences, the priorities of the national party and some degree of coordination with MEPs from the same party (Malta) or at least similarly minded parties (e.g. government parties in Luxembourg). However, the exact motivation varies from MEP to MEP, especially in the case of Luxembourg where the delegations comprise only one to two people. Thus, one MEP felt that their national party relied on them to pick up the most relevant topics for the party, but at the same time you need the approval of the European party group. Coordination with other MEPs from Luxembourg was not important for them, because they felt that the priorities of their party were clear (Interview 4). Another long-standing MEP felt that the decision should be made based on personal expertise and passion (Interview 8).

However, most other MEPs coordinated at least a bit with party colleagues or colleagues from close parties (e.g. coalition partners at home). For example, one

Luxembourgish MEP joined the EP a little later as he replaced another MEP who left. But he then realized that there were other Luxembourgers in his committees, which annoyed him, as there were so few Luxembourgers to begin with. So he moved to the IMCO, which deals with the internal market and other crucial topics. He has the impression that the Permanent Representation also approved of this decision, which led to the coverage of another important policy area (Interview 5). Interviewees 6 and 7 also coordinated among themselves to cover different issues. Similarly, according to interviewee 2, 'it was up to us to choose [the committees]. However, obviously, the direction is to try to be in as many committees as possible.' Interviewee 1 pointed out the risk of some important policies getting left out, for example, agriculture in the current term:

> You can't cover everything with a small number of MEPs. What happens usually is that you get coordinating mechanisms at party level. And coordination with the government if the party is in government in Malta. So, what we did do was that we selected what the salient committees were, e.g. ECON, BUDGET for me, Social affairs, ITRE, Juri etc. on the legal side for other people.

Of course, having your 'own' committee can also be politically advantageous, especially if the topic is of interest to the domestic audience. You can then use your expertise to stand out and make yourself better known, which would be more difficult if there were several experts (Interview 5).

As Table 3.1 shows, Luxembourg's six MEPs do indeed manage to cover 15/20 committees and 3/4 subcommittees. Among those areas that are not covered, some are clearly not among the priorities of an economically prosperous landlocked small state with currently peaceful neighbours, namely defence, fisheries and regional development. On the other hand, the one committee that three people chose as substitutes – Economic and Monetary Affairs – has an obvious relevance for a state with a strong financial sector. By contrast, the Maltese MEPs cover only 11 committees and one of the subcommittees. Of course, it has to be said that Roberta Metsola does not have a committee while she is serving as President of the European Parliament, and that Malta thus has only five MEPs who cover committee work. However, the main reason for the difference in coverage is that the Luxembourgish MEPs chose to become members of two to three committees and substitute of around two committees each, while the Maltese MEPs usually are members of only one committee and substitute for two committees.

There are different possible explanations for these different strategies. One could link this to the findings of Panke (2010) that suggest that Luxembourg is also more active in the Council due to its longer experience with EU politics and more specialized staff. However, the real explanation in this case is probably due to geography and electoral systems: First, Malta is very remote, which means that Maltese MEPs need more time to travel to Brussels and thus have less time to work. In addition, there are only a limited number of direct flights, and those are not always at a convenient time. Second, Malta uses a single transferable vote

Table 3.1 Committee coverage in 2023

	Luxembourg	Malta
Foreign Affairs	**Wiseler-Lima**	
Subcommittee Human Rights	**Goerens, Wiseler-Lima**	
Subcommittee Security and Defense		
Development	**Goerens**	
International Trade	**Hansen**	
Budgets	Goerens	Sant
Budgetary Control		
Economic and Monetary Affairs	Semedo, Angel, Hansen	**Sant**, Casa
Subcommittee Tax Matters	**Hansen**, Semedo	Sant
Employment and Social Affairs	**Semedo, Angel**	**Casa**, Agius Saliba
Environment, Public Health and Food Safety	**Metz**, Hansen	**Engerer**
Subcommittee Public Health	**Metz**	
Industry, Research Energy	Wiseler-Lima	Agius Saliba, **Cutajar**
Internal Market and Consumer Protection	Angel	**Agius Saliba**
Transport and Tourism	**Metz**	Cutajar
Regional Development		Cutajar
Agriculture and Rural Development	Goerens, Metz	
Fisheries		
Culture and Education	**Semedo**	
Legal Affairs		
Civil Liberties, Justice and Home Affairs	Wiseler-Lima	Engerer
Constitutional Affairs	**Goerens**	Engerer
Women's Rights and Gender Equality		
Petitions	**Angel**	**Sant, Agius Saliba**

This list only covers standing committees and subcommittees, not special committees or committees of inquiry. Names in bold are full members; the other names represent substitute members.

system, which means that candidates cannot rely on votes from a party list but must canvas votes for themselves. Several interviewees reported that they felt that there was a strong expectation from the voters that the MEPs should be close to the citizens, e.g., 'the combination of our electoral system plus being in the periphery is very challenging. And I cannot afford to not go home, as there will be complaints in the papers' (Interview 2). Similarly, Interviewee 3 reported that 'the other challenge, however, of being an MEP is that I'm still expected to be quite close to my constituency even if I spend most of my time away.' Thus, all three Maltese MEPs reported that they would fly to Brussels on Monday and then be available from the afternoon onwards, and that they would leave Brussels on Thursday, usually in the morning so that they could meet with people in Malta in the evening (Interview 1; Interview 2; Interview 3). This only gives them two and a half days in Brussels.

In comparison, Luxembourg is close to Brussels. MEPs can get there by train in three to four hours and by car in around two hours if the traffic is good. As a result, the Luxembourgish MEPs arrive earlier on Monday and usually spend at least part of and often the whole of Thursday in Brussels. While Luxembourg has an open list system where a substantial proportion of voters also vote for candidates rather than parties, the pressure on individual candidates is not quite as high as there is a party vote that contributes to their success. In addition, the proximity makes it possible to maintain a relatively high level of presence in both Brussels (or Strasbourg) and Luxembourg (Interview 5; Interview 7). Christophe Hansen, for example, manages to combine his post of MEP with the role of Secretary-General of the CSV, Luxembourg's Christian Democrat party. He greatly benefits from the fact that he can attend meetings in the evening in Luxembourg if necessary and drive back and forth. Other MEPs have also reported being able to attend important gatherings with constituents during the week with only a marginal impact on their work in parliament.

However, another question that is raised by the choice of committee membership is whether there is much of a difference between member and substitute. In theory, the idea is that members should actively participate in the work of a committee, whereas substitutes are meant to be replacements for members who cannot attend. However, in the context of the European Parliament, substitute members can de facto also actively participate in the work of the committee. They can even be rapporteurs, i.e., be in charge of guiding key legislative files through the committee and parliament. The main difference is that substitutes cannot vote in the committee.

MEPs are of course not obliged to actively follow the work of committees for which they are substitutes. Interestingly, though, many interviewees reported that they did follow the work of all their committees either personally (for important issues) or via their assistants, who can listen in on committee meetings (but not participate). One MEP joked that he did not know if the members of one of his committees knew that he was only a substitute. For strategic reasons, he was very present in that committee and had been rapporteur for a file, because these issues mattered domestically (Interview 5). A number of MEPs pointed towards concrete work that they had done for the committees for which they were substitutes. One MEP reported that 'literally, there is no difference between where I am a full member and where I am a substitute. I give the same energy and time to all three committees I am in. In fact, some of the most important reports I have taken care of were not in my main committee, but in the LIBE and AFCO Committees.' Another example was a Luxembourgish MEP who got to work on the Farm to Fork Strategy in the Committee for Agriculture, for which she was only a substitute (Interview 4), and one who worked on the Drinking Water Directive and the strategy for the Common Agricultural Policy (Interview 7).

On the other hand, there were also MEPs who found it difficult to cover the additional committees and who relied primarily on their assistants for this, except for a very select number of files (Interview 6). Another MEP, who already was vice chair of one committee and coordinator of another, also had no time to personally follow other committees (Interview 8). The problem is also that some committee meetings will happen at the same time. For example, one MEP who had two main committees said that he asked his assistant to monitor the committee for which he was a substitute, as he had to go to the two other ones in person as both were important (Interview 1).

Thus, while the literature on the Council pointed at 'prioritization' as a strategy for successful engagement with EU politics, Maltese and Luxembourgish MEPs generally felt that specialization was the privilege of MEPs from large states: large-state MEPs were generally perceived as focusing on their main committee, with a much lower likelihood and intensity of engagement in other committees. Some MEPs were even perceived as specializing on specific issues within their committee, as there were other MEPs from their country and party who could cover other aspects. For example, according to Interview 2, 'I would also say that [. . .] in the ENVI Committee, where I am a full member, you get Germans focusing only on the ENVI Committee, but then each one of them focuses on a separate issue. For example, climate, waste, or health.' Another MEP had the same impression for IMCO, where several Germans from the same party were dividing the work, whereas he got to speak on all issues and had more pressure to cover issues from several committees (Interview 5).

By contrast, the small-state MEPs all reported that they had to pick up issues from committees for which they were substitutes at least occasionally, because they were deemed relevant for their country, party and/or constituents. According to Interviewee 3:

it would mean that you won't have a member in a lot of committees. Despite that there are issues that affect the country that you are coming from and files that are very important actually. So that would mean that sometimes you are asked to look into issues which are part of other committees' work which we are not equipped well to have the knowledge on. And try to put the national points there too.

The voting sessions in the plenary are also a bigger challenge for small-state MEPs. The European party groups issue of course recommendations on which amendments to support. However, on some issues your national party has a different view, for example, on the nuclear energy or genetically modified organisms in the case of Luxembourg's CSV (Interview 7). If you want to know how the amendments and proposals affect your country, you sometimes have only one to two MEPs from that national party, so coordination is easy, but the workload is high (Interview 6). You can still try to coordinate with MEPs from other parties from your country that you know have a similar position on these issues. MEPs from governing parties are under more pressure, as the opposition or the media might pick up on the fact that the MEPs from coalition parties voted differently on an important file (Interview 5). Interviewee 3 also pointed out this problem:

Coming from a small member state would mean that we would have a number of files across committees where Malta's position will differ first of all due to limited resources, insularity, the limited market size, other aspects etc. Thus some rules that are meant for continental countries affect us in a

negative manner. And even when it comes to assessing how we vote at plenary stage, there are long voting lists, amendments coming up until the end
of the day that we are voting on, and we sometimes have a limited capacity.
Apart from the limited number of MEPs, which would mean that you would
have to work more – in the sense of being spread more thinly.

And, finally, their constituents and the media expect them to be able to speak about
current issues and issues that are deemed important irrespective of committee membership. It would be difficult to decline requests to comment especially if there is no
other MEP from your country who you can name as specialist in that area (Interview
3). It should be noted that both the Luxembourgish MEPs who join more committees
and the Maltese MEPs who join fewer committees agree on the need to be able to sat-
isfy the expectations of the media and constituents on all topics and pointed to the difficulty of reconciling the work in the EP which requires specialization and expertise
with the pressure to be able to speak about everything. For example, the Green MEP
from Luxembourg felt that 'as the only Green MEP for Luxembourg she could not
allow herself to not be well-informed about a core Green issue. I am not a member of
the energy etc. committee, but if somebody asks me about the new Directive, then I
have to know about that' (Interview 4). Another MEP pointed out the importance of
being able to discuss all crises, which generally interested the voters (Interview 8).

Thus, a first major impact of smallness in the context of the EP is the pressure
to cover more topics both within the European Parliament and in the relations with
national media and constituents. There is also a greater need to coordinate at least a
little bit to ensure that the most important issues are covered by the limited number of
MEPs. And, last but not least, MEPs depend more on their assistants who need to help
monitor the various committees, follow up on the many files that small-state MEPs
handle simultaneously and assist with the analysis of amendments and voting lists.

3.3.2 Securing positions of power in the EP

A second area where smallness creates a challenge is in the distribution of posts
both within the European Parliament in general and within the political groups. The
reason is that many posts depend on the weight of the national delegation, i.e., the
number of MEPs within a party group who come from a specific country. For other
positions, the larger states control the votes: 'They can gang up – two to three big
guys [delegations] together, and they can control the cake' (Interview 1). In other
words, when several big delegations agree on a distribution of certain posts among
themselves, it is extremely difficult to reverse this (Interview 5). For example, the
vice presidency of one of the party groups in the EP was lost by Malta to another
national delegation because of larger delegations agreeing to redistribute it. It took
a lot of hard lobbying to gather enough votes to reverse that decision the next time
the positions were distributed (Interview 1; Interview 6).

Indeed, the S&D was perceived as particularly difficult terrain by some of its
MEPs who pointed out that the president of the S&D is almost always from the biggest delegation, i.e., German, Italian or Spanish. The EPP was perceived as more

open (Interview 2). Indeed, the EPP's support for Roberta Metsola as President of the European Parliament was perceived very positively even by interviewees from the other parties. On the other hand, there are sometimes opportunities opening up. For example, Mark Angel became S&D Vice-President following the corruption scandals of the party group. In the brief moment of chaos that followed a resignation, there were a lot of candidates for the position, but the large states refrained from putting forward their own candidates, and he managed to build a successful coalition. The small states were particularly supportive. An advantage may have been that small delegations cannot push through their own agendas and need to build large coalitions with other states. This idea of a vice-president who has to build compromises may have appealed to the other small delegations (Interview 5). However, the additional step to becominge president of a committee would be extremely difficult to achieve mathematically, as you really need the backing of a strong delegation.

One way to overcome smallness is to get 'adopted' by a larger delegation. Some one-(wo)man delegations join a different national delegation from their party group that tends to hold similar views. That way the bigger delegation gains more weight, and the individual MEP gets some back up (Interview 4). For one MEP that worked out quite well. She wanted to become chair of the committee of inquiry on animal transports and succeeded with the help of the French delegation that had 'adopted' her. Of course, this only works if this delegation does not have its own candidate for the position (Interview 4).

3.3.3 Strategies for coping with the effects of smallness

In the case of the Council, coordination and coalition building were identified as important ways to mitigate smallness. In the European Parliament these elements are also present but used more selectively. The most important point of support is the Permanent Representation (PermRep) of the member state. Both Maltese and Luxembourgish interviewees highlighted the importance of the information received by the PermRep of their country. As noted previously, the small size of the national delegations means that a small number of people need to understand how all EP votes in all areas affect their member states. Even those MEPs who focus on the European level in their engagement feel that an understanding of the national context was important (Interview 5). Background information from the PermRep helps MEPs to accomplish that task. For the most part the PermRep would organize regular, often monthly meetings (Interview 2, Malta) or before the Strasbourg week (Interview 5, Luxembourg). Most of the time the assistants would attend these to receive background information on the current files and on how they might affect Malta or Luxembourg. However, 'if something big is going on, there is some kind of coordination with the ambassador directly. For example, when Malta had rule of law issues, we had to report back to the Ambassador directly what was being said in the EP' (Interview 1). In the case of Malta, there would often be two separate meetings, one for each of the two parties (Interview 2).

The PermRep would perform different functions: sometimes it would act as a post box that just transmits information between the EP and the Ministries.

Sometimes it would have desk officers who follow dossiers more proactively. MEPs generally appreciate the support. One MEP explained the importance of this support when you are a rapporteur: 'I am at the moment rapporteur on the Listing Act. I consulted them to check, what their position on that one is. And that is happening all the time' (Interview 1; also Interview 5). However, because of the smaller size and more limited resources of the PermRep, some interviewees were worried about receiving information on some files later than the MEPs from other states (Interview 3).

Whereas the MEPs from Luxembourg felt that the government was quite laid back and rarely asked them to defend a specific position (Interview 6; Interview 8), the Maltese Laburista MEPs, who are from the same party as their government, reported that they were often encouraged to represent the position of the government, especially on important issues (Interview 2). 'They tell us what their views are on crucial votes in the plenary – what they like, dislike etc. Basically, when they tell us to lobby on an area, we do it' (Interview 1). 'We do have a specific system, where all six MEPs can ask the Maltese government to give us the government's position on a specific file before a vote or an important debate, and that position is not only sent to the member who asks for it, but to the six MEPs' (Interview 1). An example is the green taxes on airplane kerosine, which were seen to affect Malta as an island particularly negatively. In addition, there were concerns about competition from North Africa, as those airlines did not face the same taxes.

Some Luxembourgish MEPs also coordinate with the government ministers from their party, though. For example, one MEP said that she tries to participate in the meetings of her party group from the national parliament so that she is informed about their position and tries to follow the position of the minister from her party. If she does not know what the position of her party is, she will also contact the minister's office and ask. On important issues, she might also ask the PermRep about the ministers of the other parties (Interview 4). Another government MEP also reported joining the meetings of his party's national parliamentary group as well as the meetings of the European Affairs Committee of the national parliament (Interview 5). However, another government MEP said that the government did not contact him very proactively (Interview 8), and the opposition MEPs felt that the Luxembourgish government was not very active but also pointed out that there was no real tradition of sending detailed positions to MEPs. Other states were perceived as much pushier in that regard (Interview 7).

Cross-party coalitions of MEPs from the same state do exist but are rare. While MEPs for the most part vote with their party groups rather than their countries, there are exceptions where a national cross-party consensus exists on key files: for example, the issue of tax harmonization in the EU was pushed by the S&D but was disliked by all Maltese MEPs. Another example is the move towards more qualified majority voting in the Council, where there is quite a strong consensus in favour of QMV building up on the left and on the right, but the Maltese MEPs dislike it (Interview 1). Another MEP provided the example of the Mobility Package, where the EP was divided not between parties but central countries versus Eastern countries + Malta + Cyprus. As the Maltese industry was very concerned, she decided to coordinate a common Maltese approach to the amendments in the EP. Essentially, the goal of the legislation was to introduce rest periods and the mandatory return of the trucks to their place of establishment. For Malta, the truck and driver would usually stay in Italy, and only the containers would be shipped on to Malta, which is far more practical than to ship entire trucks. The set of laws was adopted, but it remains controversial. These examples notwithstanding, it is relatively rare that the Maltese MEPs explicitly collaborate, as the two-party system tends to promote an adversarial spirit: 'We do not meet as the six of us. Unfortunately, the political situation in Malta is very much divided, where there isn't much communication between both sides' (Interview 2). In the case of Luxembourg, there are also examples for cross-party cooperation, for example, on supporting Esch-sur-Alzette on the way to become a cultural capital of Europe. Similarly, they sometimes organize visits for students jointly.

3.3.4 Does smallness have a sunny side?

While smallness is undoubtedly a challenge that can only be addressed through a broader engagement with EU politics compared to large states, it also has pleasant side effects. Several interviewees from Malta and Luxembourg highlighted the ease with which delegations consisting of two to four people could coordinate their votes (Interviews 1; 6; 7). In addition, everybody knows everybody else, and people are more prone to talk to each other when they meet in the canteen, corridors or cafes. The cordial relationship further facilitates coordination. In the case of Luxembourg, for example, MEPs often talk informally, and the assistants of different MEPs also meet for dinner in Strasbourg, whereas MEPs from larger delegations sometimes have a more distanced relationship (Interview 5).

In addition, the hard work may well pay off. According to the EU Matrix, which measures influence in the EP, three Luxembourgers and two Maltese MEPs currently rank among the top 100 most influential MEPs (Eumatrix, 2023). President of the European Parliament Roberta Metsola (Malta) is ranked second, Christophe Hansen (Luxembourg) 22nd, Alex Agius Saliba (Malta) 35th, Charles Goerens 63rd and Marc Angel 91st (both Luxembourg). As far as national delegations are concerned, once the study controls for size, Malta is the most influential delegation followed closely by Luxembourg. Both countries thus punch considerably above their weight, while many large countries are only moderately influential (Germany, Spain) or punch below their weight (France, Italy).

While not all small states do well (Cyprus underperforms, for example), the way the two states address the small state challenge might be part of the explanation for their success. Thus, the fact that the Maltese and Luxembourgish MEPs feel under pressure to cover files from multiple committees encourages a higher level of activity in general and forces them to network more. Those who are rapporteurs for files from two to three different committees in a parliamentary term have to engage with the MEPs who sit in those committees. This may later help them to obtain more easily and against the odds of their small national delegation. It is also difficult to hide behind the other MEPs when your country only has six in total. The presence of some high-performing MEPs in a small group may further increase the pressure on others to also deliver a decent performance.

Another explanation might be the relatively high level of expertise of the MEPs. Thus, out of the six Luxembourgish MEPs, three had a relatively high level of experience in politics and/or the EU: one first entered the EP in 1982 and served several terms in the EP and several years as minister in the national government, one was a member of the national parliament and committee chair and delegate to a number of parliamentary assemblies and one previously worked for the PermRep and as advisor to an MEP. Two of the other three also had a slight advantage over other newcomers, in that one of them entered the EP already several months before the election as a replacement for an outgoing MEP and thus had time to adjust before the election, and one had several years of experience at the local level and held the office of deputy mayor of Luxembourg City. Among the Maltese MEPs, one had been prime minister, leader of the opposition and MP among other offices, one had been MEP since 2004, one had worked for the PermRep and had served several terms in the EP, one was the president of the Labour Party's youth branch and a member of the party's national executive committee for a number of years, one had been deputy mayor and advisor to several ministers and one had political experience at the local level and degrees in EU law. Thus, many of the MEPs were relatively well prepared for the work in the European Parliament.

The impact of experience is also illustrated by one of the interviewees, who submitted an amendment on his second day when he replaced an outgoing MEP and created an IT problem, because he was not yet fully registered in the system. Of course, this was only possible because he already knew the file, what he wanted to do and how the EP worked (Interview 7). Similarly, it helps if MEPs already understand the importance of different roles within the EP, which roles they can realistically aspire to and how they can get them. A firm procedural understanding can determine who gets to be coordinator of a committee or vice chair of a delegation. As the European Parliament usually has a high level of turnover at election time, any kind of experience with EU politics or previous work experience in relevant jobs can be a big advantage.

3.4 Conclusion

One of the most obvious problems that MEPs from small states face is that the number of MEPs inevitably falls short of the number of committees – and the smaller the state the bigger the problem. When party politics is added to this, notably the fact that cooperation across the (national) government-opposition divide can be difficult, even the goal of covering the most important issues is a challenge. The interviews with Maltese and Luxembourgish MEPs show that the response of small-state MEPs has been to try and cover a wider range of committees per person and to focus on the most important issues within each of these committees rather than all the issues discussed in one single committee. In addition, the national public expects the MEPs to be able to discuss all important issues. These factors prevent small state MEPs from adopting a very narrow focus. In addition, MEPs from small states have a harder time fighting for posts within the European Parliament, as a number of these are determined by delegation size or votes. Some political offices in the party groups are often de facto reserved by and for large delegations. MEPs from small states thus need a firm understanding of the functioning of the European Parliament and, ideally, previous experience to position themselves well.

However, despite these challenges small states are not necessarily doomed to fail. While size does inevitably play a big role in a parliament, the higher level of experience that MEPs from Malta and Luxembourg bring to the EP, the broader range of topics and committees they cover and their higher level of activity allow them to compensate a bit and to punch above their weight. What this means for specific policies and the ability of small states to influence the position of the European Parliament is a question that goes beyond this chapter but that merits further reflection in a small states literature that has so far focused primarily on the Council. In addition, as so-called 'soft' security threats in the field of IT and energy, for example, gain importance, the relevance of the European Parliament for small state studies is also on the rise.

Bibliography

Bailes, A. and Thorhallsson, B. (2013). Instrumentalizing the European Union in small state strategies. *Journal of European Integration* 35(2): 99–113.

Björkdahl, A. (2008). Norm advocacy: A small state strategy to influence the EU. *Journal of European Public Policy* 15(1): 135–154.

Cicchi, L. (2011). Party groups in the European parliament, cohesiveness and MEPs' survey data: New evidence on voting behaviour from a new (simple) methodology? *Interdisciplinary Political Studies* 1(2): 137–147.

Eumatrix. (2023). Available at https://eumatrix.eu/en/blog/mep-influence-index-2023-top-100-most-politically-influential-meps (accessed 18 August 2023).

Eurostat. (2023). Available at https://ec.europa.eu/eurostat/databrowser/view/tps00001/default/table?lang=en (accessed 18 August 2023).

Finke, D. (2015). Why do European political groups call the roll? *Party Politics* 21(5): 750–762.

Harmsen, R. and Högenauer, A.L. (2021). Luxembourg and the European Union. In: F. Laurensen (ed.), *Encyclopedia of European Union Politics* (Oxford University Press: Oxford), pp. 1–26.

Haughton, T. (2010). *Vulnerabilities, Accession Hangovers and the Presidency Role: Explaining New EU Member States' Choices for Europe.* Center for European Studies Central and Eastern Europe Working Paper Series 68.

Högenauer, A.L. and Mišík, M. (2024). Introduction: The challenges and opportunities of EU membership for small states. In: A.L. Högenauer and M. Mišík (eds.), *Small States in EU Policy-Making: Strategies, Challenges, Opportunities* (Routledge: Abingdon-on-Thames).

Jakobsen, P.V. (2009). Small states, big influence: The overlooked Nordic influence on the civilian ESDP. *Journal of Common Market Studies* 47(1): 81–102.

Laffan, B. (2006). Managing Europe from home in Dublin, Athens and Helsinki: A comparative analysis. *West European Politics* 29(4): 687–708.

Mattila, M. (2004). Contested decisions: Empirical analysis of voting in the European Union council of ministers. *European Journal of Political Research* 43(1): 29–50.

Panke, D. (2010a): *Small States in the European Union. Coping with Structural Disadvantages* (Ashgate: Farnham).

Panke, D. (2010b). Small states in the European Union: Structural disadvantages in EU policy-making and counter-strategies. *Journal of European Public Policy* 17(6): 799–817.

Panke, D. (2011). Small states in EU negotiations: Political dwarfs or power-brokers? *Cooperation and Conflict* 46(2): 123–143.

Panke, D. and Gurol, J. (2018). Small states as agenda-setters? The council presidencies of Malta and Estonia. *Journal of Common Market Studies* 56 (S1): 142–151.

Slapin, J. (2011): *Veto Power: Institutional Design in the European Union* (University of Michigan Press: Ann Arbor).

Slapin, J. and Proksch, S. (2010). Look who's talking: Parliamentary debate in the European Union. *European Union Politics* 11(3): 333–357.

Soetendorp, B. and Hanf, K. (1998). Conclusion: The nature of national adaptation to European integration. In: K. Hanf and B. Soetendorp (eds.), *Adapting to European Integration: Small States and the European Union* (Longman: London), pp. 186–194.

Steinmetz, R. and Wivel, A. (2010): *Small States in Europe. Challenges and Opportunities* (Routledge: London).

Thorhallsson, B. and Wivel, A. (2006). Small states in the European Union: What do we know and what would we like to know ? *Cambridge Review of International Affairs* 19(4): 651–668.

Wivel, A. (2010). From small state to smart state: Devising a strategy for influence in the European Union. In: R. Steinmetz and A. Wivel (eds.), *Small States in Europe. Challenges and Opportunities* (Routledge: London), pp. 15–30.

Interviews.

Interview 1: Maltese MEP (4 July 2023).
Interview 2: Maltese MEP (27 June 2023).
Interview 3: Maltese MEP (4 July 2023).
Interview 4: Luxembourgish MEP (9 July 2023).
Interview 5: Luxembourgish MEP (14 July 2023).
Interview 6: Luxembourgish MEP (30 June 2023).
Interview 7: Luxembourgish MEP (7 June 2023).
Interview 8: Luxembourgish MEP (7 June 2023).

4 Bringing the European Union closer to the member states? The impact of the rotating EU Council presidency on small member states

Ieva Grumbinaitė

4.1 Introduction

This chapter examines the administrative challenge of preparing and holding the European Union (EU) Council presidency in six small[1] and one larger member state (MS)[2] between 2013 and 2017. With the expanding size and competence of the EU, the challenge of holding the rotating presidency of the EU has grown to brokering solutions and compromises between currently 27 Member States across a number of policy areas. On the other hand, with the Eastern enlargement, states as small as Malta with half a million of inhabitants and compact administration must manage the task that content- and effort-wise is about the same as for Germany or France with previous experience in the post and a much larger administrative capacity. The chapter explores how small states manage the challenge of steering EU decision-making process for six months and what strategies do they adopt to overcome the size-related disadvantages. In addition, the chapter explores whether there is a difference between small states that held the position before ('old' MS) and those that are faced with the challenge for the first time ('new' MS).[3]

I analyze six small MS (Ireland, Lithuania, Latvia, Luxembourg, Slovakia, Malta) presidencies comparing them to one larger MS (the Netherlands). Among them, four MS held the position for the first time (Lithuania, Latvia, Slovakia, Malta) and three had previous experience (Ireland, Luxembourg, the Netherlands). I seek to establish whether the presidency matters on a longer term and whether any of the experience and expertise gained is retained by the MS. In addition, the chapter looks at whether size- or experience-related structural disadvantages impact the quality or results of the presidency. Theoretically, the chapter introduces the concept of administrative capacity, composed of skills and resources necessary for successful participation in and coordination of EU affairs in a MS, building on new institutionalist approaches. Administrative capacity is employed as the dependent variable, while the EU Council presidency serves as the independent one. Administrative capacity is broken down to institutional memory; institutional set-up including administrative structures, resources, coordination practices as well as soft skills such as knowledge; and attitudes of civil servants involved. Each of the components is rooted in a different new institutionalist approach. Empirically, the chapter builds on 97 expert interviews with civil servants and diplomats involved in planning and conducting one of the seven rotating presidencies.

DOI: 10.4324/9781003380641-5

The chapter starts with a short literature review highlighting the contribution of this research, then introduces the institution of the rotating presidency, the theoretical framework and the methodological approach along with the case selection. I present the results in two sections – one focuses on the preparation and the conduct of the presidency, while the other analyzes the aftermath and the long-term impact. The final section summarizes the findings, which show that the presidency presents an important opportunity to the MS to (re-)engage with the EU policy-making processes and actors. Even though the rotating presidency is a neutral broker rather than a political power in the vast majority of cases, it still helps MS to 'build up muscles in Brussels'[4] allowing to better represent their interests on the EU level afterwards. The findings also highlight the additional administrative burden the position puts on small as opposed to larger MS as well as a difference between how first-time and routine presidencies are approached. However, these do not impact the quality or the results of the presidency.

4.2 Literature review

The literature on the impact of the Council presidency on the MS, and specifically the national administrations, is limited. Existing studies suggest that holding an EU Council Presidency contributes to more active and effective MS participation in EU affairs, the emergence of new methods of policy coordination, enhanced skill development and Europeanization of national public administrations (Batory and Puetter, 2013; Bunse, 2009; Hayes-Renshaw and Wallace, 2006; Jesień, 2013; Marek and Baun, 2011; Panke, 2010a). Holding the Council presidency leads to extensive political and administrative capacity building on behalf of the MS, especially if the countries are small and new to the EU and as a result have had limited resources and time to internalize EU policy-making processes (Gärtner et al., 2011; Panke, 2010c). However, apart from identifying the presidency as an opportunity for the MS, these studies do not specify what happens in national administrations and, especially, whether the governments maintain the adjustments. The literature that goes deeper into the administrative impact of the Council presidency only focuses on a small number of cases and a comprehensive comparison is missing.

The influence of the Council presidency on national governments was studied by Nuallain and Hoscheit (1985) back in the EU of 10 MS when the presidency still rotated alphabetically and had a mostly administrative function, encompassing fewer policy areas and following different legislative procedures, and so it is hardly comparable to the current presidencies. Kaniok and Gergelova Štegirova (2014) examined the impact of the Council presidency on the Czech administration, finding that it expanded the capacity and skills of national administration but was a 'wasted opportunity' in the end, since the government did not invest in maintaining the practices or staff involved. In her recent study, Galušková (2017) looks at implications of five first-time presidencies for EU policy coordination mechanisms, finding that it constituted a critical juncture for the Czech Republic and partly for Poland and Lithuania. Jensen and Nedergaard (2017) note that the presidency preparation period has barely received any attention They also raised the same question as this chapter and tested the implications of the Council presidency on the administrations of one presidency trio – Poland, Denmark and Cyprus in 2011–2012 – finding that the presidency had the most transforming effect on the small Cypriot administration holding the post for the first time (Jensen and Nedergaard, 2017). To contribute to the rather limited body of literature, I explore seven small MS presidencies as likely targets for administrative change as a result of holding the position, including both the preparation and the presidency period. This chapter adds a new dimension to the existing research by comprehensively comparing several, namely three 'old' and four 'new' MS presidencies including six small and one larger MS to explore whether and how the Council presidency contributes to Europeanization of national administrations.

4.3　The rotating presidency of the Council of the EU

The rotating presidency of the EU Council was established as a preponderantly administrative institution to share the burden of planning of the Council meetings between the six MS of the European Coal and Steel Community (Pernice, 2003). However, with a growing number of MS and the widening scope of competences of the now European Union, the presidency acquired additional obligations. It is now an important mechanism of leadership, equality and fairness in the EU, affording every MS in turn, regardless of its size or EU membership duration, a six-month period to lead proceedings of the EU Council (Bunse, 2009). The main functions of the rotating presidency include, firstly, the management of Council activity, organization and chairing of Council meetings on all levels, both in Brussels and the respective MS assisted by the Council General Secretariat (CGS). Secondly, the presidency has a limited capacity to set EU agenda by prioritizing certain issues in its programme in line with the predefined presidency trio programme drafted by three MS and the European Commission (Elgström, 2003; Warntjen, 2007; Jensen and Nedergaard, 2014). Furthermore, chairing most of the formations of Council meetings, from minister to working party level, the presidency acts as a neutral broker and as a mediator between MS. It is also a representative of the EU Council with the European Commission, the European Parliament and other EU institutions (Elgström, 2003; Hayes-Renshaw and Wallace, 2006). The Lisbon Treaty in 2009 constrained the scope of action of the presidency by introducing the permanent president of the European Council and the High Representative for Foreign Affairs to chair the respective council formation in favour of more continuity at the highest level of political leadership of the EU (Jensen and Nedergaard, 2014).

The Lisbon Treaty notably decreased the visibility but not necessarily the workload of the rotating presidency, since it only lost two Council formations. In a nutshell, instead of merely participating in the meetings of the Council of the EU, the representatives of the presiding MS must chair them,[5] act as brokers between the ministers, the diplomats and the bureaucrats of the EU-28[6] on all Council levels and represent the Council of the EU in trialogues with the European Parliament and the European Commission, steering the legislative process of the EU. Furthermore, the presidency must organize informal ministerial Council meetings in the capital (Council of the EU, 2023).

EU Council presidency is an extraordinary event in the area of international cooperation, providing unprecedented exposure to EU affairs not only to political elites but also to a large group of civil servants (Schout, 2009). None of the similar obligations in other international or regional organizations, such as a seat on the Security Council of the United Nations, the presidency of the Organisation for Economic Co-operation and Development, Višegrad, Benelux, the Baltic Sea Council or others, compare in their scope and intensity to the EU Council presidency. A handful of diplomats at the Ministries of Foreign Affairs usually handle UN or OECD matters, NATO summits only last several days, while the EU Council presidency requires the involvement of all national ministries and over a thousand of civil servants for six months, preceded by over a year of intensive preparation, which is occasionally identified as busier than the presidency itself.[7] According to civil servants from 'new' MS, the only event that compared to the Council presidency was the EU accession in 2004.[8]

Normally, regardless of the size of the administration of the MS holding a Council presidency, the scope of tasks it must perform, such as the number of working party or ministerial meetings as well as informal Council meetings in the MS, is similar, making the presidency a bigger challenge for compact administrations of small MS. However, Kirchner (1992) identified three groups of contextual factors that may impact the conduct and the scope of individual presidencies differentiating them: domestic, EU-institutional and external. Domestic factors include availability of financial and human resources, national EU policy coordination practices, public opinion towards the EU and national political context including elections or changes in the cabinet during or close to the presidency. EU-level factors relate to the institutional evolution of the EU and treaty changes, and to the legislative or budgetary cycles, meaning that the presidency agendas might be much fuller and inflexible when a new multiannual financial framework must be agreed upon, while presidencies at the beginning of the cycle have more liberty to set their agendas and priorities. External factors include unforeseen or unexpected events that can dictate or reformulate the priorities of the presidency. To illustrate these, Table 4.1 contextualizes the seven presidencies that will be analyzed in detail later.

This chapter focuses on the administrative challenge of the Council presidency largely skipping the political aspects of the institution such as agenda-setting powers or success at EU level. However, to just briefly touch upon them, the vast majority of the civil servants interviewed for this chapter underlined that their presidencies were strictly acting as neutral brokers and following the agenda outlined by the European Commission and the presidency trio, prioritizing the continuity of EU policy process over national priorities. As they noted, for small MS, the reputational losses relating to pushing their own interest instead of adhering to the norm of the neutral broker outweigh the potential benefits, especially considering that not even the largest MS manage to push their unilateral priorities during their respective presidencies without damaging their reputation.[9]

Furthermore, as noted earlier, the presidency agendas are largely predetermined by the EU legislative agenda and, to an extent, by external factors and events. For

Table 4.1 Summary of the cases

Presidency	Domestic factors	EU-level factors	External factors
Ireland 2013	Recent economic crisis; Demotivated administration; Limited human/material resources	End of EU legislative cycle; First post-Lisbon presidency	-
Lithuania 2013	Recent economic crisis; Limited material resources	End of EU legislative cycle; First presidency	Snowden scandal; Maidan events in Ukraine
Latvia 2015	National election; Limited material resources; Some Euroscepticism	First presidency	Charlie Hebdo attacks; Refugee crisis
Luxembourg 2015	Small administration; Pro-European population	First post-Lisbon presidency	Refugee crisis (quotas)
Netherlands 2016	Large administration; Euroscepticism	First post-Lisbon presidency	Refugee crisis; Brussels attacks
Slovakia 2016	Limited human resources; National election	First presidency	Refugee crisis
Malta 2017	Limited human resources; National election	First presidency	Refugee crisis; Brexit

Source: Own compilation based on interview data

instance, looking at the number of legislative acts passed, the Lithuanian 2013 presidency is an absolute leader among the seven cases, but that is to a large extent because there were just so many acts on the agenda that could not be postponed and had to be passed before the end of the financial cycle, and also the MS were respectively keener on compromising to move the process forward rather than blocking it based on their national preferences.[10]

Finally, measuring the political achievements of the Council presidency is also somewhat subjective because the Council General Secretariat (CGS) and EU as a whole is interested in maintaining a smooth legislative process, and so there are a number of checks and balances to ensure a smooth handover and negotiation of files, such as assistance from the experienced CGS staff or handover of specific portfolios to more experienced trio partners. For example, Malta took over the negotiation of many maritime issues from Slovakia, which is a landlocked country. As seen earlier, the political achievements and agendas of the rotating presidencies are a mix of a variety of factors, only a few of them controlled by the incumbent MS.

4.4 The concept of administrative capacity

Literature on small state participation in EU affairs identifies structural disadvantages faced by the small states as well as factors necessary for successful participation in the EU policy-making process (Panke, 2010a, 2010b, 2010c; Thorhallsson, 2006; Thorhallsson and Wivel, 2006). The concept of administrative capacity, employed as the dependent variable, is based on a combination of these factors as identified by Panke (2010a, 2010c). The key structural disadvantage of small states in the EU is fewer human and material resources both at the national ministries and Permanent Representations in Brussels. A lack or limited number of skilled experts and leaner EU policy coordination structures complicate the timely shaping of high-quality national positions for Council negotiations. Furthermore, for the same reason small states also have weaker networks with EU institutions and interest groups, complicating access to relevant information, and, as a result, are also less reputable. Finally, less established or stable EU policy coordination systems, lack of experience due to shorter duration of EU membership and even leaner resources constitute additional structural disadvantages for 'new' MS (Dimitrova and Toshkov, 2007; Gärtner et al., 2011; Panke, 2010a).

Administrative capacity here stands for the combination of requirements for an MS to successfully engage in EU policy-making. It serves as an aggregate dependent variable, while the EU Council presidency is the independent variable. Administrative capacity is conceptualized through a new institutionalist theory commonly used for the study of Europeanization and the impact of European integration on the MS. It combines rational choice (RCI), sociological (SI) and historical institutionalist (HI) approaches. The main logic behind RCI is that of consequentiality and cost-benefit consideration in decision-making. Actor preferences are fixed and individualistic. SI puts a strong emphasis on logic of appropriateness and behaviour led by adherence to norms and values rather than consequentiality. Actor preferences are flexible and can be changed by their environments through learning or socialization. HI emphasizes path dependency and legacy of past choices in shaping actor behaviour. Their preferences can be either fixed or flexible but also impacted and shaped by past decisions (Börzel and Risse, 2003; Checkel, 2001; Hall and Taylor, 1996; Peters, 2012). Administrative capacity here combines the institutional set-up for the presidency in the MS (explained by RCI) and soft skills of the civil servants involved (explained by SI), as well as institutional memory (reflected in HI). Institutional set-up includes material and human resources allocated for the presidency, new coordination practices between the institutions involved and creation of new institutional structures. Soft skills comprise attitudes, motivation and skills of the civil servants as well as their contact networks at national and EU levels. Institutional memory reflects EU membership duration and previous presidency experience. The concept is elaborated in Figure 4.1.

I expect that holding the rotating EU Council presidency should strengthen the administrative capacity of the respective MS, at least temporarily, but also in a long-term perspective. In addition, the impact of the presidency on the administrative capacity should be stronger in small MS with no previous presidency experience since they cannot build on institutional memory and therefore the learning effect and socialization are likely to be greater. Finally, the chapter seeks to find out which strand of institutional theory, sociological, rational choice or historical institutionalism, explains the impact of the Council presidency better and to what

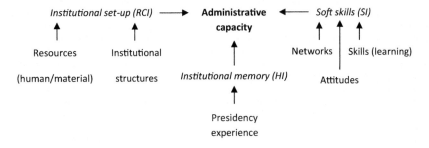

Figure 4.1 Defining administrative capacity. Source: Own elaboration

extent, as the findings might reveal that, for example, no institutional changes took place or that historical memory did not play a significant role in the preparation and conduct of the analyzed presidencies. Having only one case of a larger MS in the sample introduced in the next subsection does not allow a thorough comparison of small-large MS presidencies but it might help to flag some of the small-state-specific challenges for future research.

4.5 Case selection and data

Six cases in this comparative study, namely Ireland, Lithuania, Latvia, Luxembourg, Slovakia and Malta, were selected based on a most similar logic holding the small size of the MS as well as recent presidency experience constant (George and Bennett, 2005; Seawright and Gerring, 2008). Previous presidency experience is the variable that differs among the cases, dividing them into two 'old' and four 'new' MS. Furthermore, the focus is placed on the small MS in order to allow in-depth analysis of the cases where the impact of the Council presidency is most likely to be notable. The Netherlands was added to the sample as an example of a much larger MS with previous presidency experience to see whether a difference between small and large MS presidencies is really apparent expanding the sample of 'old' MS to three.

The empirical basis of the chapter consists of semi-structured interviews with 97 public servants from the seven countries as well as an analysis of reports, programmes, legal documents and media coverage of the seven presidencies. The interviews were conducted between March 2016 and May 2017 as well as in the summer of 2022. Interviewees were selected based on their tasks and working positions during the Council presidency: high-level diplomats at Permanent Representations in Brussels, representatives from key national ministries and representatives of presidency coordinating institutions. It should be underlined that due to the research design building mainly on expert interviews there may be a positive bias and, despite triangulation of interview findings and a large number of respondents, the impact of the Council presidency might be overstated. A breakdown of interviewees by country and target group is presented in Table 4.2.

Table 4.2 Breakdown of interviews

Country	Timing	Interviewees	By institution		
			Permanent Representation	National ministries	Coordinating institutions
Ireland	Jan 2017	14	7	6	1
Lithuania	Mar–Apr 2016	19	8	9	2
Latvia	Apr 2016	17	2	11	4
Luxembourg	Jan–Feb2017	12	3	6	3
Netherlands	Jan–Mar 2017	12	6	5	1
Slovakia	Jan, May 2017	18	8	8	2
Malta	May–Sep 2022	5	2	-	3
Total		**97**	**35**	**44**	**18**

Source: Own data

4.6 Preparation and conduct of a Council presidency

The key aspects of the preparation and conduct of the Council presidencies by the seven MS are summarized in Table 4.3 based on interview insights and respective presidency reports. The table points to a difference between the small states and the larger ones, especially when looking at human resources. In addition, there are several differences in how 'old' and 'new' MS prepare and hold their presidencies.

Overall, it is notable that the presidencies indeed entail a similar scope of tasks regardless of the size of the MS or its administration, as can be seen by roughly similar budgets with the exceptions of Malta being the least costly and Luxembourg the most. These can be explained by some country-specific decisions, such as cost-cutting event organization and transportation solutions in the small city of Valetta, or no need for separate English-language training for the Maltese civil servants, for example. The other significant aspect determining the budgets in the other MS was the extent of training needed (more elaborate and extensive programmes were organized in the 'new' MS) and the possibility to fund it from the European Social Fund (ESF), which allowed to significantly cut the costs in Lithuania and Slovakia but not in Latvia.

It is apparent that the 'new' MS invest more in the development of their administrative capacity than their 'old' counterparts from a rational choice institutionalist perspective. Most of them start preparations earlier, set up separate coordinating institutions, hire more additional staff and invest in extensive centralized training programmes for the presidency staff, instead of largely learning-by-doing and building on institutional memory and existing structures in 'old' MS. The learning-by-doing, relying on existing structures, and redeploying existing rather than hiring new staff, was also very notable in the Netherlands, the one larger MS, showing that for larger administrations the presidency indeed is a less disruptive experience than for the small ones.

During the presidency, 'new' MS seem to get greater returns from the sociological institutionalist perspective, namely in networking and institutional learning, catching up in experience and expertise with their 'older' counterparts. The Council presidency is still an important tool for re-engagement with the EU for 'old' MS but a real 'eye opener' for the 'new' ones, having a stronger overall impact on the latter and showing how the historical institutionalist component, namely previous presidency experience, influences administrative capacity building before and during the presidency to an extent. 'Old' MS had to adjust to the Lisbon Treaty changes and establish a closer working relationship with the European Parliament, but for the 'new' MS the presidency constituted a crucial learning experience, even identified as 'taking off the newcomer's hat,' 'the graduation exam' for the 'new' MS.[11]

4.7 Long-term impact of the Council presidency

This section addresses any lasting impact of the rotating EU Council presidency on national administrations. Table 4.4 provides a summary of the impact of holding

Table 4.3 Summary of the findings

	Preparation timing (years)	Presidency budget (million €)	Coordination structures	Human Resources (ministries)	Human Resources (Permanent Representation)	Training	Learning (institutional)	Coordination/ networking
Ireland 2013	3	60	Prime Minister's Office	Few staff hired, temporary redeployment of existing staff, calling experts back from retirement	From 100 to 180 people (almost doubled)	Learning on the job/CGS seminars	Introducing new generation of civil servants to EU affairs/ learning post-Lisbon processes/not a major eye opener	Re-engagement with EU institutions
Lithuania 2013	6	63	Designated temporary department at MFA	Centrally assigned quotas for additional (mostly administrative) staff at the ministries, temporary liaison officers	From 80 to 200 people (doubled to tripled)	Centralized training programme funded by ESF/CGS seminars; English and French classes	Thoroughly learning about how EU works, especially informal practices	Establishing crucial contacts with EU institutions
Latvia 2015	3	82	Independent temporary institution	Only a few administrative staff hired, liaison volunteer programme, internships	From 60 to 185 people (tripled)	Centralized training programme/ CGS seminars; English classes	Thoroughly learning about how EU works, especially informal practices	Establishing crucial contacts with EU institutions

Luxembourg 2015	3	93	EU Affairs department, MFA	About 200 people (2–3 per cent of civil service) hired on two-year contracts	From 80 to 140 people (almost doubled)	Learning on the job/CGS seminars	Learning post-Lisbon processes/not a major eye opener	Refreshing contact networks with EU institutions
Netherlands 2016	3	63	MFA	Few staff hired, temporary redeployment of existing staff, extended traineeship programme	From 100 to 180 people (almost doubled)	Learning on the job/short seminars/ CGS seminars	Learning post-Lisbon processes/not a major eye opener	Refreshing contact networks with EU institutions
Slovakia 2016	5	70	Designated temporary department at MFA	Centrally assigned quotas for additional (mostly administrative) staff at the ministries	From 70–80 to 220 people (tripled)	Centralized training programme funded by ESF/CGS seminars; English classes	Thoroughly learning about how EU works, especially informal practices	Establishing crucial contacts with EU institutions
Malta 2017	3	40	Ministry for European Affairs	Substantial number of staff hired, also internally from other ministries	N/A (substantially increased capacity)	Centralized training by external contractors/ ministry training	Thoroughly learning about how EU works, especially informal practices	Establishing crucial contacts with EU institutions

Source: Own elaboration based on interview data and presidency reports: Irish Presidency of the Council of the European Union (2013); Latvian Presidency of the Council of the European Union (2015); LR Užsienio Reikalų Ministerija (2014); Slovak Council Presidency (2016)

Table 4.4 Summary of the findings regarding the long-term impact of the Council presidency

	Rational choice institutionalism			Sociological institutionalism		
	Structures	Coordination/ communication practices	Staff	Networks	Skills	Attitudes
Ireland 2013	Capital: dismantled Only committees remained Perm rep: size back to normal	Improvement	No measures to retain additional staff; civil servants largely remained	Re-engagement (crucial after crisis)	Improvement	Motivational boost
Lithuania 2013	Capital: dismantled Perm rep: size back to normal	Improvement	No measures to retain additional staff (only competitive advantage); civil servants largely remained	Emergence	Notable improvement	Substantive change
Latvia 2015	Capital: dismantled Perm rep: size back to normal	Improvement	No measures to retain additional staff (only competitive advantage); civil servants largely remained	Emergence	Notable improvement	Substantive change
Luxembourg 2015	Capital: lean to begin with, dismantled. Perm rep: size back to normal	Marginal improvement	Hiring suspended to retain additional staff; civil servants largely remained	Re-engagement	Minor improvement	Little change

		Marginal improvement		Re-engagement (temporary)	Minor improvement	Little change
Netherlands 2016	Capital: lean to begin with, dismantled Perm rep: size back to normal	Marginal improvement	No measures to retain additional staff (only extended traineeships); civil servants largely remained.	Re-engagement (temporary)	Minor improvement	Little change
Slovakia 2016	Capital: dismantled Perm rep: size back to normal	Improvement	No measures to retain additional staff (only competitive advantage); civil servants largely remained	Emergence	Notable improvement	Substantive change
Malta 2017	Capital: dismantled (Ministry for European Affairs merged with the MFA) Perm rep: size back to normal	Little impact	No measures to retain additional staff (only competitive advantage); civil servants largely remained	Emergence	Notable improvement	Substantive change

Source: Own elaboration based on interview data

the rotating EU Council presidency on national administrations structuring it by the main RCI and SI components of the concept of administrative capacity (previous presidency experience and HI were largely discussed in the previous section).

In all the seven MS presidency coordination institutions were dismantled after the presidency. Civil servants returned from presidency coordination to their initial roles; the separate institutions established by Lithuania, Latvia and Slovakia were dismantled; in other countries EU policy coordination practices went back to normal. In Malta, the Ministry for European Affairs that coordinated the presidency was merged with the Ministry of Foreign affairs within a couple of years succeeding the event.[12] However, civil servants built up lasting personal contact networks among themselves and with the other national ministries that were valuable for several years after the presidencies. A better understanding of how other line ministries work and coordinate EU affairs emerged. Furthermore, extensive experience in logistical planning and event management obtained through the presidency was useful for similar future obligations in other international organizations (OECD or NATO), although none can quite compare to the presidency in scope and intensity.[13]

The Council presidency also contributed to capacity building in national ministries, even though to a limited extent. Only the administration of Luxembourg made conscious effort to retain staff temporarily hired and trained for the presidency in the civil service. In the other six MS, the presidency certainly served as a stepping stone into the civil service for numerous young professionals and the experience gained helped them pass civil service selection procedures.[14] Intensive work with the presidency dossiers and coordination, as well as training, led to improved competence and knowledge of EU institutions and processes among the civil servants at the national ministries. Since the presidency only repeats every 13–14 years, it is to introduce a new generation of civil servants to EU affairs in the 'old' MS.[15] More importantly, it notably changed the attitudes of civil servants in the 'new' MS holding their first presidencies. Multiple interviewees reported that only after the presidency did the understanding that EU issues are an integral part of domestic policy-making emerge.[16] The Council presidency did not change much in the institutional set-up or working practices at the national ministries apart from some adjustments in communication and information sharing practices. However, it greatly enhanced competence in EU matters and confidence among the civil servants. In the 'old' MS the presidency meant a re-engagement with the EU institutions and a re-establishment of closer contacts with them. For the first-time presidencies it was a major eye opener on how EU institutions and legislative processes work from the 'insider' perspective. They acquired knowledge of both formal and informal ways of influencing the EU agenda and built up contact networks with high-level officials at EU institutions that would be unattainable in other ways. All of these contributed to small, especially the 'new' MS obtaining more skills and tools to shape better national positions at EU level and make their voices heard.

Finally, at all the Permanent Representations, the nature and the load of work, as well as staff numbers, went back to levels that prevailed before the presidency, with the exception of the Dutch and Slovak Permanent Representations. The Dutch

Permanent Representation decreased in size due to budget cuts and the Slovak slightly expanded and restructured. All the seven MS adopted a Brussels-based presidency model giving greater autonomy to the Permanent Representations, and all returned to more capital-based practices, dropped their neutral broker roles and shifted back to representation of national interests immediately after their presidencies. However, in all the cases, new and faster communication channels with the capitals remained in place (regular videoconferences or frequent distribution of short flash notes). Furthermore, both respondents from 'old' and 'new' MS 'built up muscles in Brussels'[17] through establishing extensive and close contact networks with EU institutions and interest representatives, who normally rarely proactively approach small states if they are not holding the presidency. The diplomats acting as working party chairs improved their negotiation, brokering and coalition-building skills. The presidency was an enormous learning experience for diplomats from first-time presidencies. Having chaired Council meetings, participated in trialogues and represented the Council at the EP, they agree that only after the presidency does their country feel like a full member of equal standing of the European Union.

Overall, from the RCI perspective, in terms of changes in institutional structures, staff numbers or coordination practices are less apparent in national administrations. However, the Council presidency does constitute a crucial mechanism of socialization (SI), especially in the 'new' MS. While institutional memory (HI) is helpful in presidency preparation and conduct, it does not impact the results or the achievements.

4.8 Conclusion

Connecting the findings to the theoretical argument and the concept of administrative capacity, it is notable that the presidency fulfils a strong socialization function in national administrations, rather than leading to any lasting institutional change in coordination structures and practices. It is 'not the structure, but the quality of EU issue coordination that changes after the presidency.'[18] These findings point out that long-term Europeanization of national administrations through holding the EU Council presidency is predominantly apparent through the sociological institutionalist perspective. On the rational choice side, only minor adjustments of administrative capacity, such as communication practices between the institutions, have lasting value. In that sense, capitalizing on the aftermath of the presidency can be seen as a wasted opportunity to an extent. From a historical institutionalist perspective, there is a difference between 'old' and 'new' MS, with the latter reporting greater returns from the presidency and a stronger impact on administrative capacity, along with more investments into the preparation process.

In terms of size, it is evident that the presidency poses a bigger challenge for small MS if one compares the effort and energy the Netherlands invested in covering all the dossiers and tasks to what the smaller administrations did. The Dutch presidency largely made do with own resources while the smaller administrations needed to plan more extensively, hire more staff or rely on external support.

However, with a number of mitigation strategies in place, size did not seem to impact the quality of small state presidencies in any way. If anything, it might have served as an advantage, since smaller states are used to collaboration and coalition building and therefore make better neutral brokers, which is a crucial role for a successful and effective Council presidency.

Furthermore, the Council presidency is an unprecedented experience for both 'old' and 'new' MS. However, it certainly contributes more to capacity building in the 'new' MS. A common experience among the first-time presidencies is that 'you only become a normal EU Member State after the presidency [. . .], there certainly is an effect of taking off a newcomer hat in all countries.'[19] Civil servants from the 'new' MS agreed that it is impossible to fully understand how EU institutions function, especially behind the scenes, without having held the Council presidency.[20] While respondents from experienced MS also reported learning a lot about cooperation with the EP and the changes introduced by the Lisbon Treaty, the effect of the presidency was weaker than in the countries that held the position for the first time.

These findings provide a contribution to the long-going debate about the necessity and the use of the institution of the rotating EU Council presidency. Both academics and policy-makers criticized the chair held by a different party every six months as an unsuitable leadership structure for the European Union of 28 MS, for lacking accountability, disrupting the continuity of policy-making and being a costly burden for the MS, or a powerless institution since the Lisbon Treaty reforms (Crum, 2009). However, the findings of this research indicate that, despite being costly and very occasional experience, the Council presidency still fulfils an important socializing function within the national administrations bringing the allegedly remote 'Brussels affairs' closer to the MS. As noted by one of the interview respondents, 'The presidency is an important piece in turning the "they" to "we".'[21]

Notes

1 I define small states as those having a lesser than average population of the EU. This relative definition of smaller than average in a regional construct in question was adopted from Panke and Gurol (2019).
2 Following my definition of a small state having a lesser than average population of the EU, the Netherlands constitutes the smallest large state falling at just above the EU-27 average of 16.5 million with its 17.5 million inhabitants.
3 Since the 'old' and 'new' member state distinction may appear outdated at this day, two decades after the Eastern enlargement of the EU, I opt for quotation marks to simply and quickly distinguish between member states that joined the EU before and after May 2004.
4 Interview, with representative from LT.
5 Except for the Foreign Affairs Council as of Lisbon Treaty reforms in 2009.
6 As it was still EU-28 at the time of research, it was left unchanged here.
7 Interviews with representatives from IE, LT, LV, LU, SK, NL.
8 Interviews with representatives from IE, LT, LV, SK.
9 Interview with representatives from IE, LT, LV, LU, MT.
10 Interview with representative from LT.
11 Interviews with representatives from LT, LV, SK.

12 Interview with representative from MT.
13 Interviews with representatives from IE, LT, LV, LU, NL, SK.
14 Interviews with representatives from LT, LV, SK.
15 Interview with representative from IE.
16 Interviews with representatives from IE, LT, LV, LU, SK.
17 Interview with representative from LT.
18 Interview with representative from LT.
19 Interviews with representatives from LT, LV.
20 Interview with representative from LV.
21 Interview with representative from IE.

Bibliography

Batory, A. and Puetter, U. (2013). Consistency and diversity? The EU's rotating trio council presidency after the Lisbon treaty. *Journal of European Public Policy* 20(1): 95–112.

Börzel, T.A. and Risse, T. (2003). Conceptualizing the domestic impact of Europe. In: K. Featherstone and C.M. Radaelli (eds.), *The Politics of Europeanization* (Oxford University Press: Oxford), pp. 57–80. http://www.oxfordscholarship.com/view/10.1093/0199252092.001.0001/acprof-9780199252091-chapter-3.

Bunse, S. (2009). *Small States and EU Governance: Leadership through the Council Presidency* (Palgrave Macmillan: London).

Checkel, J.T. (2001). *International Institutions and Socialization in the New Europe* (ARENA).

Council of the EU. (2023). The presidency of the Council of the EU. Available at https://www.consilium.europa.eu/en/council-eu/presidency-council-eu/ (accessed 1 August 2023).

Crum, B. (2009). Accountability and personalisation of the European council presidency. *Journal of European Integration* 31(6): 685–701. https://doi.org/10.1080/07036330903199853.

Dimitrova, A. and Toshkov, D. (2007). The dynamics of domestic coordination of EU Policy in the new member states: Impossible to lock in? *West European Politics* 30(5): 961–986.

Elgström, O. (ed.). (2003). *European Union Council Presidencies: A Comparative Perspective* (Routledge: London).

Galušková, J. (2017). The influence of the EU council presidency on national coordination mechanisms for European Agenda. *Romanian Journal of European Affairs* 17(1): 16–39.

Gärtner, L., Hörner, J. and Obholzer, L. (2011). National coordination of EU policy: A comparative study of the twelve "new" member states. *Journal of Contemporary European Research* 7(1): 77–100.

George, A.L. and Bennett, A. (2005). *Case Studies and Theory Development in the Social Sciences* (MIT Press: Cambridge).

Hall, P. and Taylor, R. (1996). Political Science and the Three New Institutionalisms. *Political Studies*, *44*(5), 936-957.

Hayes-Renshaw, F. and Wallace, H. (2006). *The Council of Ministers* (2nd ed.) (Palgrave Macmillan: London).

Irish Presidency of the Council of the European Union. (2013). *Results of the Irish Presidency of the Council of the European Union*, January–June (Irish Presidency of the Council of the European Union: Dublin).

Jensen, M.D. and Nedergaard, P. (2014). Uno, duo, trio? Varieties of trio presidencies in the council of ministers: Varieties of trio presidencies in the council of ministers. *Journal of Common Market Studies* 52(5): 1035–1052.

Jensen, M.D. and Nedergaard, P. (2017). *EU Presidencies between Politics and Administration: The Governmentality of the Polish, Danish and Cypriot Trio Presidency in 2011–2012* (Routledge: Milton Park).

Jesień, L. (2013). *The European Union Presidency: Institutionalized Procedure of Political Leadership* (Peter Lang: Brussels).

Kaniok, P. and Gergelova, Š. (2014). Presidency and state administration in the Czech Republic: Planting a seed or a shattered chance? *Journal of Contemporary European Research* 10(3): 337–354.

Kirchner, E.J. (1992). *Decision-Making in the European Community: The Council Presidency and European Integration* (Manchester University Press: Manchester).

Latvian Presidency of the Council of the European Union. (2015). *Results of the Latvian Presidency of the Council of the European Union*. Available at https://www.mod.gov.lv/sites/mod/files/document/EU2015LV_results_en.pdf.

LR Užsienio Reikalų Ministerija. (2014). *Lietuvos Pirmininkavimo Europos Sąjungos Tarybai 2013 m. Liepos 1 d. – Gruodžio. 31 d. Programos Įgyvendinimas* (LR Užsienio Reikalų Ministerija: Vilnius).

Marek, D. and Baun, M.J. (2011). *The Czech Republic and the European Union* (Routledge: Milton Park).

Nuallain, C.O. and Hoscheit, J.-M. (1985). *The Presidency of the European Council of Ministers. Impacts and Implications for National Governments* (Croom Helm: London).

Panke, D. (2010a). *Small States in the European Union: Coping with Structural Disadvantages* (Ashgate: Farnham).

Panke, D. (2010b). Good instructions in no time? Domestic coordination of EU policies in 19 small states. *West European Politics* 33(4): 770–790.

Panke, D. (2010c). Small states in the European Union: Structural disadvantages in EU policy-making and counter-strategies. *Journal of European Public Policy* 17(6): 799–817.

Panke, D. and Gurol, J. (2019). Small states in the European Union. In: F. Laursen (ed.), *Oxford Encyclopaedia of European Union Politics* (Oxford University Press: Oxford).

Peters, B.G. (2012). *Institutional Theory in Political Science: The New Institutionalism* (3rd ed.) (Continuum: London).

Schout, A. (2009). Organizational learning in the EU's multi-level governance system. *Journal of European Public Policy* 16(8): 1124–1144. https://doi.org/10.1080/13501760903332613.

Seawright, J. and Gerring, J. (2008). Case selection techniques in case study research: A menu of qualitative and quantitative options. *Political Research Quarterly* 61(2): 294–308.

Slovak Council Presidency. (2016). Budget. Available at SK EU2016 http://www.eu2016.sk/en/about-the-presidency/budget (accessed 4 June 2017).

Thorhallsson, B. (2006). The role of small states in the European Union. In: C. Ingebritsen, I. Neumann, S. Gstöhl and J. Beyer (eds.), *Small States in International Relations* (University of Washington Press: Seatle), pp. 218–227.

Thorhallsson, B. and Wivel, A. (2006). Small states in the European Union: What do we know and what would we like to know? *Cambridge Review of International Affairs* 19(4): 651–668.

Warntjen, A. (2007). Steering the Union. The impact of the EU presidency on legislative activity in the council. *Journal of Common Market Studies* 45(5): 1135–1157.

5 Small states coalition building in EU policy-making

The cases of the Nordic and Baltic countries

Tobias Etzold

5.1 Introduction

Forming coalitions of like-minded countries in various forms and shapes – institutionalized or ad hoc without any permanent structures, territorially constituted, i.e., consisting of countries from one region, or more theme based - has become an important tool for EU member states to promote and implement their national interest over time. The number of coalitions within a European Union (EU) context increased significantly since the block's big enlargement from 2004. Coalition building is not only but in particular useful for small- and medium-sized EU member states in order to increase their otherwise limited political weight and impact in EU policy-making in cooperation with other like-minded countries.

The three Baltic countries – Estonia, Latvia and Lithuania – the three Nordic EU members – Denmark, Finland and Sweden – and the two Nordic non-EU but EEA (European Economic Area) members, Iceland and Norway, are examples of small(er) countries that know a long tradition of aligning with each other and/or other like-minded countries in international and European cooperation contexts. The countries cooperate in formal, i.e., institutionalized, and informal ways and in various settings of which most prominently: Nordic (formal and informal), Baltic (formal and informal), Nordic-Baltic 8, Nordic-Baltic 6 (NB6) (just EU members) and groups also involving other countries such as the New Hanseatic League (originally NB6 plus the Netherlands, Ireland and later also the Czech Republic and Slovakia) as well as the Frugal Four (Denmark, Sweden, Austria and the Netherlands) and consecutive variations of these. With the United Kingdom having been an important like-minded partner for all these countries, coalitions with other small/er but also bigger like-minded countries bear an even bigger weight for the Baltics and the Nordics since Brexit in order to counterweight the positions of the remaining big members, mainly Germany and France, more effectively.

Informed by theoretical and conceptual approaches on small states and coalition building within the EU as well as various definitions of terms, this chapter takes an analytical look at several examples of formal and informal groupings with Nordic and/or Baltic participation, establishing the type of coalition and examining their effectiveness in pursuing the Nordic and Baltic countries' interests in EU policy-making addressing the first research question of this volume how small states can overcome the challenge of size and influence in EU decision-making:

DOI: 10.4324/9781003380641-6

what purpose and impact do these formal and informal coalitions of and for small(er) EU members have? Which settings, more formal and institutionalized or more informal and ad hoc, regional or theme based, are best suited and useful for what specific purpose(s) and policies and which one(s) are currently preferred by these countries?

The chapter builds on a qualitative content analysis of scholarly secondary literature on coalition building in the EU, for example, Elgstroem et al. (2001) and Klemencic (2011); the role of small states within the EU including coalition building, such as Panke (2010) and Thorhallsson and Wivel (2006); the Nordic and/or Baltic countries' role in coalition building and Nordic-Baltic cooperation within an EU context, for example, Ruse (2013, 2014) and Kuusik and Raik (2018a, 2018b); Baltic cooperation (Busygina and Klimovich, 2017); Nordic cooperation (Etzold, 2020; Strang, 2016; Ruse, 2015), and newer coalitions such as the New Hanseatic League (Korteweg, 2018; Schöller, 2021) and Nordic cooperation in combination with the New Hanseatic League and the Frugal Four (Schulz and Henökl, 2020).

The next section provides a conceptual framework for the analysis with an overview of purposes and means of coalition building in general and for small states in particular and the various forms of coalitions and differences among them. The third section briefly introduces the Nordic and Baltic states as member states of the EU and analyzes several examples of formal and informal groupings/coalitions within the EU in which the Nordic and/or the Baltic states participate, followed by a comparative discussion and conclusions.

5.2 Conceptual framework: Coalition building in the EU and the role of small states

Coalition building among EU member states has always played an important role in the EU decision-making process in order to exert greater influence considering national interests. According to Janning and Zunneberg (2017), coalition building serves three major purposes. Firstly, it is a tool of governance in a largely intergovernmental EU: government coalitions can assist in agenda shaping, driving issues forward and bridging cleavages between the interests of member states (ibid.). Within smaller settings, governments can coordinate their policies and positions more easily and strengthen their positions by gaining support from other states (Lang and von Ondarza, 2018: 2). Secondly, coalitions can be helpful in majority building as they represent clusters of consensus on various issues (or vice versa in building a minority being big enough to block a decision in the EU's qualified majority voting system). Thirdly, coalitions are also useful in creating flexibility and differentiation of integration (Janning and Zunneberg, 2017).

Thus, coalitions as exclusive groups have advantages. Based on the common interests of their members, they can make important contributions to the further development of the EU and of specific policy areas and even initiate and drive forward closer cooperation in certain fields, for example, infrastructure development (Lang and von Ondarza, 2018: 6). On the other hand, they can potentially cause complications and create destructive competition among country groups, delay decision-making as well as render the decision-making process fuzzy (ibid.). Nonetheless, especially for small- and medium-sized member states it is important to form groups with like-minded countries in order to make themselves heard and to increase their political weight within the EU. A coalition can provide them with some protection from dominant big members and with a higher probability not to be ignored (ibid.: 5). Small states have a special incentive to form or join coalitions, and they behave differently within them than bigger countries (Busigyna and Klimovich, 2017: 6). In a coalition they can share the burden of losses with other members or respond to external challenges more effectively as a group: 'As part of a coalition, small states increase their chances of formulating and implementing a successful policy in the changing external conditions and insist on decisions that they could not secure if they acted on their own' (ibid.). Thus, when small states have succeeded in influencing EU policy along the lines of their national interests and/or have been able to find a majority for their own initiatives, then coalition building has been decisive (Thorhallsson and Wivel, 2006: 660). Limited bargaining capacities of small member states can potentially be counterbalanced with either institutionalized coordination on a regional basis or strategic partnerships with bigger countries. Such counterbalancing strategies 'can help small states to, at least, partially compensate for the disadvantages they face in day-to-day negotiations owing to their limited votes, fewer financial resources, smaller economies and undersized staff' (Panke, 2010: 802).

Influencing the decision-making process in the EU through coalition building is done by means of consultation, informal coordination and cooperation among members states' representatives before and during official negotiations (Advisory Council on International Affairs, 2018: 10). Since EU enlargement, coalition building and informal consensus building have even increased in importance and number because with more members the weight and impact of each have become smaller and their interests more diverse. An increased use of qualified majority voting, growing politicization of EU matters and various crises affecting various groups of member states in different ways add to the picture (Kuusik and Raik, 2018a: 1).

Coalitions can take various forms and types while the categories and also their definitions differ among scholars. The most useful ones in the context of this chapter are by Korteweg (2018) and Ruse (2013). Korteweg identifies three types of coalitions within the EU: lead groups, ad hoc coalitions and alliances. Lead groups are loose partnerships at official level aimed primarily at putting certain initiatives on EU level in motion. Ad hoc coalitions are more political but either created for a single occasion or focused on just a single issue. Finally, 'alliances emerge at the political level, are structural in nature and usually cover multiple issues' (Korteweg, 2018). Ruse (2013: 85 ff.) differs mainly among ad hoc and institutionalized coalitions. She defines the former as 'issue-based aggregations of member states that coordinate their action in order to achieve short-term goals.' Their composition is not fixed and can change depending on the particular issue. In addition, such coalitions are not supported by a permanent procedural and/or structural basis. In contrast, institutionalized coalitions are 'more stable (in terms of membership) and quite fixed alignments (in terms of durability)' usually bound together by geographical proximity (Ruse, 2013: 86). But there are also differences among institutionalized coalitions. Some occur outside a specific EU context in the form of regional organizations with firm organizational structures, for example, a secretariat and committees, others are less institutionalized but, for example, still have a rotating chairmanship. Generally, institutionalized groupings with a long-term basis are more stable than ad hoc coalitions and profit from good knowledge of each other and well-functioning communication structures (Lang and von Ondarza, 2018: 5). Other scholars use different categories, for example, Klemencic (2011: 3), distinguishing more broadly between coalitions and alliances, or Panke (2010), differing between strategic partnerships of small with big member states and institutionalized coordination arrangements on a regional basis.

Ruse (2013: 85) further identified four types of institutionalized coalition-building patterns: interest based, culture and identity based, ideological affinity based and territorially constituted, with the first and the fourth being the most relevant and common categories. Territorial coalitions emerge on the basis of a geographical proximity of their member states, sharing political and cultural features as well as identity and history (Advisory Council on International Affairs, 2018: 13). They often stem from pre-existing regional cooperation, based on a joint regional identity, shared history and common values (Ruse, 2013: 88), for example, Nordic and Baltic cooperation (see next section). Thus, the aforementioned patterns, culture and identity and ideological affinity can also play a role in territorial coalitions. Theme-based (Advisory Council on International Affairs, 2018: 17) or interest-based and task-specific (Ruse, 2013: 87) coalitions gather member states beyond one particular region that share similar interests and preferences and cooperate systematically on specific EU dossiers and policy areas usually over a longer period of time which distinguishes them from ad hoc coalitions. Examples, including all or some of the Nordic and/or Baltic countries, are the Group of Net Contributors, the Copenhagen Group on financial and competition policy, a trade policy group promoting free trade and the Northern Lights Group for a general exchange of information (Advisory Council on International Affairs, 2018: 17–19). Such groups work mainly behind the scenes and are hardly known to the wider public. There are however also theme-based or task-specific ad hoc coalitions such as the New Hanseatic League or the Frugal Four (see below).

As shown, coalitions in the EU can take on different types and can be driven by various motives. But in general, 'coalitions in the EU tend to be open, flexible and issue-based, with member states operating nimbly to find partners in the process of informal negotiations and pre-cooking of decisions' (Kuusik and Raik, 2018a: 1). "Coalition patterns are fluid, rather than stable", governments tend to come together and consult on different issues in varying constellations (Elgstroem et al., 2001: 117). Still, following certain coalition patterns, some countries are more likely to form coalitions with certain states than with others. Supported by geographical and cultural considerations stemming from the cases of the Nordic countries and the United Kingdom, coalition patterns tend to be surprisingly fixed (Elgstroem et al., 2001: 126). This assumption still seems valid today by and large as the examples of the coalitions of the Nordic and/or Baltic countries will show.

However, that there is some more variation today due to a larger number of member states and therefore more choice can also be verified by the examples of coalitions of some Nordic and/or Baltic states with other EU members.

From the above, the assumption can be derived that alliances (Korteweg, 2018) or institutionalized coalitions, both territorial and interest based, (Ruse, 2013), are the most advanced forms of coalition building. But are they also the most influential and most desired forms of coalitions for the Baltic and Nordic EU members in an EU context, or do they prefer more (single) issue-based ad hoc coalitions?

5.3 The Nordic and Baltic states and EU coalitions

5.3.1 The Nordic and the Baltic countries in the EU

The Nordic and the Baltic states are all small countries albeit to different extents – populations between 372,520 (Iceland) and 10 million (Sweden) and 1.3 (Estonia) and 2.8 (Lithuania) million – and are all to differing degrees integrated in the European cooperation and integration structures. Of the five Nordic countries, generally often considered as somewhat reluctant and EU sceptical, Denmark (since 1973), Sweden and Finland (since 1995) are members of the EU. However, only Finland is fully integrated, participates in all areas of cooperation and is a member of the Eurozone. Denmark has obtained optouts from the Maastricht Treaty for four cooperation areas, Economic and Monetary Union (EMU), Justice and Home Affairs, the European Citizenship and, until 2022, the Common Security and Defence Policy. Sweden does formally not have any opt-outs but remains outside the Eurozone regardless, due to a negative people's referendum in 2003. Norway and Iceland decided to stay out of the EU but entered the newly established European Economic Area (EEA) as members of the European Free Trade Area (EFTA) in 1994 and are cooperating closely with the EU in many policy areas. Through the EEA they gained access to the European Single Market but are in return bound to a big part of EU legislation without being able to co-decide on it.

Estonia, Latvia and Lithuania joined the EU in 2004. Membership was one of their foremost foreign policy objectives since regaining their full independence from the Soviet Union in 1991. They participate in all policy areas and even joined the EMU and introduced the Euro despite the aftermath of the financial and economic crises in 2011, 2013 and 2015, respectively. The Nordic countries supported the Baltic states since independence strongly in their political, economic and societal transition process. They can also be considered as an important link connecting the Baltic states to other Western EU members (Janning and Raik, 2020: 11). Despite several differences in their political and socio-economic structures and EU relations, both groups of countries cooperate closely in many policy areas and on various levels. They jointly form the core of various formal/institutionalized and informal coalitions in a regional setting and on an EU level.

The Nordic EU countries, but even more Estonia, Latvia and Lithuania, belonging to the smallest EU members, have been forced to find opportunities to participate in intra-EU coalitions and to team up with the leading and other countries while simultaneously building up a reputation of reliable partners (Busigyna and

Klimovich, 2017: 11). For forming a blocking minority in the qualified majority voting system in the Council of the EU, 35 per cent of the total EU population is required. Even together the six constitute only 5.4 per cent, thus they need partners. Therefore, they are all perceived as fairly active and effective in vocalizing their preferences in EU decision-making (Panke, 2010) and hence in developing EU-related network and coalition-building capabilities. But there are differences as to the actual activities and their connectedness depending on their capacities. According to the European Council on Foreign Relations EU Coalition Explorer of 2020, showing potentials for coalition building among EU member states, Sweden was ranked 5th, Finland 9th, Denmark 12th, Estonia 14th, as a country with both Baltic and Nordic characteristics playing a special role in connecting the two groups, Lithuania 19th and Latvia 21st, in the overall ranking (combination of most contacted, most responsive, most influential, shared interests, deeper integration, most disappointing, punch above weight and punch below weight) (European Council on Foreign Relations, 2020). Sweden is regarded as the most influential Nordic country in an EU context and as one of the EU members mastering the art of punching above one's weight best (Zerka, 2020).

5.3.2. Nordic cooperation

The five Nordic countries cooperate closely in many policy fields both in formal/institutionalized and informal settings. The Nordic Council (NC), established as early as 1952, serves as a forum for promoting cooperation among the Nordic countries' national parliaments. In order to foster a more regular and structured cooperation among governments, the Nordic Council of Ministers (NCM) was inaugurated in 1971 as a separate intergovernmental institution. As a general rule, Nordic cooperation 'never goes further than the interests of each country permit' (Nordiska Rådet, 1973). Nordic cooperation takes place in many fields of public administration with however a focus on culture (based on a common Nordic identity and values), education, research and environment. The Nordic cooperation structures developed fairly advanced capabilities for problem-solving in policy areas such as environment, energy, consumer protection, technology and regional development (Schumacher, 2000: 15).

Generally, Nordic cooperation, especially its more informal settings such as meetings of prime ministers, foreign ministers and officials in an EU context, can be seen as an arena for EU-related debate, sharing information and informally testing arguments. Formats such as lunch meetings of the Nordic prime ministers, including Norway and Iceland, prior to important European Council summits are well established mainly for the exchange of views. However, they are not so much a place where coalitions are built and specific policy positions are agreed on (Grøn and Wivel, 2018: 276).

For the NCM, the picture looks different. Despite having increasingly promoted intra-Nordic EU cooperation and included EU matters on its agenda since the early 2000s and even more after the Brexit referendum in the United Kingdom, the NCM's role remains less clear and effective (Schulz and Henökl, 2020: 412). Both the NCM and NC have ambitions to coordinate Nordic positions on EU-related issues. EU-related Nordic activities include projects with EU funds, direct EU involvement or the coordination of the implementation of EU directives, for example, in relation to labour market-, environment- and consumer rights-related questions. Already since 1995, all Nordic Ministerial Councils and committees have EU issues on their agenda. However, they deal with them unsystematically, in different forms and to different extents (Ottoson, 2008: 26). Despite efforts to improve this, not much has changed so far. Thus, the NCM has never evolved into an arena or an instrument for the coordination of EU policies, establishing a joint Nordic agenda on the European level (Olesen and Strang, 2016: 36) and this way influencing EU decision-making. At least the NCM, together with the NC, is used for monitoring and analyzing the effects of EU legislation on national legislation in the Nordic countries and for finding ways to harmonize the implementation of EU legislation. This way, unnecessary differences among the Nordic countries and the emergence of so-called border obstacles, for example, different taxation, are to be prevented. The NCM-Secretariat principally regards itself as a facilitator, as a meeting place and as an instrument which could be used to complement the member states' EU policies but in practice seems reluctant to take on a more proactive role. The old idea to establish a NCM representation in Brussels did not find any support among the governments at any point and has hence never materialized (Etzold, 2020).

Overall, the Nordic countries never intended to establish a Nordic bloc within the EU, both through formal and informal ways, but rather to strive for closer cooperation wherever possible and feasible. The Nordic countries are too small and too different to act as a Nordic bloc (Maertens, 1997: 43). They desired to be flexible, also having the opportunity to ally with bigger member states to promote their interests. After Finland and Sweden joined the EU, the Nordic EU members even developed some sort of rivalry by seeking rather individually than jointly for more national influence in EU decision-making

(Ruse, 2013: 99). Also, not all EU-related topics are suited to be considered on a Nordic level because the countries' interests are partly different, for example, in relation to the development of the Eurozone, security and defence and migration, rendering comprehensive coordination and joint positioning in all policy areas unfeasible. The biggest hinder for a more efficient and effective Nordic EU policy influencing EU decision-making, driven by the NCM and NC, is however that two of its members, Iceland and Norway, remain outside the EU. For them, the formal and informal cooperation structures can be seen as an additional backdoor into EU circles, but their, in much respect, different interests as non-members prevent more joint positioning.

Thus, the formal and informal forms of Nordic cooperation can overall be regarded as a territorially constituted regional alliance, somehow culture and identity based, featuring some common interests but then mainly in a regional context. While on the EU level it is good for some exchange of information, coordination and harmonization, it has never fully evolved into a strong permanent institutionalized coalition suitable for influencing EU decision-making on a great scale.

5.3.3 Baltic, Nordic-Baltic and Baltic Sea

The three Baltic countries (B3) alone form in some way a permanent institutionalized coalition within the EU, for example, in the form of informal meetings among the prime ministers or ministers of foreign affairs. The three also know institutionalized cooperation within the Baltic Council of Ministers and the parliamentary Baltic Assembly. But both informal and formal forms of cooperation ever became so close as Nordic cooperation. The group is far too small to exert any major impact alone but renders useful for information exchange and policy coordination. As a subgroup within the bigger group of the Nordic-Baltic countries, it appears sensible to first coordinate among each other and to formulate possible common interests before entering bigger coalitions and tangible negotiations with other countries. This way the Baltic voice could be stronger. In the early 1990s, the Nordic countries made close cooperation and establishing intra-Baltic cooperation structures even a pre-condition for entering closer interaction with them.

Consequently, the *Nordic-Baltic Eight* (NB8) started as an informal setting in 1992 and has slowly been formalized and to some extent institutionalized. Its main purpose was to discuss important regional and international issues in an informal atmosphere, fostering regional cooperation in a wider sense. Typical topics of discussion include regional security, cyber, connectivity, including regional energy and transport projects and digital cooperation, climate change, environment, cultural and health. The group is chaired and coordinated by one of its members on a rotational basis but does not have a permanent secretariat. According to the Latvian Ministry of Foreign Affairs, the cooperation among the Baltic and Nordic countries, based on shared values and political and economic interests, has become even more important since the beginning of Russia's war against Ukraine (The Baltic Word, 2023). The current focus is on strengthening the region's overall security, i.e., military security and deterrence capabilities.

Out of this group, the *Nordic-Baltic 6* (NB6) emerged as a highly informal and mainly consultative setting within an EU context, consisting of the three Baltic and the three Nordic EU members. This group was established on a Swedish initiative after the Baltic countries' EU accession in 2004. It provides a framework for informal meetings discussing EU-related matters without following any formal guidelines on how to proceed with the institutionalized coordination of EU policy, depending on the policy area (Ruse, 2013: 102). Unlike in NB8, there is no formal head or rotating chairmanship. The group meets, for example, in person of the prime ministers prior to European Council gatherings and the foreign ministers before EU General Affairs and EU Foreign Affairs Council meetings but also on the level of the countries' permanent representatives in COREPER. Cooperation among the latter is based on 'thick trust' (Ruse, 2013: 12). The significance of this group has increased over the years (Janning and Raik, 2020: 8). The NB6 format can be regarded as a family 'within which the members can raise new ideas and shifting positions, seek support, and ask questions' (Kuusik and Raik, 2018b: 9). The cooperation among the NB6 is issue based, which implies that there is cooperation only when there is common ground (Kuusik and Raik, 2018a: 6) and when there is a specific issue of common interest. But the countries are not obliged to agree or engage with initiatives by their fellow members (Kuusik and Raik, 2018b: 4). Important issues discussed in NB6 are, for example, democratic values and the rule of law, free trade, digitalization and security and defence (Kuusik and Raik, 2018a).

The biggest success of the group so far has been the adoption of the EU Strategy for the Baltic Sea Region in the European Council in 2009 (Ruse, 2014: 237–239). The six pushed hard for this but required the support of the big Baltic Sea littoral EU states, Germany and Poland. For this, the existing structures of institutionalized Baltic Sea cooperation including all eight countries were useful. But the latter, especially the intergovernmental Council of the Baltic Sea States (CBSS), has never intended to materialize as an EU lobby group mainly because they include also non-EU members, Iceland, Norway and, until its suspension and then withdrawal in spring 2022, Russia. Instead, the CBSS focussed purely on regional affairs and intended to effectively foster regional cooperation outside an EU setting while there always has been an interest to involve the EU in its work, manifested by the EU's membership in the body.

Overall, Nordic-Baltic cooperation can be characterized as a territorial constituted permanent partly institutionalized coalition, pre-dominantly interest based. It is mainly about exchange, consultation and coordination among the countries in order to find acceptance for their positions and to test them (Ruse, 2013: 108). This way, Nordic-Baltic cooperation forms a stable basis for more interest-based coalitions with other countries on mainly an ad hoc basis (see below). This common basis is required when wishing to influence decision-making in the EU effectively as being too small on their own. According to Ruse (2014: 243), NB6 expresses a regional voice in the EU but as in the case of the Nordic countries there is no persistent regional Nordic-Baltic bloc in EU decision-making.

5.3.4 Nordic-Baltic Plus

With all or several of the Nordic and Baltic countries at their core, several coalitions including other EU members, mostly small but in some formations also big(ger) ones, have formed over the years. Among the first was the *Northern Future Forum* consisting of the NB8 plus the United Kingdom, meeting regularly between 2010 and 2016 and exchanging views on European, international and security-related issues. The NB8 also held several meetings with the four *Visegrad* countries (Czech Republic, Hungary, Poland and Slovakia) since 2013 but this has not developed into a firm structure. The three Baltic states also participate in the *Three Seas Initiative* together with the Visegrad Four, Austria, Bulgaria, Croatia, Romania and Slovenia, connecting the Baltic Sea, the Black Sea and the Adriatic Sea. Through promoting cooperation, the initiative aims at contributing to economic growth and energy security and fostering cohesion and unity across Europe. The three Nordic EU members have inaugurated their own informal coalition with Germany on foreign ministers' level, N3+1, in 2013, to exchange information positions on important EU items, however on a very unregular basis and without being able (or willing) to develop a more permanent structure out of this.

An interesting example of a new coalition is the *New Hanseatic League*. Inaugurated in March 2018, it originally consisted of the NB6 plus Ireland and the Netherlands. The latter initiated the group and took some sort of leadership position, trying to pursue its own EU agenda, which however the NB6 countries did not feel too comfortable with as equality is a key characteristic within the group and any bid of leadership is seen as unnatural (Kuusik and Raik, 2018b: 7). Later that year the Czech Republic and Slovakia joined as well. The group, in person of the countries' finance ministers, met regularly for informal dinners and issued several position papers, also seeking the attention of the public for its proposals. Their main message was that the responsibility for Europe's economic and monetary policy as well as economic reforms should remain in the member states. Within this context, the countries opposed a Eurozone budget, a European minister for finances and major far-reaching Eurozone reforms as proposed by France's president Emmanuel Macron. Furthermore, consisting of both Eurozone members and non-members, they strongly advised to include non-members in efforts to reform and develop the Eurozone further on an equal basis. The group has been successful when the European Council in December 2018 agreed instead on a Eurozone budget on a 'Budgetary Instrument for Convergence and Competitiveness' (BICC), the group's counterproposal, which was much weaker and lacked all the risk-sharing features than originally intended by France but was dropped during the COVID-19 crisis requiring new measures and instruments (Schöller, 2021: 11). While the group has been criticized for its hardly constructive agenda (Korteweg, 2018) – for obvious reasons especially France accused them of dividing the EU – and the lack of own proposals (Janning quoted in ORF 2019), Schöller (2021: 16) hailed the league for being successful in replacing issues with counterproposals in form of the BICC. Such a coordinated opposition by smaller member states was rather atypical for EMU politics (ibid.: 2) and showed that they were able to pursue their own preferences and prevent the proposal of a powerful coalition led by France with South European and at least some German support (ibid.: 16).

The league had also sought Germany's support. Although the Federal German government's reactions on Macron's proposals have been lukewarm and parts of the country's political spectrum even sympathized with the objections of the league, Germany officially did not become a part of the group. In this particular case it would have been difficult for the German government to take sides and to dismiss the French ideas too openly and frankly due to the importance of the French-German axis. Without Germany or any other big member, the group, however, was too small to form a blocking minority within the EU and to achieve a lot in the long term (Beundermann, 2019; Schulz and Henökl, 2020: 413). Also, among its members natural differences existed since the group includes Eurozone members and non-members as well as net payers and net recipients. They also differed in opinion whether the league should remain focussed on Eurozone and economic issues or open up and adopt a broader agenda.

Korteweg (2018) labelled the New Hanseatic League an ad hoc coalition rather than a proper alliance. Indeed, the group seemed to have fulfilled its main purpose when in form of a compromise the original reform proposals for the Eurozone were watered down (see above). For exerting any major impact in the negotiations on the Multiannual Financial Framework (MFF) 2021–2027 that started in 2019, the league was not regarded as suitable as the interests among the net payers (the Netherlands, Denmark and Sweden) and net receivers (Baltic states, Czech Republic and Slovakia) diverged. The same division applied in the case of the COVID-19 Recovery Funds that were negotiated after the outbreak of the pandemic in Europe in spring 2020. Finland left the group after a government change in spring 2019, wishing to be more flexible with whom to cooperate on what issue (Ojanen, 2020).

After its preliminary end, a new group of four like-minded countries formed in late 2019, consisting of only net payers. Denmark, the Netherlands and Sweden were joined by Austria that although a Central European country had sympathized with the New Hanseatic League and pursued similar interests. In that sense, the group is an interesting example for a formation in which geographical proximity and thematic interests mix. Finland joined the group for aforementioned reasons on an occasional basis only, preventing a strong Nordic unity on this matter. This group became known as the *Frugal Four/Five* and managed to steer the directions of negotiations on the MFF and the COVID-19 Recovery Funds (Next Generation EU) in 2020 and forced the rest of the EU into compromises. The four countries' prime ministers made clear in February 2020 that 'our budget contribution must remain stable, taking into account inflation and economic growth. This requires the budget to remain at 1 percent of EU gross national income and a system of permanent corrections to protect individual states from having to shoulder excessive budgetary burdens' (Government Offices of Sweden, 2020). In the budget negotiations each member state has a veto right, so each of them could have prevented the budget and the Funds by its own but the countries joined forces in order to make their case stronger and to make changes through increasing their bargaining power. It seems that coalition building and hard negotiating for their objectives paid off for the group. The four obtained rebates from the budget for themselves, and they managed to get the desired reduction of the size of grants as opposed to loans in the Recovery Funds worth €750 billion, of which 390 billion in grants and 360 billion in loans – the European Commission had proposed a 500/250 division while the Frugal Four originally demanded an even lower share of grants – and pushed hard for conditionality in member states' access to the funds (Zerka, 2020). However, they were not successful in their bid to reduce the overall EU budget framework, as especially Germany did not support this and declared willingness to increase its own contributions to the budget. This shows that the small(er) countries even when acting as a group need the at least silent support by Germany to be successful (Schulz and Henökl, 2020: 415).

Still, with the end of the negotiations the original mission of the Frugal Four has been accomplished but there were discussions whether the group should continue. Denmark, for example, wanted the four to cooperate also in the future on similar and possibly also other issues, while it was clear that in policy areas in which member states do not have a veto right it might be more difficult for them to exert the same level of impact (Sørensen, 2020). However, the group has not continued as such, but variations emerged which however did not accomplish the same power and influence so far. In September 2021, a group of finance ministers from Austria, the Czech Republic, Denmark, Finland, Latvia, the Netherlands, Slovakia and Sweden took position in talks about post-pandemic changes to the EU's budget rules. Regarding its members, working method and policy areas this group showed some resemblance to the Hanseatic League. In a joint paper, they promoted improvements to the EU's Stability and Growth Pact but insisted that reforms should not jeopardize fiscal sustainability, as this creates confidence and fiscal space for political priorities, or weaken debt reduction targets but instead making the rules simpler, more transparent and consistently applied (Fleming, 2021).

All these cases are good examples for theme- and interest-based ad hoc coalitions as they centre around a specific single issue in which several countries wish for a certain outcome along their national interest and a territorial core, have some substance and make at least some achievement. In these coalitions the membership varies along needs and interests. For the Nordic and Baltic states as small countries these ad hoc coalitions seem to be useful instruments in EU negotiations.

5.4 Discussion and conclusions: Which coalition for what purpose?

As the analysis has shown, within an EU context Nordic and Baltic EU members' governments seem overall to prefer flexible, issue-specific intergovernmental ad hoc coalitions consisting of a smaller number of like-minded countries in order to defend their interests. This can also involve countries outside the Nordic-Baltic region (New Hanseatic League, Frugal Four), preferably with the inclusion of some bigger ones, that are on more or less the same line regarding the very same issue. They seem most effective in countries' attempts to block or at least water down important EU decisions, although the analyzed cases have not managed to do so throughout but at least to some extent. For this, the geographical context of the coalition is not decisive, although it might help the effectiveness of the group when there is a common cultural and political understanding and when some trust and good communication lines already exist.

For mainly information exchange, consultation and some sort of coordination among geographically close and culturally like-minded countries the regional permanent institutionalized coalitions seem to be appropriate and useful, for implementing hard interests in the EU decision-making process less so. Schulz and Henökl (2020: 415) confirmed that Brexit has not altered the Nordic countries' preferences for ad hoc coalitions over the long established Nordic institutions. In contrast, regional permanent institutionalized coalitions can be less useful when there are institutional and thematical dividing lines among its members, for example, EU versus non-EU members and Eurozone members versus Eurozone outsiders, as these lines bear a potential to split the group. This could then hamper the cooperation in other policy areas in which they have common interests. Unlike ad hoc coalitions (or also even institutionalized coalitions) that have emerged within an EU context, consist of EU members only, have an explicit EU agenda and solely attempt at influencing EU decision-making, mostly in particular policy areas, regional organizations' primary goal is to foster independent regional cooperation in various policy areas more generally. They also do attempts to drive regional issues onto the EU agenda and to make an explicit regional impact but with usually not all their members also being part of the EU their possibilities are limited to exert impact on particular policy outcomes. Through their activities, they mainly promote regional interests and the respective region, in some cases also within the EU, to a lesser extent national ones. In contrast, ad hoc coalitions of like-minded states mainly promote national interests which one country just on its own would not be able to obtain. A case in between is the institutionalized NB6 as a permanent but hardly institutionalized and more informal format which deals with regional interests and coordinates national interests in an EU setting but is less used for hard negotiating as the group is too small.

Thus, while some of the academic literature labels institutionalized coalitions and alliances as the highest category of coalitions, in practice they do not seem to be preferred by the governments of the Nordic and Baltic countries for influencing decision-making along their national interests in an EU context. Although they provide the necessary infrastructure, they might not be flexible enough and/or have clear disadvantages such as being too small in terms of members or having not only EU member states on board in order to be able to do so.

References

Advisory Council on International Affairs. (2018). *Forming Coalitions in the EU after Brexit. Alliances for a European Union That Modernizes and Protects.* The Hague.

Busigyna, I.M. and Klimovich, S.A. (2017). A coalition within a coalition: The Baltics in the European Union. *Political Science* 9(1): 4–17.

Elgström, O., Bjurulf, B., Johansson, J. and Sannerstedt, A. (2001). Coalitions in European Union negotiations. *Scandinavian Political Studies* 24(2): 111–128.

Etzold, T. (2020). The Nordic council of ministers: Aspirations for more political relevance. *Politics and Governance* 8(4): 11–20.

European Council on Foreign Relation. (2020). EU coalition explorer. Available at https://ecfr.eu/special/eucoalitionexplorer/.

Fleming, S. (2021). EU hawks set tough terms for talks on reform of fiscal rules. *Financial Times.* Available at EU hawks set tough terms for talks on reform of fiscal rules | Financial Times (ft.com).

Government Offices of Sweden. (2020). *The 'Frugal Four' Advocate a Responsible EU Budget, Opinion Piece by Sebastian Kurz,* eds. M. Fredriksen, M. Rutte and S. Löfven. Available at https://www.government.se/opinion-pieces/2020/02/the-frugal-four-advocate-a-responsible-eu-budget/.

Grøn, C.H. and Wivel, A. (2018). Scandinavia and the European Union: Pragmatic functionalism reconsidered. In: P. Nedergaard and A. Wivel (eds.), *The Routledge Handbook of Scandinavian Politics* (Routledge: London), pp. 269–280.

Janning, J. and Raik, K. (2020). *Estonia's Partner in the EU Coalition Machinery* (International Centre for Defense and Security/Estonian Foreign Policy Institute: Tallinn).

Janning, J. and Zunneberg, C. (2017). The invisible web – from interaction to coalition-building in the EU, European council on foreign relations. Available at ecfr.eu/publication/the_invisible_web_from_interaction_to_coalition_building_in_the_eu_7289/.

Klemencic, M. (2011). Formal intergovernmental alliances in the European Union: Disappearing or still alive?. EUSA Twelfth Biennial International Conference Boston.

Korteweg, R. (2018). *Why a New Hanseatic League Will Not Be Enough* (Clingendael Spectator: The Hague).

Kuusik, P. and Raik, K. (2018a). *The Nordic-Baltic Region in the EU* (International Centre for Defence and Security/Estonian Foreign Policy Institute).

Kuusik, P. and Raik, K. (2018b). *The Nordic-Baltic Region in the EU: A Loose Club of Friends, European Policy Analysis* (Swedish Institute for European Policy Studies: Stockholm).

Lang, K.O. and von Ondarza, N. (2018). Minilateralismen in der EU. Chancen und Risiken der innereuropäischen Diplomatie. *Stiftung Wissenschaft und Politik, SWP-Aktuell* 7, pp. 1–8.

Maertens, M. (1997). 'Norden in der EU: Jeder kämpft für sich allein'. Nordeuropaforum. *Zeitschrift für Politik, Wirtschaft und Kultur* 1: 43.

Marc, B. (2019). Machtfaktor Hansegruppe. *Frankfurter Allgemeine Zeitung*, 15 April.

Nordiska Rådet. (1973). *The Role of the Nordic Countries in European Cooperation* (Nordisk Utredningsserie: Stockholm), p. 27.

Ojanen, H. (2020). Why Finland never joined the frugal four, European council on foreign relations, 4 September. Available at https://ecfr.eu/article/commentary_why_finland _never_joined_the_frugal_four.

Olesen, T.B. and Strang, J. (2016). European challenge to Nordic institutional cooperation. In: J. Strang (ed.), *Nordic Cooperation: A European Region in Transition* (Routledge: Oxon), pp. 27–47.

ORF. (2019). EU Staaten: Brexit mischt Machtblöcke neu, 25 May. Available at: https://orf .at/stories/3121146.

Ottosson, S. (2008). *Nordiska Ministerrådet - Fortsättning på reformen*, Rapport 2008-12-02 (Regeringskansliet, Utrikesdepartementet: Stockholm).

Panke, D. (2010). Small states in the European Union: Structural disadvantages in EU policy-making and counter-strategies. *Journal of European Public Policy* 17(6): 799–817.

Ruse, I. (2013). *(Why) Do Neighbours Cooperate?: Institutionalized Coalitions and Bargaining Power in EU Council Negotiations* (Budrich Unipress).

Ruse, I. (2014). Nordic-Baltic interaction in European Union negotiations: Taking advantage of institutionalized cooperation. *Journal of Baltic Studies* 45(2): 229–246.

Ruse, I. (2015). Nordic cooperation in the EU Council: Does institutional embeddedness matter?. In: C. H. Grøn, P. Nedergaard, and A. Wivel (eds.), *The Nordic countries and the European union: Still the other European Community?* (Routledge: Abingdon), pp. 53–67.

Schöller, M.G. (2021). Preventing the Eurozone budget: Issue replacement and small state influence in EMU. *Journal of European Public Policy* 28(11): 1727–1747.

Schulz, D.F. and Henökl, T. (2020). New alliances in post-Brexit Europe: Does the new Hanseatic League revive Nordic political cooperation? *Politics and Governance* 8(4): 409–419.

Schumacher, T. (2000). *The Emergence of the New Nordic Co-Operation*. Working Paper No. 6 (Dansk Udenrigspolitisk Institut: Copenhagen).

Sørensen, C. (2020). How the frugal four could grow in number and influence. *European Council on Foreign Relations*, 7 September. Available at https://ecfr.eu/article/ commentary_how_the_frugal_four_could_grow_in_number_and_influence/.

The Baltic Word. (2023). Latvia will be coordinating cooperation in the format of the Nordic-Baltic eight. Available at https://balticword.com/latvia-will-be-coordinating -cooperation-in-the-format-of-the-nordic-baltic-eight/.

Thorhallsson, B. and Wivel, A. (2006). Small states in the European Union: What do we know and what would we like to know? *Cambridge Review of International Affairs* 19(4): 651–668.

Zerka, P. (2020). *The Swede Spot: Why Stockholm Needs Flexible Coalitions* (Commentary, European Council on Foreign Relations). Available at: https://ecfr.eu/artice/commentary _the_swede_spot_why_stockholm_needs_flexible_coalitions.

6 Small-state veto power in the European Union? National interests and coalition-building capacity of the member states in Central and Eastern Europe

Boyka Stefanova

6.1 Introduction

In November 2020, in an effort to prevent the link between access to EU funding and adherence to rule-of-law principles, Hungary imposed a veto on the adoption of the EU's 2021–2027 Multi-annual Financial Framework (MFF), despite its position of a major beneficiary of structural funds from the EU budget. Also in November 2020, Bulgaria blocked the Negotiating Framework for the accession of the Republic of North Macedonia, despite the fact that two years prior to that, Bulgaria's 2018 Presidency of the Council of the EU had advanced the European perspective of the Western Balkans as a central priority. The Czech Republic and Slovakia in turn blocked the Council Conclusions on EU enlargement to the Western Balkans in disagreement with Bulgaria's conditions, effectively imposing a veto on Bulgaria's veto on the same issue, thus stalling the accession negotiations of Albania and the Republic of North Macedonia.

Instances of member state veto in the past have sometimes preserved policy stability and prevented reform and sometimes have been resolved by side payments or opt-outs as the common approach to collective action problems in the EU. This chapter explores veto rights as a less discussed aspect of the international behaviour of small states on the example of selected EU member states in Central and Eastern Europe (CEE). The negotiation strategies of small states, implemented to overcome the challenge of size, and the effectiveness of those strategies represent principal areas of investigation in this volume, outlined by Högenauer and Mišík in the Introduction. As the editors point out, experience, cooperation and prioritization in building up capacity, rather than size, are at the centre of this analysis.

The member states in CEE are a prominent case for the workings of shelter theory that posits the dependence of small states on the protection, resources and rules-based order of international institutions. These countries are in principle more dependent on EU resources than small EU members in general. Furthermore, they are a notable example of the socialization of the member states into the values, norms and policy principles of EU decision-making. Small states should be expected to maintain a consensus-seeking posture within the EU institutions. A veto on an EU agenda item, imposed by a small state from CEE, would be a puzzle

DOI: 10.4324/9781003380641-7

for the workings of shelter theory. How does veto power feature in the negotiation strategies of the small states from CEE? How effective is a small-state veto in influencing EU negotiation outcomes? What are the implications of veto rights for the model of bargaining and decision-making in the EU that relies on multiple coalitions across the East/West divide in EU politics?

Analytically, the chapter posits shelter theory as a principal explanatory framework for the relationship between small states and international organizations. As the literature accepts that, despite their dependence on the resources and protection of international institutions, the behaviour of small states is not predetermined. They are capable of agency embedded in the complexity of the institutional context. The chapter sets out to examine how small states negotiate and whether they are effective negotiators. It draws on theories of negotiation and bargaining, in order to examine the connections between structural disadvantages, small-state influencing strategies and the scope conditions for their success, first outlined in Panke (2012b). Methodologically, the chapter traces such connections in selected case studies of veto power applied by member states in CEE and their ad hoc coalitions in EU decision-making. The cases are based on European Commission proposals on different policy areas, negotiated and voted on in the Council between July 2015 and December 2022.

The chapter contributes to two literatures: on the international behaviour of small states and on the politics of veto rights in EU negotiations. It expands upon the preceding chapters in this volume that focus on the social practices, networks and persuasion capacities of small states. Analysis builds on arguments that focus on small-state preferences for issue prioritization, networking in a socially thick environment and ability to claim competence and wield influence as successful negotiation strategies overcoming the challenges of size in EU decision-making.

The chapter brings in an added dimension. It contends that, in parallel to being selective in their ability to launch system-relevant initiatives, participating in networks and positioning themselves as effective and persuasive negotiators, small states apply rationalist strategies as veto players affecting both the immediate outcomes of EU-level decision-making and its systemic coherence.

The chapter proceeds as follows. The next section explores the negotiation strategies of small states and the place of the member states from CEE in EU decision-making. It proceeds to identify the key features of veto politics in the EU as a form of executive dominance dependent on access to EU-based resources. The chapter traces the evolution of small-state veto politics on the frontier of EU governance on the example of the veto positions adopted by selected small states in CEE and their capacity to affect the EU's systemic coherence. Cases under examination include the 2015 refugee crisis during which individual small states in CEE rejected EU-mandated distribution of refugee quotas, Hungary's opposition to the principle of political conditionality in the 2021–2027 Multi-Annual Financial Framework (MFF) and the structuring of EU emergency funding, as well as Bulgaria's veto politics in European Council deliberations on a negotiating framework for the EU accession of the Republic of North Macedonia.

6.2 The international behaviour of small states

The concept of 'smallness' with regard to state size is not a coherent analytical category. According to power-based theorizing, states are defined by their material resources, such as population size, economic power and military capabilities (Steinmetz and Wivel, 2010: 5). Realism posits small states as vulnerable. They take international outcomes for granted and need protection and coalitions for either bandwagoning or balancing hegemonic powers. Keohane (1969: 296) suggests that small states are 'system ineffectual' states: they can do little to influence the system (Theys, 2022: 85).

The clustering of states based exclusively on their size-induced vulnerabilities is one-dimensional and does not represent the variety of preferences and initiatives that guide the international behaviour of small states (Thorhallsson and Wivel, 2006). In order to address such limitations, scholars have defined small states also in relative terms, evoking their asymmetry with respect to great powers and their capacity to participate in alliances (Keohane, 1969: 296; Long, 2017). A relational perspective is relevant to the EU, as the latter has adopted the typology of large states, middle-tier powers and small states defined as states with population size below the EU average (Panke, 2012b: 315).

Liberal theory holds a number of propositions relevant to the international position of small states. It brings in institutionalist and domestic politics perspectives. Neoliberal institutionalism not only acknowledges the asymmetry of capabilities between large and small states but also accepts that small states can exert influence in international politics. According to Panke (2010), the international behaviour of small states is driven both by domestic constraints and international factors. The domestic constraints proposition suggests that small states will have divergent strategies, reflecting different domestic interests and dimensions of political conflict: urban/rural, exporters/importers, majority/minority, centre/periphery, etc. Katzenstein (1985) and, more recently, Bohle and Jacoby (2017) point to the flexibility of small states to adapt to the international environment by creating consensual domestic arrangements as 'domestic buffers' against the constraints of a fluctuating international economy (Thorhallsson, 2011).

Preferences for multilateralism and institutional embeddedness do not mean that small states are power neutral. According to Bailes and Thorhallsson (2013: 105), small states are a part of the postmodern power play. Long (2017) and Panke (2010) have found that small states are diverse, possessing different material, ideational and relational resources. As a result, there is a wide variation in the interests, strategies and goals they pursue. An intersubjective definition of the concept of smallness is warranted, due to its socially constructed and contested nature (Theys, 2022). Long (2017) has argued that small states are most successful when they apply three types of power: derivative, collective and particularistic-intrinsic. This typology shows that power is relational, embedded in structures, agendas and connections. Derivative power relies upon the relationship with a great power. Collective power involves building coalitions of supportive states, achieved through institutions. Particular-intrinsic power relies on the assets of the small state seeking to wield influence.

Thorhallsson and Wivel (2006) contend that the institutionalized policy environment benefits small states. Within a given institutional context, they adopt a variety of roles. Small states are free riders as consumers of security in defence alliances. They tend to support a stronger role for international organizations in agenda setting and the resolution of coordination and distributional conflicts (Keohane, 1969; Panke, 2010, 2012a, 2012b; Steinsson and Thorhallsson, 2017). Theoretically, therefore, small states are likely to seek multilateral frameworks, compromise, conflict resolution and coalition building.

Shelter theory (Thorhallsson, 2011, 2019) constitutes the main explanation of the relationship between small states and international institutions. Shelter cannot be reduced to the dynamics of alliance politics. It defines a relationship of protection and assistance across political, economic and social domains based on sustained cooperation, alignment and socialization. In an EU context, those values are captured by the concept of Europeanization and represent a thick social environment (Johnston, 2001). In that relationship small states are not simply recipients of institutional protection. They deploy a plethora of strategies to advance their interests, 'punching above their weight' (Panke, 2012a; Wivel and Crandall, 2019).

Panke (2012b: 318) posits two types of small-state strategy: capacity building and shaping strategies. The former do not directly influence negotiations; they create the conditions for that. The latter are designed to influence negotiation outcomes by applying either constructivist persuasion strategies (e.g. framing, expertise, references to the common good, leader-based communication or arguing) or rationalist bargaining strategies (such as the exchange of threats, concessions and demands, support trading and coalition formation). Panke (2010, 2012b) notes that persuasion- and bargaining-based strategies coexist, as one and the same actor may shift between a rationalist and a constructivist mode of action when seeking influence.

6.3.1   *The special place of small states in the EU*

The very creation of the European Union (originally, of European Economic Community of 1957) reflects a compromise between large and small states in Europe. Small states form the majority of EU member states. The EU provides a framework for small states to be under its protection when their political and economic interests are pursued in its institutional contexts. The EU thus validates the workings of shelter theory (Bailes and Thorhallsson, 2013: 105; Thorhallsson, 2019). It acts as a broad form of shelter, providing existential and soft security guarantees (Bailes and Thorhallsson, 2013).

The deepening of European integration through EU treaty reform has had a complex influence on the relative positioning of small states. The Nice and Lisbon treaties have been conducive to rebalancing the power of large and small EU member states. Changes to the decision-making procedure in the Council, such as new voting rules, the creation of permanent posts for an EU president and a High Representative for External Affairs and the increased use of ad hoc coalitions among large member states have removed traditional unanimity and simple majority mechanisms that had favoured the interests of small states. At the same time, treaty reform has strengthened the EU's rule-based order, making power capabilities less important (Howard Grøn and Wivel, 2011: 528). Furthermore, the member states have continued to reserve certain fields to unanimous decision-making. Such areas include adoption of the EU's seven-year financial framework, foreign policy, the EU's own resources as well as enlargement of the Schengen Area, among others.

The position of the small states, therefore, is not predetermined. Long (2017: 15) contends that they can enjoy certain latitude and advance individual preferences by means of influence over agenda setting and bargaining. Depending on the institutional context, small states may place a higher value on autonomy relative to external protection. Long (2017), Panke (2010, 2012b) and Thorhallsson (2011), among others, have found that small states apply a variety of strategies as a mix of cooperation and confrontation, including multiple asymmetries, veto power, networks and persuasion. Empirical analyzes reveal that, according to behavioural trajectory, the 19 small EU member states form a heterogeneous group (Panke, 2010; Schoeller, 2022; Sotirov et al., 2021). Panke (2010) reports substantial variation in small-state participation in the EU, operationalized as a mix of capacity building and shaping strategies, and discusses the possibility of shifts between rationalist and normative behaviour. While conventional theorizing would explain such outcomes with country size, membership experience and domestic factors, the literature concludes that the negotiation success of small states is achieved by being active, using diverse arguing and persuasion strategies, presenting initiatives for the common good and acting as norm entrepreneurs (Howard Grøn and Wivel, 2011: 529; Ingebritzen, 2002; Panke, 2010, 2012b).

Long (2017) conceptualizes the diverse trajectories of small-state behaviour as agency. It follows that shelter theory is permissive of the agency of small states. Analytically, we may open the black box of their international behaviour and its outcomes through the lens of bargaining theory. This perspective examines the capacity of small states to advance their interests, participate in networks and gain international influence through social dynamics. In line with shelter theory we expect persuasion, based on normative arguments and logic of appropriateness, to be the essential modus operandi of small states, rather than coercion, associated with rationalist logics and implemented as veto or exit threats.

Still, veto rights and the threat of exit continue to exist as small-state bargaining strategies. In the EU, as well as international institutions in general, they represent a tool for preserving member state autonomy and a negotiating strategy in policy reform. Both principles are essential to the international behaviour of small states.

6.3 Veto power in EU politics

Veto rights are embedded in the legislative history of European integration as a result of the 'empty chair crisis' of 1965 that strengthened the ability of the member states to protect individual interests from changing along regional goals. Veto power is also an element of the bargaining position of small states, as they shift between persuasive and rationalist strategies. The EU member states may individually use veto to reflect coherent domestic interests or the preferences of influential social actors. They may participate in adversarial coalitions whereby veto power is amplified and more likely to maintain policy stability (see Schoeller, 2022).

There are two competing theories of bargaining power in EU decision-making: institutionalism and intergovernmentalism (Slapin, 2011). Institutionalism holds that bargaining power is related to the rules governing negotiations; for example, that the support of all member states is necessary for a treaty to come into effect. Thus, institutionalism implies that states with preferences close to the status quo (wishing to prevent change) should be able to veto a treaty or a policy proposal. Intergovernmentalism posits bargaining power as derived from member state size and resources, meaning that large states should prevail at negotiations regardless of their proximity to the status quo.[1] According to Slapin (2011), small states are as capable of preventing policy change as large states.

Member state bargaining strategies within the EU are amenable to the premises of veto players theory applicable to decision-making processes in the domestic political system (Tsebelis, 2002), whereby member states may be conceptualized as multiple veto players. The theory traces the impact of individual or collective actors, whose agreement is required for a policy decision and who may veto the process when they have diverging or opposing preferences. The theory is relevant to assessing the capacity of political systems to produce policy change. The number of players, congruence (similarity) of the positions of the parties and internal cohesion of collective veto players (e.g. executive dominance or positions *within* a veto player) influence the capacity for change (Buti and Polli, 2021). Policy stability/ inertia increases when the number of veto players and/or their cohesion increases and when their congruence decreases (Buti and Polli, 2021). Shifting coalitions reduce the capacity of veto rights to block decision-making and are thus permissive of policy change (Sotirov et al., 2021: 2154).

Tracing the evolution of EU treaty reform, Slapin (2011) finds that such nominal references to veto rights, veto players and adversarial coalitions do not adequately measure the effectiveness of veto power from a rational choice perspective. Slapin's (2011) veto theory posits an interaction between exit rights from the EU, the possibility to threaten member states with exclusion and veto power. Member states opt for a veto or an exit regime depending on the costs associated with leaving the organization relative to maintaining membership while accepting policy change. For the remaining states, it similarly depends on relative costs: whether it is more costly to retain veto rights, allowing member states to block future proposals, or allow status quo states to either exit the organization by absorbing reputational costs or threaten to exclude them from the regime (Slapin, 2011: 134). The trade-off between veto rights and exit threats depends on the bargaining leverage the two options provide. Slapin's (2011) argument is that for veto rights to matter in an international organization, leaving the organization must cease to be a viable option for member states. States that wish to remain in the EU, but also wish to block deeper integration, may not be able to cast a veto if other member states can credibly threaten to exclude them if they do. As the Lisbon Treaty introduced the option of leaving the EU, we should expect veto politics, and especially the veto power of small states, to be in decline.

In reality, the small EU member states have been in a strong bargaining position to maintain veto rights. They have prevented further institutional change by preserving the number of EU commissioners and voting rights on the Council. Individually, Greece maintained a veto over Macedonia's EU accession negotiations between 2009 and 2018. Cyprus vetoed all rounds of negotiations pertaining to Turkey's EU accession. The Netherlands has blocked the Schengen membership of Bulgaria and Romania since 2011.

Analyzing small-state strategies in response to Brexit, Wivel and Thorhallsson (2018: 272) find that small states are likely to use hedging strategies as a combination of shelter seeking and preferences for elite autonomy, benefiting from EU and large-state support while seeking to form 'coalitions with like-minded states' on specific aspects of decision-making. Similar findings are reported in Schoeller (2022) with regard to small-state coalitions in the Economic and Monetary Union. In order to understand the diverging preferences driving small-state veto politics, Csehi and Kaniok (2021) test whether increased levels of politicization affect the capacity of small states to influence EU decision-making and, especially, how the greater centrality of identity, sovereignty-related issues and challenger parties affect the argumentative and bargaining powers of small states in EU-level negotiations. The authors find that 'small state' nature is a causal factor, as small-state identities influence their behaviour more profoundly than the level of domestic contestation with regard to European integration.

'Smallness,' therefore, remains a factor in the international strategies of states. It is in line with institutionalist bargaining theory (Slapin, 2011) and propositions of small-state agency (Long, 2017). We should expect small states to act as status quo powers in international negotiation, supporting established institutional rules to the detriment of power-based preferences for policy change. We should also expect these states to be able to build adversarial coalitions, apply veto and exit threats and obtain concessions. How effective are such rationalist strategies, given the fundamentally consensus-oriented culture of small states and their proactive persuasion and networking power? The application of veto power on behalf of individual small states in CEE is a challenging case for shelter theory due to the pronounced dependence of these member states on EU protection, resources and socialization.

6.4 Small-state shelter theory and veto politics in practice: The countries of Central and Eastern Europe as veto players

In line with shelter theory (Thorhallsson, 2011, 2019), the national preferences of the small states in Central and Eastern Europe (CEE) for more integration have been coterminous with their EU membership (Mišík, 2019). These countries have supported the European Commission as the guardian of the regional interest, ensuring that small states are represented in interstate bargaining relative to the interests of large states.

Boehle and Jacoby (2017) contend that the member states in CEE have a limited capacity to act as a permanent coalition. In reality, there has been no cohesive East European coalition in the EU with the capacity to act as a veto player. The most prominent subregional format, the Visegrád Group (V4),[2] is a pragmatic ad hoc coalition with variable participants and bargaining mechanisms. However, in the context of major policy decisions affecting critical areas of EU governance, such as budget, foreign policy, crisis management and asylum, individual CEE member states have done just that. They have acted based on their own preferences, vetoed or threatened to veto EU-level decisions, formed adversarial coalitions and affected the dynamics of EU policy-making.

The proposition about the Europeanization and adaptability of the small states has worked in contradictory ways in CEE. On the one hand, Europeanization has produced significant socialization outcomes in the domestic political systems of the member states (Schimmelfennig and Sedelmeier, 2005). It has increased the capacity and confidence of the small states from CEE to work with the EU institutions and consolidated their long-term dependence on the EU structural policies (Hanf and Soetendorp, 2014). On the other hand, coterminous with the growth of the material capabilities and argumentative resources of the small states has been the aggrandizement of the executive in several states in CEE, embedded in populist efforts to preserve state autonomy by diluting the very principles of Europeanization they have embraced. The coexistence of the two premises of resource dependence and executive autonomy (Stefanova, 2021) marks a departure from the principles of small-state influence in the EU prevalent in the literature.

6.4.1 *Diverging policy preferences in the East?*

How do the bargaining strategies of the small states in CEE balance their preferences for elite autonomy with dependence on EU resources and legitimacy? Questions pertaining to the alignment of the policy preferences of small states in CEE (cohesion), proximity between the policy positions of individual veto players (congruence) and number of veto players (adversarial coalitions) are central to understanding the evolving dynamics of their veto power.

The EU Coalition Explorer (EUCE)[3] maps out the policy preferences of the EU member states and their coalition-building capabilities. Figure 6.1 captures the diversity of policy preferences of selected small states in CEE relative to the EU27 average of ranked preferences as well as the policy preferences of Poland, the largest state in CEE, often considered a middle EU power. The figure shows that, in terms of policy preferences, CEE is neither a homogenous region nor a cohesive collective actor, despite the conventional clustering of EU member states in an East-West dichotomy. The data reveal that the national preferences of the analyzed small states in CEE vary widely and have low visibility relative to the EU average. Such premises point to their limited coalition-building potential, the expectation being that they pitch 'below capacity.'

The figure demonstrates that neither consistent clustering nor overlap with prevalent EU averages is typical of national preferences in CEE. For example, the

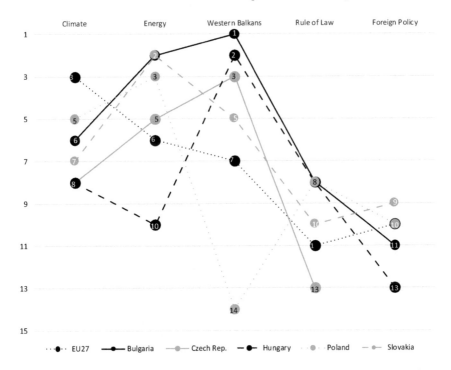

Figure 6.1 Comparing small-state policy preferences. Source: EU Coalition Explorer (EUCE), https://ecfr.eu/special/eucoalitionexplorer/

policy positions of the V4 members differ significantly. The policy intentions of Hungary, the Czech Republic and Slovakia, often assumed as allies in a number of issue areas, show low levels of convergence as potential veto players. National rule-of-law preferences are of low intensity (Ranks 8, 10 and 13 for Hungary, Slovakia and the Czech Republic, respectively), making veto politics in this issue area less likely. The intensity of the policy preferences of the Czech Republic (Rank 3) and Slovakia (Rank 5) for the EU accession of the countries in the Western Balkans similarly shows low cohesion and coalition potential.

The EU Coalition Explorer further notes that, while small states have an opportunity to act as norm entrepreneurs, mediators and coalition builders, the member states in CEE have lagged behind the EU's West European members. Figure 6.2 demonstrates that they are not perceived by their peers to possess such assets and are not typically valued as coalition partners.

The figures collectively reveal that the coalition-building potential of the small states in CEE is limited. EUCE expert assessments refer to individual East European elites as disappointing low-initiative coalition partners, suggesting that the opportunities for participation in small-state blocking coalitions are limited. Due to their divergent interests, these countries may be expected to resort to veto politics when isolated. Propositions about the cooperative, consensus-driven

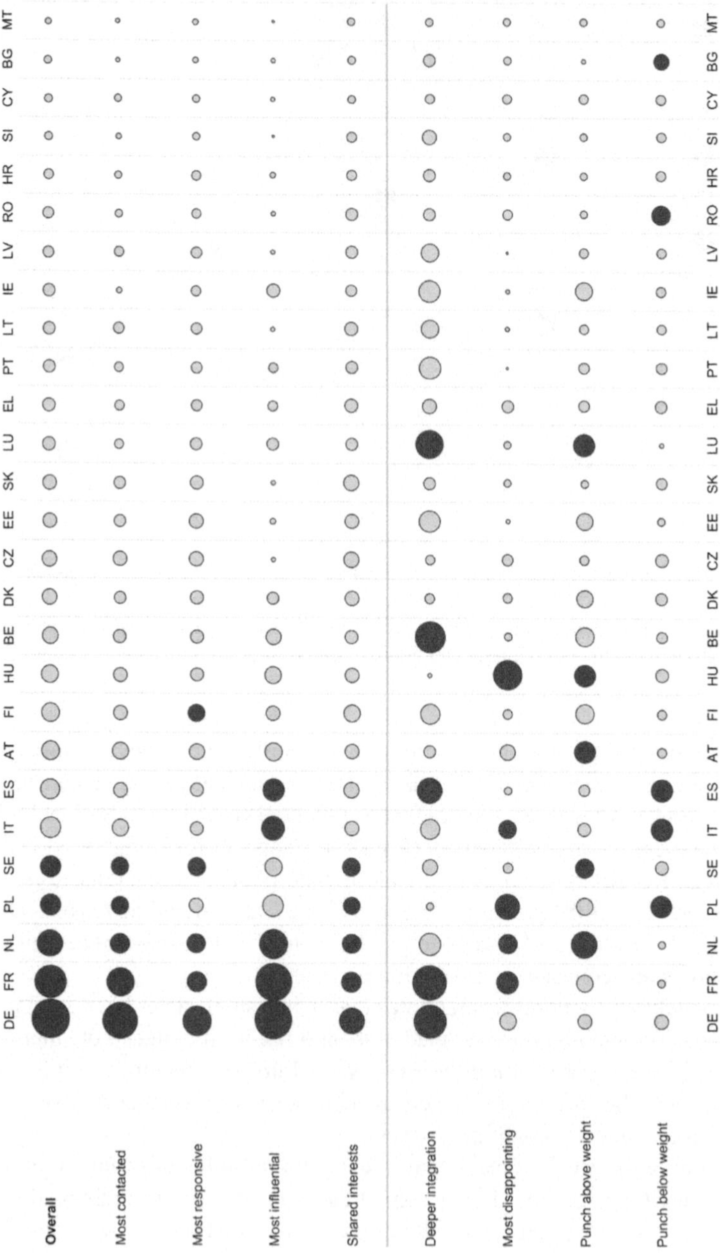

Figure 6.2 The coalition-building relevance of the small states in EEC: Comparative positioning within the 27 EU member states. Source: EU Coalition Explorer (EUCE), https://ecfr.eu/special/eucoalitionexplorer/

culture and persuasion-based strategies of small states, therefore, are not a theoretical necessity. An empirical examination of the negotiating behaviour of the small states in CEE will permit to determine whether they challenge or validate the EU shelter model.

6.5 Bargaining power of the small states in CEE in EU decision-making
This section examines the selective application of adversarial coalitions and veto power on behalf of individual small states in CEE in key instances of decision-making in the Council of the EU/European Council since 2015, with a view towards establishing their effectiveness and capacity to affect EU policy reform.

6.5.1 Small-state adversarial coalitions in the 2015 EU asylum crisis and negotiations of the 2021–2027 Multi-Annual Financial Framework and Emergency Recovery Fund

According to Sarapuu et al. (2021), the 2015 European migrant crisis made it obvious that the classical shelter strategy valid for the small EU member states within the EU was suboptimal. The crisis marked the first test of the ability of a small-state sustainable adversarial coalition to form in CEE (Joensen and Taylor, 2021).

The tensions between the V4 and the majority of EU member states in favour of policy change started in September 2015, when the European Council approved quotas for the relocation of refugees, overruling the dissenting votes of the Czech Republic, Hungary and Slovakia.[4] These counties emerged as status quo powers. They insisted on maintaining asylum measures on a voluntary basis, preventing mandatory rules and permanent quotas (Visegrad Group, 2016). Hungary and Slovakia turned to the Court of Justice of the EU (CJEU) questioning the Council decision over procedural mistakes and, namely, approving relocation with a qualified majority.

In line with institutionalist bargaining theory, given the status quo position of the three countries, we should expect an adversarial coalition to consolidate, at odds with the premises of shelter theory. The evolution of the case demonstrates, however, that a blocking coalition did not hold. Slovakia effectively withdrew from the coalition, signalling a preference in favour of the common good and granting temporary entry to 1,200 asylum seekers (Brady, 2021: 82).

A CJEU judgement of April 2020 concluded that Hungary and the Czech Republic were noncompliant with the temporary mechanism for relocation of refugees and in breach of their obligations under EU law. In 2023, the European Commission launched an infringement procedure against them, confirming that the 2015 Council decision on relocation remained valid.[5] Despite the proceedings, the Czech Republic and Hungary did not take any action to meet their obligations. This outcome points to the capacity of small states to adopt issue-specific strategic positions based on diverging national preferences even if they continue to rely on EU resources for economic growth and government legitimacy.

A similar stream of evidence of fragmented adversarial coalitions in the Council on behalf of the small states from CEE and of the inherently contradictory process of small-state veto under the EU shelter model emerged during the negotiations on the 2021–2027 Multi-Annual Financial Framework (MFF), along with the agreed *Next Generation EU* temporary recovery instrument following the COVID-19 crisis.

The negotiation of the €1.8 trillion financial package of the 2021–2027 MFF marked the first instance of post-Brexit distributional policy. Along the premises of intergovernmentalism, Germany, supported by other member states, proposed a conditionality mechanism making the distribution of EU funds dependent on the adherence to rule-of-law principles. The proposed policy change applied directly to Hungary as a major beneficiary of EU structural funds whose domestic politics have experienced democratic backsliding (Guérin, 2023). In line with the institutionalist negotiation framework, we expect small states to prefer the status quo of old rules precluding a new structure and, consequently, policy reform.

Hungary imposed a veto on the MFF seeking to prevent the proposed conditionality mechanism.[6] It insisted that the EU budget and the rule of law should be treated as separate domains. In December 2020, the German Presidency achieved a compromise, providing assurances that politically targeted conditionality would be excluded by creating an explicit role for the CJEU in the implementation of rule-of-law criteria for access to EU funding.

The depoliticization of the conflict, achieved by legal means, recognized the precedence of the rule of law as a legitimate interest in the EU. Based on the CJEU's decision, the European Commission withheld funding for Hungary, although it did not block the full amount of cohesion funds.[7] Hungary's use of veto was not successful.

Although the unanimity of EU member states was preserved, as a veto player, Hungary emerged isolated in the process of generating a compromise. The European Commission and the EU member states prepared options for implementing the financial framework and recovery package by sidelining a potentially persisting veto. In the context of Council negotiations Germany, along with other member states, expressed a preference for the removal of the principle of unanimity in the Council, suggesting a possibility for policy reform to pre-empt veto rights.[8]

Hungary failed to impose a sustainable veto or create a coherent adversarial coalition in the MFF bargaining process. Initially, the Czech Republic and Slovakia were prepared to participate in a joint position. They did not support Hungary in its objections, however, as the rule of law conditionality was not a significant issue for them (demonstrated in Figure 6.1). The choice not to maintain a CEE-based coalition shows the relative isolation of small-state populist elites and their ideological coalitions from broader coalition-building processes in EU decision-making.[9]

The possibility of exclusion from the regime weakened Hungary's (along with Poland's) bargaining position. The opportunity for the member states to move ahead with an exclusion rule meant that, as a veto player, Hungary remained isolated. The outcome validates Slapin's (2011) bargaining theory suggesting that if there is an opportunity of exclusion, the threat of exit is less credible, leading to a weaker bargaining position for the veto player (Slapin, 2011: 144). At the first stage of the negotiation game of the MFF, the member states opted to exclude Hungary from negotiation due to noncompliance with the values and norms of the EU. The European Commission suspended payments for Hungary (albeit not completely). The member states signalled that they were prepared to remove the veto option altogether by accepting majority voting in budget issues. They also allowed access to EU funding to substate actors in Hungary, in order to differentiate between the government and social actors, revealing that the veto player's position lacked public support.

The failure of an adversarial coalition to form showed the limited capacity of small-state elites in CEE to hedge their positions in EU-level decision-making (Wivel and Thorhallsson, 2018) by preventing policy change while drawing on shelter theory to protect their interests and maintaining legitimacy.

The case of a single-member veto in the EU enlargement policy further validates changes in the trade-off between veto rights and exclusion threats in the direction of marginalization of veto power in EU decision-making.

6.5.2 Small-state veto rights: Bulgaria and the negotiating framework on North Macedonia in the Council

The Republic of North Macedonia was granted the status of a EU candidate country in 2005. The European Commission first recommended the launch of accession negotiations in its Progress Report of November 2009. Due to a name dispute, Greece maintained a veto on Macedonia's NATO and EU membership between 2009 and 2018. Greece and Macedonia signed the Prespa Agreement on 17 June 2018 whereby Macedonia adopted the name Republic of North Macedonia (February 2019). The European Council adopted Conclusions on the opening of accession negotiations with the Republic of North Macedonia on 25 March 2020 (Council of the European Union, 2020).

The Conclusions did not list preliminary conditions for North Macedonia at the time. Bulgaria outlined its position in a memorandum to the EU member states in August 2020. It did not seek to build a supporting coalition.[10] At the December 2020 Council, Bulgaria imposed a veto on the decision to establish a negotiation framework for the Republic of North Macedonia by including conditions pertaining to bilateral issues and by invoking Macedonia's non-compliance with the 2017 friendship and good neighbourliness treaty between the two countries.[11]

At the same Council meeting, the Czech Republic and Slovakia issued a statement objecting to Bulgaria's rationale for including conditions in the Council Conclusions (Permanent Representation of the Czech Republic to the European Union, 2020). As Bulgaria did not withdraw its veto, the negotiating framework was blocked by a de facto double veto, combining substantive and procedural aspects of the negotiating framework.

The double veto of the EU negotiating framework with the Republic of North Macedonia was a puzzling outcome, especially in the context of a German Presidency of the Council, as Germany is the preferred coalition partner for the countries in CEE. The veto stalled the agenda of the EU enlargement policy and threatened to set a precedent, as more countries from the Western Balkans could potentially relate to bilateral issues in accession negotiations. In July 2022, France's

EU Presidency negotiated with Bulgaria to lift the veto. According to the French proposal, Bulgaria unblocked the EU's accession negotiations with the Republic of North Macedonia in exchange for including Bulgarians 'on an equal footing' with other peoples recognized in the Republic of North Macedonia's constitution, signing a bilateral protocol, and the 'effective implementation' of the 2017 bilateral friendliness and good neighbourliness treaty (Agence Europe, 2022).

The case shows that small states do not automatically enjoy derivative power (Long, 2017: 196) by convincing fellow large states to adopt their agenda. The consensus-seeking proposal of France's Council Presidency sought to neutralize the veto while lending support to North Macedonia's accession negotiations. It was the Republic of North Macedonia – a small state, candidate for EU membership – that was able to use derivative power. In an unprecedented move, the German Bundestag adopted a resolution recognizing a North Macedonian language, iden- tity and culture (Sofia News Agency, 2023).[12] Both small states applied ration- alist strategies. Bulgaria used coercion while the Republic of North Macedonia pursued lobbying. Rationalist strategizing took precedence over persuasion-based interactions.

Bulgaria's veto was only partially effective, insofar as it succeeded in 'Europeanizing' the bargaining process on the issue but not the issue itself. Bulgaria's position as a veto player was unsustainable. It placed the country in iso- lation, thus raising the costs for national elites to maintain a veto without changes in their shelter-seeking behaviour. Furthermore, Bulgaria failed to mobilize a sup- porting coalition and obtained only limited concessions likely to disappear over time. Lifting the veto validated the prevalence of shelter theory as a model of small-state behaviour in the EU.

6.6 Conclusion

Examined with regard to the principal questions on small-state strategies dis- cussed in this volume, the findings from the three cases of veto power, applied by EU member states in CEE, suggest that small states are likely to use rationalist strategies depending on the institutional context. Due to its diverse applications across policy areas spanning migration, budget management, foundational norms and values and enlargement policy, small-state veto has emerged as a recurrent feature of EU decision-making. At the same time, in line with the premises of shelter theory, the analysed cases show that small states maintain a relationship based on protection by and dependence on the EU. The cases confirm prior find- ings in the literature (Panke, 2010; Long, 2017) that point to the capacity of small states to shift their strategies between rationalist and normative premises. The application of veto rights therefore remains a valid behavioural trajectory, despite theoretical expectations about the compromise-seeking preferences of small states in general.

The analysis of small-state veto on the example of countries in CEE shows that the strategy is applied as a populist-statist reaction that departs from the conven- tional use of veto politics in EU decision-making, as the latter assumes a coherent value-neutral national preference. Such differences narrow down the political definition of member state veto to an actor-centred (*statist*) phenomenon. The application of veto rights, as demonstrated in the cases of Hungary and Bulgaria, may be interpreted as an elite reaction to the detriment of universal claims of member state (*sovereign*) veto that should reflect the popular will (Stefanova, 2021). The potential differences between member-state veto in CEE and conventional cases of veto politics on behalf of West European member states present an opportunity for comparative research on small-state strategies in the EU.

With regard to the second research question posed by this volume (Högenauer and Mišík, Introduction), that of the effectiveness of small-state strategies in EU-level decision-making, it may be concluded that when seeking to preserve their national interests at the expense of the majority preference, the member states in CEE have been unsuccessful. Furthermore, the use of veto rights has largely failed to consolidate as a compensatory strategy for participation in EU decision-making.

In terms of visibility in EU decision-making, the three cases demonstrate a build-up of potential for institutional reform. The cases provide important evidence validating propositions about a weakening veto regime in the EU, originally hypothesized by Slapin (2011: 146). Every application of veto by the small states in CEE has led to a substitution of consensus-oriented negotiations in the Council of the EU by preferences for majority voting effectively overriding small-state veto or exit threats. On the contrary, threats of exclusion within the Council have intensified, implemented as withholding of funds, infringement procedures and peer isolation. The negotiating power of the veto players has declined due to rising costs of maintaining a veto for fear of being excluded.

The cases of Hungary's disregard for EU norms in a growing number of issue areas, from asylum rights to budget rules, and Bulgaria's veto on the EU negotiating framework for the Republic of North Macedonia reinforce the contested nature of consensus-based decision-making with the potential to aggravate, rather than transcend, the East-West division in the EU.

Notes

1 Intergovernmentalism, outlined in Slapin (2011), should be distinguished from liberal intergovernmentalism, the general theory of European integration (Moravcsik, 1998). It is a theory of international negotiation that does not include preference formation, a principal component of liberal intergovernmentalism.
2 The Czech Republic, Hungary, Poland and Slovakia are members of the Visegrád Group.
3 The EU Coalition Explorer represents an elite survey conducted by the European Council on Foreign Relations in the 27 member states of the European Union. It maps out the potential for future coalition building among the EU member states across 20 policy areas. Online at https://ecfr.eu/special/eucoalitionexplorer/.
4 See Goran Gotev, 'Visegrad countries trigger crisis ahead of EU refugee summit.' *Euractiv,* 22 September 2015. https://www.euractiv.com/section/justice-home-affairs/news/visegrad-countries-trigger-crisis-ahead-of-eu-refugee-summit/ (accessed 22 July 2023).
5 European Commission, 2023. 'Relocation: Commission launches infringement procedures against the Czech Republic, Hungary and Poland.' *Press Release.* Document IP/17/1607.

6 Poland also imposed a veto in the process. Hungary and Poland initially attempted a coalition as like-minded states.

7 In line with the rule-of-law conditionality mechanism, the European Commission withheld the larger part of the original cohesion funds, planned for Hungary: 6.3 billion euros, instead of 7.5 billion euros, remained suspended over corruption concerns related to the use of EU money. Payments to Hungary from the EU's pandemic recovery fund in the amount of 5.8 billion were subject to strict criteria (Guérin, 2023).

8 See *Euronews*, 'Germany calls for abolition of "paralysing" EU Member States foreign policy veto.' 8 June 2021, https://www.euronews.com/my-europe/2021/06/08/germany-calls-for-abolition-of-paralysing-eu-member-states-foreign-policy-veto (accessed 12 May 2023).

9 See Tomáš Valášek, 'Can the V4 survive Hungary and Poland's veto.' *Politico*, 9 December 2020. https://www.politico.eu/article/can-the-v4-survive-hungary-and-polands-veto/ (accessed 1 June 2021).

10 A French veto on the negotiating framework, initially imposed in 2019, was lifted by that time. Denmark and the Netherlands also have previously vetoed accession talks with the Republic of North Macedonia.

11 The treaty of friendship, good-neighbourliness and cooperation between the Republic of Bulgaria and the Republic of Macedonia was signed in Skopje on 1 August 2017. The text of the treaty is available at https://treaties.un.org/doc/Publication/UNTS/No %20Volume/55013/Part/I-55013-08000002804f5d3c.pdf.

12 The existence of a North Macedonian identity was not a part of Bulgaria's veto. Identities are not an element of and do not depend on international recognition. The Bundestag also mandated that the German executive work to prevent Bulgaria from introducing additional conditions on the Republic of North Macedonia's accession.

Bibliography

Agence Europe. (2022). *Bulgarian Parliament Votes in Favour of Lifting Veto on North Macedonia's Accession to EU*, 24 June (Brussels). Available at https://agenceurope.eu/en/bulletin/article/12979/7 (accessed 13 May 2023).

Bailes, A. and Thorhallsson, B. (2013). Instrumentalizing the European Union in small state strategies. *Journal of European Integration* 35(2): 99–115. DOI: 10.1080/07036337.2012.689828.

Beribes, A. (2021). The misunderstood? The Visegrád States and the conference on the future of Europe. *Facts & Findings* 439(July) (Berlin: Konrad-Adenauer-Stiftung e. V).

Bohle, D. and Jacoby, W. (2017). Lean, special, or consensual? Vulnerability and external buffering in the small states of East-Central Europe. *Comparative Politics* 49(2): 191–212.

Brady, H. (2021). Openness versus helplessness: Europe's border crisis, 2015-2018. In: T. Joensen and I. Taylor (eds), *Small States and the European Migrant Crisis* (Palgrave Macmillan: Cham), pp. 67–85.

Buti, M. and Polli, O. (2021). Veto player theory and the governance of the Recovery and Resilience Facility. VoxEU Center for European Policy Research (CEPR). *Facility*. Available at https://voxeu.org/article/veto-player-theory-and-governance-recovery-and-resilience- (accessed 20 May 2021).

Council of the European Union. (2020). *Enlargement and Stabilisation and Association Process: The Republic of North Macedonia and the Republic of Albania*. Council conclusions. Document COM (2020) 57 final, SWD(2020) 46 final and SWD(2020) 47 final (Council of the European Union: Brussels).

Csehi, R. and Kaniok, P. (2021). Does politicization matter? Small states in East-Central Europe and the Brexit negotiations. *East European Politics and Societies: and Cultures* 35(1): 136–155.

Guérin, A. (2023). "The rule of law: The uncertain gamble on conditionality." European Issue No. 660, 13 March 2023. Available at https://www.robert-schuman.eu/en/european-issues/0660-the-rule-of-law-the-uncertain-gamble-on-conditionality.

Hanf, K. and Soetendorp, B. (2014). Small states and the Europeanization of public policy. In: K. Hanf and B. Soetendorp (eds), *Adapting to European Integration: Small States and the European Union* (Routledge: Abingdon and New York), pp. 1-13.

Howard Grøn, C. and Wivel, A. (2011). Maximizing influence in the European Union after the Lisbon Treaty: From small state policy to smart state strategy. *Journal of European Integration* 33(5): 523–539. DOI: 10.1080/07036337.2010.546846.

Ingebritsen, C. (2002). Norm entrepreneurs: Scandinavia's role in world politics. *Cooperation and Conflict* 37(1): 11–23.

Joensen, T. and Taylor, I. (2021). *Small States and the European Migrant Crisis: Politics and Governance* (Palgrave Macmillan: Cham).

Johnston, A. (2001). Treating international institutions as social environments. *International Studies Quarterly* 45(4): 487–515.

Katzenstein, P. (1985). *Small States in World Markets: Industrial Policy in Europe* (Cornell University Press: Ithaca NY).

Keohane, R. (1969). Lilliputians' dilemma: Small states in international politics. *International Organization* 23(2): 291–310.

Long, T. (2017). Small states, great power? Gaining influence through intrinsic, derivative, and collective power. *International Studies Review* 19(2): 185–205.

Mišík, M. (2019). *External Energy Security in the European Union: Small Member States' Perspective* (Routledge: Abington and New York).

Moravcsik, A. (1998). *The Choice for Europe: Social Purpose and State Power from Messina to Maastricht* (Cornell University Press: Ithaca NY).

Panke, D. (2010). *Small States in the European Union: Coping with Structural Disadvantages* (Ashgate: Farnham).

Panke, D. (2012a). Negotiation effectiveness: Why some states are better than others in making their voices count in EU negotiations. *Comparative European Politics* 10(1): 111–132.

Panke, D. (2012b). Dwarfs in international negotiations: How small states make their voices heard. *Cambridge Review of International Affairs* 25(3): 313–328. DOI: 10.1080/09557571.2012.710590.

Permanent Representation of the Czech Republic to the European Union. (2020). Joint statement by the ministers of foreign affairs of the Czech Republic and the Slovak Republic on the Council conclusions on enlargement, 14 December 2020. Available at https://www.mzv.cz/representation_brussels/en/news_and_media/joint_statement_by_the_ministers_of.html (accessed 31 May 2021).

Sarapuu, K., Thorhallsson, B. and Wivel, A. (2021). Analyzing small states in crisis: Fundamental assumptions and analytical starting points. In: T. Joensen and I. Taylor (eds), *Small States and the European Migrant Crisis* (Palgrave Macmillan: Cham), pp. 19–40.

Schimmelfennig, F. and Sedelmeier, U. (eds) (2005). *The Europeanization of Central and Eastern Europe* (Cornell University Press: Ithaca NY).

Schoeller, M. (2022). Centrifugal forces in a hegemonic environment: The rise of small-state coalitions in the Economic and Monetary Union. *European Political Science Review* 14(1): 1–17.

Slapin, J. (2011). *Veto Power: Institutional Design in the European Union* (University of Michigan Press: Ann Arbor).

Sofia News Agency. (2023). Germany recognized the Macedonian language, identity and culture. *Novinite.com*, 16 June 2023. Available at https://www.novinite.com/articles/220532/Germany+Recognized+the+Macedonian+Language%2C+Identity+and+Culture (accessed 20 July 2023).

Sotirov, M., Winkel, G. and Eckerberg, K. (2021). The coalitional politics of the European Union's environmental forest policy: Biodiversity conservation, timber legality, and climate protection. *Ambio* 50(12): 2153–2167.

Stefanova, B. (2021). Sovereigntism meets post-Westphalian sovereignty: The EU experience. *Ideology and Politics Journal* 1(17): 161–181.

Steinmetz, R. and Wivel, A. (2010). Introduction. In: R. Steinmetz and A. Wivel (eds.), *Small States in Europe: Challenges and Opportunities* (Ashgate: Surrey and Burlington), pp. 3–14.

Steinsson, S. and Thorhallsson, B. (2017). *Small State Foreign Policy. The Oxford Research Encyclopedia of Politics* (Oxford University Press: Oxford).

Theys, S. (2022). Small states reconsidered: Small is what we make of it. *Journal of International Affairs* 74(2): 81–96.

Thorhallsson, B. (2006 [2000]). The role of small states in the European Union. In: C. Ingebritsen, I.B. Neumann, S. Gstöhl and J. Beyer (eds.), *Small States in International Relations* (University of Washington Press: Seattle), pp. 218–226.

Thorhallsson, B. (2011). Domestic buffer versus external shelter: Viability of small states in the new globalised economy. *European Political Science* 10(3): 324–336. https://doi .org/10.1057/eps.2011.29.

Thorhallsson, B. (ed.). (2019). *Small States and Shelter Theory: Iceland's External Affairs* (Routledge: London).

Thorhallsson, B. and Wivel, A. (2006). Small states in the European Union: What do we know and what would we like to know? *Cambridge Review of International Affairs* 19(4): 651–668.

Tsebelis, G. (2002). *Veto Players: How Political Institutions Work* (Princeton University Press: Princeton).

Visegrad Group. (2016). Joint declaration of the Visegrad group prime ministers. *Visegradgroup.eu*, 8 June 2016. Available at http://www.visegradgroup.eu/documents/ official-statements/joint-declaration-of-the-160609 (accessed 23 July 2023).

Wivel, A. and Crandall, M. (2019). Punching above their weight, but why? Explaining Denmark and Estonia in the transatlantic relationship. *Journal of Transatlantic Studies* 17(3): 392–419. https://doi.org/10.1057/s42738-019-00020-2.

Wivel, A. and Thorhallsson, B. (2018). Brexit and small states in Europe: Hedging, hiding or seeking shelter? In: P. Diamond, P. Nedergaard, and B., Rosamond (eds),*The Routledge Handbook of the Politics of Brexit* (Routledge: London), pp. 266–277.

Section II

Small states in foreign, security and trade policy

7 The economic diplomacy of Luxembourg within the European Union framework

Between agility and stability

Helen Kavvadia

7.1 Introduction

Small states are, by necessity, open economies, due to the absence of self-sufficiency. Therefore, they rely on their economic diplomacy to optimize both the demand and supply sides of their economies. Their international economic relations are of existential significance and are at par with their security needs. The post–World War II order intensified the opportunities as well as the necessity of increased international cooperation. This trend has been further strengthened due to globalization, which has exacerbated the interdependence of states, while also spurring competition and spreading successive crises at the global level. Small states are now being challenged more than ever within the currently prevailing multifocal world order and the 'polycrisis' – a cluster of related global risks with compounding effects (Torkington, 2023) on climate, energy, health and, thereby, at an economic and political level. Constituting the majority of the European Union (EU)[1] member states, small states are increasingly finding 'shelter' (Thorhallsson, 2011; Bailes et al., 2016) within the EU framework, which offers them opportunities to promote their defensive and offensive economic interests at national, regional and global levels. On the one hand, internationally small states can stretch their economic presence globally as part of the EU and sheathed with the EU's international might, while being parallelly in the position to influence the EU's overarching policies to reflect their interests. On the other hand, internally within the EU, small states can benefit from the single market's size and increased economic efficiency engendered by the four fundamental freedoms for the movement of goods, services, capital and labour (Bublitz, 2018; Thirion, 2017). Furthermore, within the EU framework, member states can drive and shape policies to best meet their needs. The way to promote state objectives through economic vectors, policies and activities involving state and non-state actors defines economic diplomacy.

Practised since ancient times, and despite being at the nexus of trade, foreign policy and security, economic diplomacy gained scholarly interest only in the aftermath of the globalization. The academic literature focuses on aspects of economic diplomacy, such as conceptualization (Wayne, 2019; Bayne and Woolcock, 2017; Woolcock, 2012; Melissen et al., 2011; Okano-Heijmans, 2011; Lee and Hudson, 2004), vectors and tools (van Veestra et al., 2011; van Bergeijk and Moons, 2009) and country-specific analyzes (Wang, 2020; Lai, 2017; Rana, 2018)

DOI: 10.4324/9781003380641-9

focusing though on larger players, such as the United States (Parkinson, 2015), the EU (Bouyala Imbert, 2017) and China (Heath, 2016). Small states, and especially smaller EU member countries, have not attracted enough attention, as their policies and activity have minor impact in the globalized world, although being the majority of states, the policies developed in relation to their economic diplomacy and the impact some of them can have are of prime interest to the rest. Luxembourg, having developed into the EU's wealthiest country despite its smallness, is therefore a case to study.

Except for Kavvadia et al. (2018), who analyzed the vectors of Luxembourg's economic diplomacy and confirmed their efficiency and effectiveness, scholarly works argue that the country's success is partly due to different factors, including Luxemburg's capacity in international affairs (Hey, 2003), 'size-overcompensation' within the European institutions (Bailie, 2005; Majerus, 2008; Harmsen and Högenauer, 2021), multilateral policy orientation of a 'multiplier of power' (Bourbaki, 2016), contribution in significant policy development (Hirsch, 2016; Frentz, 2010; Harmsen and Högenauer, 2021), diplomatic style as an 'honest broker' (Hirsch, 2016; Frentz, 2010; Harmsen and Högenauer, 2021) and networking and lobbying capacity (Croisé-Schirtz, 1996; Hirsch, 2016; Frentz, 2010; Harmsen and Högenauer, 2021). Academic works on Luxembourg frequently use the country as a case study to understand small states, from a foreign policy angle (Chong and Maass, 2010), Frentz, 2010) and especially from a security perspective (Archer, 2016; Bailes et al., 2016; Thorhallsson, 2011; Enrikson, 2001; Mastanduno, 1998; Baker Fox, 1969), as part of the increased research interest on small states.

Adding to existing works on small states, this chapter discusses the policy dynamics between Luxembourg and the EU in terms of the Grand Duchy's economic diplomacy. It contributes to the book's second overarching aim of studying specific policy cases in order to address the book's third overall research question of how do small states influence individual EU policy areas. In particular, this chapter takes an historical institutionalism approach to answer the following research question: Under what conditions can Luxembourg's economic diplomacy within the EU framework be best understood?

The use of historical institutionalism in a retrospective analysis can reveal the factors that enabled policy formation over time. The identification of the critical junctures assists the exploratory analysis (DuPont et al., 2020) in order to understand whether Luxembourg's economic diplomacy has evolved through gradual changes or changes introduced at historical turning points (Bell, 2011). In this way, critical historical situations can be identified and their role in breaking, catalyzing or continuing pre-existing trends in Luxembourg's economic diplomacy can be understood.

The understanding of Luxembourg's past economic diplomacy can also hint at future perspectives. Additionally, focusing on Luxembourg as a case study allows for an in-depth study due to the country's smallness (Veenendaal and Corbett, 2015) and allows the replicability of results to other small states.

This chapter approaches the research question mainly using secondary works. It contends that Luxembourg's economic diplomacy objectives, strategies and tactics have changed at critical junctures. The three critical junctures identified reflect meg-atrends' turns that influenced not only Luxembourg but equally the EU (Mariniello et al., 2015). At these critical junctures Luxembourg did not always change in order to follow the EU. In some cases, Luxembourg preceded the EU in planning its eco-nomic and diplomacy policies by several years. In these cases, Luxembourg used these years to prepare and hone its objectives and ways to achieve them, includ-ing the strategies and tactics to influence the overarching EU framework. While Luxembourg's economic diplomacy strategies and tactics show several paradigm shifts, the country's economic diplomacy approach demonstrates a path depend-ency by remaining 'niche' in the sense of prioritizing a limited number of policy areas, in order to match Luxembourg's quasi mono-intensive economic models, increase its impact and overcome its size-related limitations through higher effi-ciency. In this sense, the analysis of Luxembourg's economic diplomacy legacy elucidates its mediation between stability and change (Thelen, 1999).

The structure of the chapter starts with a first section that grounds the analysis in a historical institutionalism perspective. The next section provides an overview of the historical evolution of Luxembourg's economic diplomacy in order to showcase long-established policy patterns based on the country's integration in several larger agglomerations and unions overtime. It reviews also Luxembourg's ever-evolving economic model identifying changes at critical junctures that are seen as identical with the critical junctures of the country's concomitant economic diplomacy and its evolving objectives. Luxembourg's economic and economic diplomacy evolu-tion is subsequently juxtaposed against the EU evolution in order to understand as possible enabling factor whether the country preceded or followed European devel-opments. The third section analyzes Luxembourg's economic diplomacy approach, strategies and tactics within the EU framework and demonstrates path dependency and paradigm shifts, respectively. The last section summarizes the major findings and concludes.

7.2 Economic diplomacy of Luxembourg from an historical institutionalist perspective

Historical institutionalism offers a unique methodological vantage point to understand the long-term trends and evolution of the economic diplomacy of Luxembourg within the EU framework. While predominantly applied in studying institutional aspects, Ikenberry (1998), Cortell and Peterson (1999) and Fioretos (2011) applied historical institutionalism in international relations, while others (Rixen and Viola, 2016; Simmons and Martin, 2002) showcased its exploratory potential in the field. Through temporal concepts, such as path dependency and critical junctures (Viola, 2019), historical institutionalism can explain inertia or change (Ebbinghaus, 2005). Change, if not continuous, is generated at critical junc-tures that are understood as fluidity points when the selection among alternatives opens within windows of opportunity, possibly leading to policy paradigm shifts (Mahoney et al., 2016; Capoccia and Kelemen, 2007; Stinchcombe, 1975). Critical junctures are turning points that interrupt extended periods of stability or more gradual change at opportune moments and offer prospects for innovation (Cortell and Peterson, 1999) by reshaping policy (Thelen, 2002). Through the basic features of historical institutionalism, such as the subsequent process (Arthur, 1994; David, 1985), the self-reinforcing processes and path dependence in the form of sequenced contingent decisions (Rokkan, 1999), a failure to innovate at a critical junction implies a future legacy of either reform or redundancy. Alternatively, the increased returns of a policy change at a critical juncture (Pierson, 2000) reinforce the propensity for future policy to change through positive feedback. For the purposes of this chapter, policy reforms in Luxembourg's economic diplomacy can be both procedural and normative.

Under an historical institutionalism lens the chapter identifies the critical junctures that brought about changes to Luxembourg's economic diplomacy within the EU framework. Despite a background historical overview, the analysis focuses therefore after the establishment of the EU in 1957. The chapter also applies the concept of path dependence (Pierson, 2015; Ebbinghaus, 2005; Mahoney, 2000) to assess 'the dualism between stability and change' (Kay, 2005: 567), in order to explain the absence of shifts in Luxembourg's economic diplomacy approach, which has steadily been a 'niche' economic diplomacy, in the sense that the country has focused its economic diplomacy to a limited number of areas for higher efficiency (Smith, 1999; Henrikson, 2005). In its analysis, the chapter studies also 'how the past impacts the present, with past actions, commitments and change serving to influence, constrain and shape future change'. Beyond identifying critical junctions, the chapter therefore studies what were the changes, in terms of objectives and how changes were implemented in terms of strategies and tactics within the EU framework for achieving national interests. Through historical institutionalism, the chapter tests the following hypothesis to answer the question presented earlier: Luxembourg's economic diplomacy evolution reflects a steady niche approach and paradigm shifts in its objectives and implementation strategies and tactics that occurred around critical junctures engendered primarily by national interests related to EU priorities.

In analogy with the five elements provided by Collier and Munch (2017), this chapter concentrates on examining the following: (1) antecedent conditions, including the historical background in relation to Luxembourg's economy and economic diplomacy; (2) the points in time that triggered the occurrence of critical junctures in the country's economic diplomacy as a result of internal or external factors; (3) the critical mechanisms of production, in the sense of the approach, objectives, strategies and tactics in economic diplomacy used by the Grand Duchy to responded to the critical junctures; and (4) the legacy that results from the mechanisms of production, resulting in path dependency or paradigm shift. The legacy demonstrates whether critical junctures triggered self-reinforcing, self-undermining or reactive responses, which either strengthen or weakened the existing set-up, network or cognitive effects (Viola, 2019) of Luxembourg's economic diplomacy overtime. With regard to Luxembourg's economic diplomacy within the EU framework, the chapter emphasizes the importance of interaction effects, which describe how policies become embedded in a broader framework through the introduction of new add-on or parallel policies and the impact of such embeddedness (Viola, 2019), by studying the strategies and tactics used by Luxembourg in support of its economic diplomacy. Recognizing the broader influence Luxembourg has in the EU framework – seen as a network in which the country is embedded – reveals how the country has been responding internally to critical junctures and the external consequences of the country's reaction (Thelen, 2002), preceding or following EU priorities related to its economic diplomacy. Critical junctures are therefore examined in connection with external and internal impetuses that nonetheless crystallize only through internal responses by affecting the country's economic diplomacy policy formation (Skocpol, 1992; Knight, 1992). This chapter argues that Luxembourg's economic diplomacy has been evolving around critical junctures triggered internally, as well as externally, in response to changing megatrends or external shocks. It identifies the critical junctures and the triggering factors. Furthermore, it explains Luxembourg's economic diplomacy approach, objectives, strategies and tactics, level of ambition, policy change sequencing in relation to EU major turning points.

The analysis of Luxembourg's economic diplomacy legacy elucidates its mediation between stability and change (Thelen, 1999). In this sense, the understanding of Luxembourg's past economic diplomacy can also hint at future perspectives.

7.3 Brief overview of Luxembourg's economic diplomacy over time

This section starts with a longer-term overview of Luxembourg's economic diplomacy, outside the period under review. However, in this way, the chapter records the ever-evolving integration of the country in larger agglomerations and economic unions, which set the basis for patterns of policy choices used by the Grand Duchy after 1957.

7.3.1 The historical roots of Luxembourg's 'belonging experience'

Luxembourg was part of ever-changing larger entities as a result of wars fought by the then great powers and dominion marriages, and inheritances, due to its 'geostrategic importance' (Peporté, 2022: 12). After centuries of foreign dominion, Luxembourg saw the dawn of its independence at the Vienna Congress in 1815. Further to the collapse of the Napoleonic Empire and as a result of a rebalancing attempt by the great powers of the time, in addition to containing France, Luxembourg was attributed to the Netherlands for creating a greater Dutch kingdom while simultaneously becoming a member of the German Confederation (Lodhi, 2019) and later following a Dutch initiative o dilute the French and Belgian cultural and economic influence in Luxembourg' (Calmes, 1989: 326), was forced into the German Customs Union (Zollverein) with Prussia in 1842.

The Zollverein membership constituted a decisive step in Luxembourg's economic development as it integrated an otherwise isolated small country 'closely surrounded by borders, [with] its main roads [. . .] in poor condition and [. . .] only one navigable river' (Peporté, 2022: 18) into an incomparably larger economic area. In this sense, Zollverein membership has also been the onset of the Grand Duchy's economic diplomacy, as the country began introducing policies for its integration into economic networks while parallelly developing two prime economic diplomacy vectors, trade and foreign direct investment (FDI). Trade has been a vector of development in the country's modern era. Imports secured necessary production and living resources, and exports offered market opportunities to Luxembourg-based producers. FDI follows and builds upon trade and has been directed predominantly in the steel industry by German companies, such as the Stinnes group and the Gelsenkirchener Bergwerks-AG, contributing to the growth and know-how transfer not only in technical but also in social issues to ensure a level playing field for fair competition. The introduction of social security legislation, through the laws of 1904 and 1911, regulated 'sick pay, accidents at work, disability and pensions were drafted on the Prussian model' (Peporté, 2022 : 18). Coupled with the construction of physical road and rail links (Biel et al., 2024), Luxembourg's first successful international economic steps created a growth-enabling environment, on which the country built up further growth using its economic diplomacy for stepping up trade and FDI to assure Luxembourg's survival and independence, in response to the country's smallness and its landlocked location, at the centre of Europe.

After the end of World War I, as a consequence of its bitter occupational experience by the ultimately defeated Germany and recognizing the apt benefits of belonging to an economic union, Luxembourg turned from Germany to France with a similar cooperation proposal. The proposal, having been met with disinterest from France, was presented to Belgium later, leading ultimately to an economic union – the Belgium–Luxembourg Economic Union (BLEU) concerning a customs and currency union – in 1922 till World War II. During World War II, the Netherlands joined the two countries and signed the Benelux Union Treaty in 1958, which marked the official continuation of the historic dynastic bonds between the reigning houses of Belgium, the Netherlands and Luxembourg and interlinked the three countries over time. However, it placed their cooperation on a new condition, concentrating on economic bonds and exchanges. Due to its successful judicious blend of political and economic cooperation, the treaty was renewed in 2008, functioning not only parallelly but also synergically with European integration efforts within the EU, converging often to a common stance.

7.3.2 ...continued with Luxembourg's EU membership

The early talks among the three Benelux members allowed them to 'polish' their policy and negotiation tactics before the treaty to create the European Coal and Steel Community (ECSC), which was completed in early 1951 and whose inaugural session of the High Authority and the first session of the Special Council of Ministers Luxembourg offered to host in the following year (Deschamps, 2010). Following this inaugural meeting in Luxembourg, the ECSC established its seat in the country in 1952. In addition to past economic union's participative experience, the benefits of the ECSC creation and membership initiated the Grand Duchy's internationalization and 'Europeanization' path, as they led the country to become one of the founding members of the European Union in 1957. Using this window of opportunity to develop an autonomous economy spearheaded by the emergence of its steel industry while parallelly increasingly integrating within the ever-enlarging EU, Luxembourg benefited economically and socially by using the European internal market to resource its economy and promote its output. Additionally, bandwagoning behind the European political and economic might at an international level, Luxembourg gained access to further resources and market opportunities that would otherwise have been impossible due to its smallness.

Following the usual path of development from the secondary to the tertiary sector of economic production, Luxembourg found plenty of manoeuvring space within the EU for carving out the financial services sector as a niche area of priority for specialization and growth. The development of the finance sector has been a prime Luxembourg objective because of its contribution to economic growth (Bekaert et al., 2005; Gehringer, 2013; Gourinchas and Jeanne, 2006). In order to develop its financial sector, Luxembourg benefited to a large extent from the overarching EU framework. Using its negotiating skills in the run-up to the Merger Treaty establishing a Single Council and a Single Commission of the European Communities (European Union, 1967) in 1965, Luxembourg became the site for most European credit and investment activities and the seat of the European Investment Bank (EIB), which, after ten years of operations in Brussels and as part of a deal for the transfer of ECSC to Brussels, moved to Luxembourg in 1968 despite its strong objections (EIB, 1964). The establishment of the EIB in Luxembourg (in the former ECSC building) was seen by the Luxembourg authorities as an engine for the development of a financial cluster. The objective was successfully promoted by the renowned Luxembourgian stateman Pierre Werner, who served at different ministerial posts and as prime minister for over 30 years. Strategically pursuing the creation of Luxembourg's 'place financière', Werner offered fiscal incentives to attract foreign holdings and banking institutions in Luxembourg (Grosbois, 2009). Furthermore, Werner's main contribution to the EU, 'the Werner Report of 1970 that served as the official blueprint for [Economic and Monetary Union] EMU' (Danescu, 2016: 94), proposed the free movement of capital, which in turn retrofitted in Luxembourg's financial sector's further development.

As briefly shown in the earlier analysis, Luxembourg's economy has been adapting to the ever-evolving international economic structure and context, by changing its economic model and the concomitant economic diplomacy policy in its support.

7.3.3 Luxembourg's ever-evolving economic model

Within this historical backdrop, Luxembourg has been adapting its economy to the prevailing international political and economic context by modifying the prime orientation and structure of its internal production possibilities, crystallized in its ever-evolving economic model. The evolution of the economic model is correlated with the evolution of the country's economic diplomacy, which aims at supporting the prevailing model at any given point in time. The critical junctures in the country's economic model evolution can therefore be considered also as critical junctures for Luxembourg's economic diplomacy.

After the industrial revolution, the Grand Duchy's economic model evolved away from the primary economic sector, by shifting its priorities at three critical junctures that triggered three distinct waves in the country's quasi mono-intensity economic development: the *first wave* (1836–1980s) was based on the secondary sector and characterized by the dominance of steel manufacturing, which represented 25 per cent of employment; the *second wave* (1980s–2010s), during which the financial sector with 11 per cent of employment had the lead role; and the *third wave* (since 2010s) transitioning towards some digitization and innovation, with already some 5 per cent of employment in the information and communication technologies (ICT) of the quaternary sector alone. Containing a range of new technologies that are fusing the physical, digital and biological worlds, the country's third wave development can be seen as a quasi mono-intensity model aiming at the country's 'economic development and diversification . . . through a wide fabric of innovative and dynamic companies [having] . . . a head start on other regions that are considering a similar route' (Sustainability Magazine, 2015: 27, 29). With the latter statement, Luxembourg emerged as part of what is broadly known as the 4th industrial revolution (4IR) or Industry 4.0 (EP, 2016: 22–23) race, despite Luxembourg's coining as the '3rd industrial revolution' (TIRLUX, 2016: 6).

The strategic lead sectors constituting Luxembourg's ever-evolving economic model have been successively developed, securing distinctive top ranks for the country, with steel initially reaching 1.3 per cent of global steel production in 1975 (Casali, 2013), subsequently becoming the most important financial centre in the EU – twelfth in the world – in 2020 (Wardle and Mainelli, 2020), with innovation placing Luxembourg 5th out of the 28 EU member states in the Digital Economy and Society Index in 2017 (Larosse, 2017), 3rd out of 130 countries in 2020 in creative outputs and 6th out of 100 countries in 2015, in Patent Cooperation Treaty resident applications (WB, 2021). The sectors corresponding to the three economic development waves have been chosen to build up the country's prosperity edifice in an additive stepwise manner, whereby the achievements during the first wave constitute the foundation for the second wave; this, in turn, sets the basis for the third wave. This approach allows for a focused prioritization, hence the efficient use of all the country's resources and specialization – rather limited due to its size – in the selected lead sectors to ensure competitive positioning at the international level. In turn, the country's progressively improved positioning allowed for 'safeguarding and supporting existing industries and creating an environment conducive to helping establish new industrial activities, support industrial actors active on the international market, and identify new activity niches' (TIRLUX, 2016: 85). Success at each wave subsequently led through retrofit to the attainment of the next wave. In this way, the country achieved a stepwise progression of its economic model and its diversification overtime.

The Grand Duchy's prime economic sectors have been strategically selected to follow changing overarching megatrends of the wider political, economic and

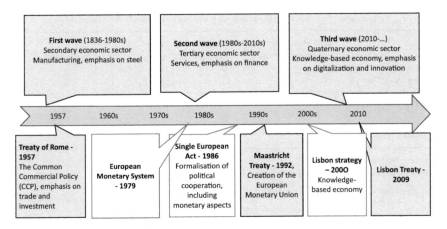

Figure 7.1 Luxembourg's economic model evolution within the EU context

social context at the international and EU level or external shocks, such as the global economic and financial crisis (GEFC). Nonetheless, the country's lead sectors always followed, but in some cases preceded, EU developments, as shown in Figure 7.1. Luxembourg selected its lead sectors 'adapted to the particular conditions' (Sustainability Magazine, 2015: 27) of the country in order to build on the Grand Duchy's strengths while also aiming at mitigating weaknesses and threats for increasing the country's resilience. Luxembourg's lead sectors, therefore, have often suggested EU evolutions. As it will be shown in the next section, the country then used its economic diplomacy to guide and shape the EU framework to support its national priorities.

The three-wave stepwise evolution of Luxembourg's economic model corresponds to the three-wave evolution of the country's economic diplomacy, which at three critical junctures changed its objectives to best support the Grand Duchy's political and economic priorities in support of the lead sector of every wave with an approach, strategies and tactics that will be analyzed in the next section.

7.4 Luxembourg's economic diplomacy strategies and tactics within the EU
    framework

Luxembourg's ever-evolving economic model has been bolstered at all times by the country's domestic and international policies, processes, instruments and corresponding channels in an 'orchestrated' manner, given that for a small country such as Luxembourg, national interests are mainly of an economic nature (Katzenstein, 1985). The sectors selected for 'surfing' on the three waves of the Grand Duchy's development have been promoted strategically internally through the country's fiscal, legal and administrative policies (IMF, 2017) and externally, to a great extent, through the country's economic diplomacy, especially within the EU framework. This section studies Luxembourg's economic diplomacy strategies and tactics within the EU framework through a historical institutionalist analysis by drawing insights from the three-wave path of the Grand Duchy's economy and

Table 7.1 Luxembourg's economic diplomacy at various economic development stages

	Economic diplomacy strategies and tactics		
	Persuasion-based	Bargain-seeking	Power-exercising
First wave (1836–1986*)+	V	V	-
Second wave (1980–2010*)	V	V	V
Thirs wave (2010*–…)	V	V	-

Source: Author's elaboration
*Indicative dates, + The chapter focuses after 1957

V = Strategies and tactics used, - = Strategies and tactics not used

economic diplomacy. The strategies and tactics used by the Luxemburgish authorities for promoting the ever-changing economic diplomacy objectives within the EU framework have been of a wide array, including persuasion-based, bargain-seeking and power-exercising methods, as shown in Table 7.1. Additionally, the country promoted its economic diplomacy objectives through a wide variety of unofficial ways, such as networking and lobbying (Croisé-Schirtz, 1996; Hirsch, 2016; Frentz, 2010; Harmsen and Högenauer, 2021) and a conciliatory diplomatic style as 'honest broker' promoting consensual stances (Hirsch, 2016; Frentz, 2010; Harmsen and Högenauer, 2021).

While economic diplomacy objectives changed in co-relation with Luxembourg's three-wave economic development, the country's economic diplomacy approach followed a steady niche approach, prioritizing its ever-changing lead sectors of the mono-intensity economic models of every economic development wave. The niche approach is typical and appropriate for small states (Thorhallson, 2015; Criekemans and Duran, 2016), for higher impact of their economic diplomacy through efficiency, specialization and best use of resources. While following steadily a niche economic diplomacy approach, within the EU framework Luxembourg did not only vary its economic diplomacy strategies and tactics but also its ambition level. The Grand Duchy's confidencegot of a higher level, as the country's economic development progressed along the three-wave path and its image and positioning strengthened. As shown in Table 7.2, the ambition level progressed from catching up with other EU countries in the first wave, to achieving a level playing field and being on par with other EU member states later in the second wave, to aiming at a lead position within the EU in the third wave.

Historically and in particular in the first wave of economic development, Luxembourg has been 'frequently [applying] persuasion-based or bargaining-based shaping strategies' (Panke, 2016: 2) while 'seeking to secure specific derogations where particular national circumstances posed potential problems [including] immigration [especially from Italy] . . . demanded the right to impose restrictions. Given its small size, Luxembourg has been granted these rights and was again granted the right after the enlargement to Portugal' (Harmsen and Högenauer,

Table 7.2 Luxembourg's economic diplomacy paradigm shifts

	Economic model focus	Luxembourg (versus EU) sector and/or specialization initiatives' sequencing	Ambition level to achieve for sector and/or specialization development	Economic diplomacy strategies and tactics change	Critical juncture triggering factor
First wave (1836–1986*)+ Secondary economic sector Steel manufacturing	Mono-intensity	Preceding	Catch up	V	Internal
Second wave (1980–2010*) Tertiary economic sector	Mono-intensity	Preceding	On par/lead	V	Internal
Third wave (2010*–...) Quaternary economic sector	Quasi mono-intensity	Succeeding	Lead	V	External

Source: Author's elaboration

*Indicative dates, + The chapter focuses after 1957

V = Strategies and tactics used

2021: 5). Derogations – such as a special mention in ECSC Treaty Art. 31, recognizing the importance of the steel sector for the Grand Duchy and pronouncing that serious disturbances to its economy should be avoided. In addition to persuasion and bargaining methods, during the second and third waves, Luxembourg exercised equally power strategies and tactics. 'Fights' escalating to veto rights (Hirsch, 2016) during the second and third waves were about safeguarding banking secrecy and avoiding a Europe-wide tax on big technology companies, respectively. Additionally, 'battles that have been fought' without directly resulting in Luxembourg-promoted settlements have not been really lost. Endowed with deep knowledge of intergovernmental governance mechanisms, processes and people, stemming from its belonging to greater agglomerations experience and its founding role in the European project, Luxembourg was a skilful economic diplomacy negotiator. Further negotiating gains in economic diplomacy were achieved due to the country's role as an 'honest broker' (Hirsch, 2016: xii; Frentz, 2010: 140; Harmsen and Högenauer, 2021: 10). Furthermore, Luxembourg's economic diplomacy was efficient as a result of its small-sized public administration with cross-sectoral knowledge and developed personal networks (Wivel, 2016; Frentz, 2010; Harmsen and Högenauer, 2021). Although efficiency is typical for small states (Arter, 2000; Howard Grøn and Wivel, 2011; Henrikson, 2005), Luxembourg has been acknowledged as one of a small number of EU small states that are particularly active in deploying shaping strategies within the EU framework, among others, due to their highly motivated bureaucrats characterized by a sense of ownership.

In the case of banking secrecy, Luxembourg used its economic diplomacy skills to tactically delay the EU regulatory framework decisions in order to provide to the banks located in the Grand Duchy – and their international clientele – extra time for adapting to the prospective banking secrecy conditions or for devising alternatives. Likewise, extra time has been used for Luxembourg's complete subsequent pivot from banking secrecy to banking transparency in an effort to secure a lead position in the new banking set-up era (Raizer, 2018). The same 'switch' tactics have also been followed in the case of the EU Banking Union, for which Luxembourg's initial reluctance, on grounds of over-prescriptive regulations, has turned to an exponent of full alignment and compliance (Howarth and Quaglia, 2015). Such complete turnarounds, converting a lost claimed position into a proponent position for championing the prevailing arrangement, have been hailed by market actors as 'resilience and ability to rapidly comply with changing regulations' (PwC, 2019: 4). This enabled Luxembourg not only to maintain but also to further strengthen its position as a world financial centre. Similar tactics have also been followed in the case of the EU taxation issue after the so-called Lux Leaks affair in 2014. Notwithstanding that Luxembourg departed from a disadvantageous position, being classified in the OECD's tax-heavens grey list for having offered 'illegal tax benefits to Amazon' (Moncada, 2017), the country maintained its opposition to the EU proposals for a European-wide tax on big technology companies (Luxembourg Times, 2017). Negotiating for its national interests 'to preserve its tax privileges' (Thorhallson, 2018: 24) and aiming at the establishment of an international rather than EU playing field, the country counter-proposed a global OECD framework approach, which was finally adopted by the European Commission (Strupczewski, 2021). Subsequently, the Luxembourg-proposed international framework has been achieved through the US-led efforts for an agreement on a global minimum corporate tax applicable in the 135 states negotiating under the 'inclusive framework' (Giles and Politi, 2021) concluded in the G7, in 2021 (Karnitschnig, 2021).

Beyond using its economic diplomacy to vividly defend its positions, as shown earlier, on immigration, banking secrecy and transparency, as well as taxation, as important economic diplomacy goals corresponding to the critical junctures initiating each of the three waves of its economic diplomacy, Luxembourg has chosen to launch its 'Lëtzebuerg 3.0', or rather 4.0, during its presidency of the Council of the EU in 2015. Using its presidency, it aimed at *'positioning* the Grand Duchy as a country that wishes [. . .] to take pride in one of the *highest standards* of living through *sustainable economic development'* (Sustainability Magazine, 2015: 31). As described by Etienne Schneider, former vice prime minister and minister of the economy, for the country's 'economic development and diversification . . . through a wide fabric of innovative and dynamic companies [having] . . . a head start on other regions that are considering a similar route' (Sustainability Magazine, 2015: 27, 29). With the latter statement, Luxembourg emerges as part of the race for what is broadly known as the 4th industrial revolution (4IR) or Industry 4.0 (EP, 2016: 22–23), despite coining it as the '3rd industrial revolution [sic] [. . .] for transforming the country into the first nation-state of the smart green era [. . .] of global interconnectivity and accompanying planetary stewardship of the Earth's ecosystems – the Biosphere Valley model' (TIRLUX, 2016: 6). The term '3rd industrial revolution' has been adopted by actors and scholars who follow the model visioned by the economist-prospectivist Rifkin (Rifkin, 2011; Région Hauts-de-France, 2020) instead of the more mainstream term – Industry 4.0 – and hints to the country's integration with plans, values and ideas developed by some of its immediate neighbours at a sub-EU level.

From an historical institutionalism perspective, the overview of the historical evolution of Luxembourg's economic diplomacy and economic model, their juxtaposing against the EU evolution in conjunction with the analysis of Luxembourg's economic diplomacy strategies and tactics within the EU framework, demonstrates that Luxembourg changed its economic diplomacy three times around critical junctions triggered by overarching megatrends, which also shaped turning points in the country's economic model. These megatrends include, for the first wave, the emphasis on trade and investment in Europe after World War I, the emphasis on the tertiary sector and the beginnings of the EMU for the second wave and the European and national need to move to a knowledge-based economy to increase its global competitiveness through digitalization and innovation. In the first two waves, Luxembourg was driven by its existing or attainable production development possibilities. The Grand Duchy opted for mono-intensity economic models spearheaded by lead sectors for which the country disposed of indigenous resources, such as the steel sector in the first wave, or had since long started to create an enabling environment for their development through its regulatory and labour mobility system to attract investments and talent as in the financial sector during the second wave. For both of these waves, Luxembourg often preceded EU decisions and even contributed to their development in order to best promote its national objectives. The situation is different in the third wave. Luxembourg changed its economic model following the Lisbon strategy for achieving a knowledge-based economy by 2010 (European Council, 2000) albeit with a ten-year delay. As seen earlier, it was the GEFC that surfaced the country's economic vulnerabilities opening simultaneously an opportunity window grasped by Étienne Schneider, then Minister of Defence and Minister of Economy, to turn Luxembourg to digitalization and innovation (SWG, 2020), when 'Luxembourg was looking for ways to diversify its economy and explore new sectoral avenues' (Carey, 2017). Building on its financial system and its established ability to entice talent in the country, Luxembourg, during the third wave, is continuing to attract capital and labour to develop a cross-sectoral digitalized and innovative, as well as a sustainable, economy. Luxembourg's level of ambition also changed around the three critical junctures, ranging from the country's will to catch-up in manufacturing with its EU partners in the first wave to becoming an equal partner initially, and with higher aspirations later concerning the finance sector in the second wave, and the ambition to be among the leaders in digitalization and innovation in the third wave.

In the period under review, Luxembourg has developed and adapted its economic diplomacy policies within the EU framework. Changes in economic diplomacy strategies and tactics to reflect the *Zeitgeist*, the nature of its national objectives, the level of the country's economic development and the capacity of Luxembourg to influence EU governance at any given critical juncture point. In parallel, as mono-intensity economic models result in specialization and a consequent niche economic diplomacy that focuses on each of the lead sectors of the country's three-wave economic development, there is a clear path dependence in Luxembourg's niche economic diplomacy approach. Exercising a niche economic diplomacy over time presents increasing returns (Henrikson, 2005; Pierson, 2000; Arthur, 1994) to Luxembourg by efficiently utilizing its limited number of officials, who over the years have developed a high degree of specialization and know-how in representing the country's interests in its lead sectors. Furthermore, the analysis showed that Luxembourg sticks to internal norms and its entrenched culture, which delimits its economic diplomacy to correspond to the country's size and economic models.

7.5 Conclusions

Taking an historical institutionalism approach to examine Luxembourg's economic diplomacy, this chapter contributes to the book's overall goal to better understand small EU states in relation to their strategies, specific interests and motivations in particular policy areas. It demonstrates that Luxembourg has an agile economic diplomacy, which has changed its objectives over time at three critical junctures. These critical junctures correspond to changes in the country's economic model that occurred in order to adapt to megatrends that influenced not only the Grand Duchy but also the EU as a whole. Nonetheless, Luxembourg has not been a 'follower' of EU and megatrends' development at world level. Whereas in the first wave, steal and coal, Luxembourg's lead sectors, were a shared priority for all ECSC establishing countries, the country's long-term planning, in order to develop an economic model matching its own interests within the EU framework, is evidenced in the second wave and the promotion of finance as the country's lead sector. Contrarily, in Luxembourg's third wave of economic development, the country followed adopted EU economic strategies with a ten-year delay, only when the GEFC unveiled the vulnerabilities of the Grand Duchy's finance-based mono-intensity economic model.

As Luxembourg's economic models evolved step-wise, by each new wave adding on to the previous one, the country's economy, positioning and influence within the EU framework increased over time. As a result, Luxembourg increased the level of ambition of its economic diplomacy, from aiming at catching up with other EU member states in the steel sector, to being an equal and later lead in the finance sector, to being set to race in the digitalization and innovation sectors. In addition to changing the objectives and level of ambition of its economic diplomacy, the country varied also its strategies and tactics applied in order to influence and shape EU policies, which ranged from persuasion-based to bargain-seeking, without shying away to use power exercising as its image and position within the EU progressed.

Applying an historical institutionalist analysis, the chapter argues that while observing paradigm shifts in Luxembourg's economic diplomacy objectives, level of ambition, strategies and tactics at critical juncture triggering changes in the country's economic model, there is a path dependence in the country's economic diplomacy niche approach that prioritized a small number of key areas at a time and in particular the lead sectors in each wave. The Grand Duchy's economic diplomacy approach remained sticky due to the country's quasi mono-intensity economic models and its smallness.

Note

1 The term is used throughout for convenience, rather than also using the terms 'European Economic Community' and 'European Community.'

Bibliography

Archer, C. (2016). Small states and the European security and defence policy. In: R. Steinmetz and A. Wivel (eds.), *Small States in Europe. Challenges and Opportunities* (Routledge: Abington), pp. 47–62.

Arter, D. (2000). Small state influence within the EU. *Journal of Common Market Studies* 38(5): 677–697.

Arthur, W.B. (1994). *Increasing Returns and Path Dependence in the Economy* (University of Michigan Press: Ann Arbor, MI).

Baker Fox, A. (1969). The small states in the international system, 1919–1969. *International Journal* 24(4): 751–764.

Bailes, A.J.K., Thayer, B.A. and Thorhallsson, B. (2016). Alliance theory and alliance 'Shelter': The complexities of small state alliance behaviour. *Third World Thematics: A TWQ Journal.*

Bailie, S. (2005). The seat of the European institutions. An example of small-state influence in the EU. In: G.Trausch (ed.), *Le rôle et la place des petits pays en Europe au XXe Siècle* (Nomos: Baden-Baden), pp. 465–478.

Bayne, N. and Woolcock, S. (2017). What is economic diplomacy? In: N. Bayne and S. Woolcock (eds.), *The New Economic Diplomacy: Decision-Making and Negotiation in International Economic Relations* (Routledge: London), pp. 1–14.

Bekaert, G., Harvey, C.R. and Lundblad, C. (2005). Does financial liberalization spur growth? *Journal of Financial Economics* 77(1): 3–56.

Bell, S. (2011). Do we really need a new 'constructivist institutionalism'to explain institutional change? *British Journal of Political Science* 41(4): 883–906.

Biel, V.J.P., Erpelding, J.-P., Gehring, J.M. and Lambert, V. (2024). Luxembourg. *Encyclopedia Britannica*, 18 February. Available at https://www.britannica.com/place /Luxembourg.

Bourbaki, R. (2016). End of paradise? Le Luxembourg et son secret bancaire dans les filets du multilatéralisme. *Critique Internationale* 2(2): 55–71. https://doi.org/10.3917/crii .071.0055.

Bouyala Imbert, F. (2017). EU economic diplomacy strategy. European Parliament. Directorate-general for external policies. Policy department. DG EXPO/B/PolDep/ Note/2017_66 EN, March 2017-PE 570.483. Available at https://www.europarl.europa .eu/RegData/etudes/IDAN/2017/570483/EXPO_IDA(2017)570483_EN.pdf.

Bublitz, E. (2018). The European single market at 25. *Intereconomics* 53(6): 337–342.

Calmes, C. (1989). *Gründung und Werden eines Landes. 1815 bis heute. (The Making of a Nation from 1815 up to Our Days)* (Saint-Paul: Luxembourg).

Capoccia, G. and Kelemen, R. (2007). The study of critical junctures: Theory, narrative, and counterfactuals in historical institutionalism. *World Politics* 59(3): 341–336.

Carey, M. (2017). Luxembourg was looking for ways to diversify its economy and explore new sectoral avenues. Interview by Étienne Schneider. *Happen*, November 16. Available at https://gouvernement.lu/fr/actualites/toutes_actualites/interviews/2017/novembre/15 -schneider-happen.html.

Casali, S. (2013). *Le Luxembourg 1960–2010* (STATEC: Luxembourg). Available at https:// statistiques.public.lu/fr/publications/series/luxembourg/2013/02-13/index.html.

Chong, A. and Maass, M. (2010). Introduction: The foreign policy power of small states. *Cambridge Review of International Affairs* 23(3): 381–382.

Collier, D. and Munck, G. (2017). Building blocks and methodological challenges: A framework for studying critical junctures. *Qualitative and Multi-Method Research* 15(1): 2–9.

Cortell, A.P. and Peterson, S. (1999). Altered states: Explaining domestic institutional change. *British Journal of Political Science* 29(1): 177–203.

Criekemans, D. and Duran, M. (2016). Small state diplomacy compared to sub-state diplomacy: More of the same or different? In: R. Steinmetz and A. Wivel (eds.), *Small States in Europe. Challenges and Opportunities* (Routledge: Abington), pp. 31–45.

Croisé-Schirtz, E. (1996). La bataille des sièges (1950–1958). In: G. Trausch, E. Croisé-Schirtz, M. Nies Berchem, J.M. Majerus and C. Barthel (eds.), *Le Luxembourg Face à la Construction Européenne/Luxemburg und die Europäische Einigung* (Centre d'études et de Recherches Européennes Robert Schuman: Luxembourg), pp. 67–104.

Danescu, E. (2016). Pierre Werner: A visionary European and consensus builder. In: K. Dyson and I. Maes (eds.), *Architects Ofthe Euro Intellectuals in the Making of European Monetary Union* (Oxford University Press: Oxford), pp. 93–116.

David, P.A. (1985). Clio and the economics of QWERTY. *American Economic Review* 75(1): 332–337.

Deschamps, E. (2010). Luxembourg, un destin européen. De la Déclaration Schuman à l'installation des institutions de la CECA Luxembourg, a European destiny. From Schuman Declaration to the establishment of the ECSC institutions. Available at https://www.uni.lu/wp-content/uploads/sites/9/2023/08/edic-Expose-du-Dr-Etienne -Deschamps.pdf.

Dupont, C., Oberthür, S. and von Homeyer, I. (2020). The Covid-19 crisis: A critical juncture for EU climate policy development? *Journal of European Integration* 42(8): 1095–1110. https://doi.org/10.1080/07036337.2020.1853117.

Ebbinghaus, B. (2005). *Can Path Dependence Explain Institutional Change? Two Approaches Applied to Welfare State Reform.* MPIfG Discussion Paper, 2 (Max-Planck-Institut für Gesellschaftsforschung: Köln). Available at https://hdl.handle.net/10419/19916.

Enrikson, A.K. (2001). A coming 'magnesian' age? Small states, the global system, and the international community. *Geopolitics* 6(3): 49–86.

European Council. (2000). *Presidency Conclusions* (Lisbon European Council), 23 and 24 March 2000. Available at https://www.consilium.europa.eu/uedocs/cms_data/docs/pressdata/en/ec/00100-r1.en0.htm.

European Investment Bank (EIB). (1964). T r a n s f e r t éventuel du siège de la B . E . I . à Luxembourg (The eventual transfer of the seat of EIB to Luxembourg). Available at https://www.eib.org/attachments/general/archives/57_fr.pdf.

European Parliament (EP). (2016). *Industry 4.0. Directorate General for Internal Policies. Policy Department A: Economic and Scientific Policy (IP)/A/ITRE/2015-02*, February 2016 PE 570.007 (European Parliament: Brussels). Available at https://www.europarl.europa.eu/RegData/etudes/STUD/2016/570007/IPOL_STU(2016)570007_EN.pdf.

European Union, The Merger Treaty, OJ 152, 13.7.1967. pp.2-17. https://eur-lex.europa.eu/legal-content/EN/ALL/?

Fioretos, O. (2011). Historical institutionalism in international relations. *International Organization* 65(2): 367–399.

Frentz, J.M. (2010). The foreign policy of Luxembourg. In: R. Steinmetz and A. Wivel (eds.), *Small States in Europe* (Ashgate Publishing: Farnham), pp. 131–146.

Gehringer, A. (2013). Growth, productivity and capital accumulation:the effects of financial liberalization in the case of European integration. *International Review of Economics and Finance* 25(C): 291–309.

Giles, C. and Politi, J. (2021). G7 close to agreement on corporate tax rules. *Luxembourg Times*. Available at https://www.luxtimes.lu/en/business-finance/g7-close-to-agreement-on-corporate-tax-rules-60ab6b1ede135b9236088ac2.

Gourinchas, P.-O. and Jeanne, O. (2006). The elusive gains from international financial integration. *Review of Economic Studies* 73(3): 715–741.

Grosbois, T. (2009). Werner Pierre. In: P. Gerbet, G. Bossuat, and T. Grosbois (eds.), *Dictionnaire historique de l'Europe unie (The History Dictionary of the United Europe)* (André Versaille : Bruxelles), pp. 1140–1143.

Harmsen, R. and Högenauer, A.-L. (2021). Luxembourg and the European Union. In: F. Laursen (ed.), *The Oxford Encyclopedia of European Union Politics.* Available at https://oxfordre.com/politics/page/european-union-politics/the-oxford-encyclopedia-of-european-union-politics, https://doi.org/10.1093/acrefore/9780190228637.013.1041.

Heath, T.R. (2016). China's evolving approach toEconomic diplomacy. *Asia Policy* 1(22): 157–191. Available at http://asiapolicy.nbr.org.

Henrikson, A.K. (2005). Niche public diplomacy in the world public arena: The global 'corners' of Canada and Norway. In: J. Melissen (ed.), *The New Public Diplomacy: Soft Power in International Relations* (Palgrave Macmillan: London), pp. 67–87. https://doi.org/10.1057/9780230554931_4.

Hey, J.A.K. (2003). Luxembourg's foreign policy: Small size help or hinder? Luxembourg's foreign policy: Small size help or hinder? *The European Journal of Social Science Research* 15(3): 211–225.

Hirsch, M. (2016). About the resilience of small states. In: R. Steinmetz and A. Wivel (eds.), *Small States in Europe. Challenges and Opportunities* (Routledge: Abington), xi–xvi.

Howard Grøn, C. and Wivel, A. (2011). Maximizing influence in the European Union after the Lisbon Treaty: From small state policy to smart state strategy. *Journal of European Integration* 33(5): 523–539. https://doi.org/10.1080/07036337.2010.546846.

Howarth, D. and Quaglia, L. (2015). The new intergovernmentalism in financial regulation and Banking Union. Authors' pre-print version, to appear. In: C.J. Bickerton, D. Hodson and U. Puetter (eds.), *The New Intergovernmentalism States and Supranational Actors in the Post Maastricht Era* (Oxford University Press: Oxford), pp. 146–162. Available at https://core.ac.uk/download/pdf/189612959.pdf.

Ikenberry, G.J. (1988). Conclusion: An institutional approach to American foreign economic policy. *International Organization* 42(1): 219–243.

International Monetary Fund (IMF). (2017). Country report – Luxembourg, No. 2017/122. Available at https://www.imf.org/en/Publications/CR/Issues/2017/05/15/Luxembourg-Financial-System-Stability-Assessment-44907

Karnitschnig, M. (2021). G7 seals breakthrough deal to tax global companies. *Politiko*, 5 June. Available at https://www.KARNITSCHNIGpolitico.eu/article/g7-seals-breakthrough-deal-to-tax-global-companies/.

Kavvadia, H., Adam, M.C., Clemons, K., Devenyi, V., Girotto, E., Lisova, Y., Mo, F. and Vojta, Z. (2018). The economic diplomacy of small states. A case study of the Grand Duchy of Luxembourg: Trade and services, Official Development Assistance (ODA), foreign direct investment (FDI). *Review of Decentralisation, Local Government and Regional Development* 90: 96–129.

Katzenstein, P.J. (1985). *Small States in World Markets: Industrial Policy in Europe* (Cornell University Press: Ithaca, NY).

Kay, A. (2005). A critique of the use of path dependency in policy studies. *Public Administration* 83(3): 553–571.

Knight, J. (1992). *Institutions and Social Conflict* (Cambridge University Press: New York).

Lai, C. (2017). Acting one way and talking another: China'scoercive economic diplomacy in East Asia and beyond. *The Pacific Review*. https://doi.org/10.1080/09512748.2017.1357652.

Larosse, J. (2017). *Analysis of National Initiatives on Digitising European Industry. Luxembourg, Digital4Industry* (European Commission: Brussels). Available at https://ec.europa.eu/futurium/en/system/files/ged/lu_country_analysis.pdf.

Lee, D. and Hudson, D. (2004). The old and new significance of political economy in diplomacy. *Review of International Studies* 30(1): 343–360.

Lodhi, N. (2019). The birth of the grand duchy as a nation. *RTL Today*. Available at https://today.rtl.lu/culture/exhibitions-and-history/a/1363846.html.

Luxembourg Times. (2017). Bettel refuses to tax large internet companies on turnover. Available at https://www.luxtimes.lu/en/luxembourg/bettel-refuses-to-tax-large-internet-companies-on-turnover-602e34f3de135b92361c27fd.

Mahoney, J. (2000). Path dependence in historical sociology. *Theory and Society* 29(4): 507–548.

Mahoney, J., Mohamedali, K. and Nguyen, C. (2016). Causality and time in historical institutionalism. In: O. Fioretos, T.G. Falleti and A. Sheingate (eds.), *The Oxford Handbook of Historical Institutionalism* (Oxford University Press: Oxford), pp. 71–88.

Majerus, J.M. (2008). Luxemburg und die Europäische Union—Entwicklung der Europapolitik. In: W.H. Lorig and M. Hirsch (eds.), *Das Politische System Luxemburgs: Eine Einführung* (VS Verlag für Sozialwissenschaften: Wiesbaden), pp. 311–329.

Mariniello, M., Sapir, A. and Terzi, A. (2015). *The Long Road towards the European Single Market*. Bruegel Working Paper No. 2015/01, March. Available at https://www.bruegel.org/working-paper/long-road-towards-european-single-market.

Mastanduno, M. (1998). Economics and security in statecraft and scholarship. *International Organization* 52(4): 825–854. Available at http://www.jstor.org/stable/2601359.

Melissen, J., Okano-Heijmans, M. and van Bergeijk, P.A.G. (2011). Economic diplomacy: The issues. *The Hague Journal of Diplomacy* 6(1): 1–6.

Moncada, R. (2017). EU-logos: The European Union and the GAFA issue. Eyes on Europe. Available at https://www.eyes-on-europe.eu/the-european-union-and-the-gafa-issue/.

Okano-Heijmans, M. (2011). Conceptualizing economic diplomacy: The crossroads of international relations, economics, IPE and diplomatic studies. *The Hague Journal of Diplomacy* 6(1–2): 7–36.

Panke, D. (2010). *Small States in the European Union. Coping with Structural Disadvantages* (Ashgate: Farnham).

Panke, D. (2016). *Small States in the European Union. Coping with Structural Disadvantages* (Routledge: Abington).

Parkinson, M. (2015). *US Economic Diplomacy – A View from Afar, Griswold Center for Economic Policy Studies*, Working Paper No. 246,Princeton, NJ September.

Péporté, P. (2022). The Historyof Luxembourg. Information and press service of theLuxembourg government. Available at https://gouvernement.lu/lb/publications.gouv _sip%2Bfr%2Bpublications%2Bminist-etat%2Bsip%2Bbrochure%2Ba-propos%2BA _propos_Histoire.html.

Pierson, P. (2000). Increasing returns, path dependence, and the study of politics. *American Political Science Review* 94(2): 251–267.

Pierson, P. (2015). Power and path dependence. In: J. Mahoney and K. Thelen (eds.), *Advances in Comparative-Historical Analysis* (Cambridge University Press: Cambridge), pp. 123–146.

PricewaterhouseCoopers (PwC). (2019). Banking in Luxembourg 2019: Live long and prosper. Available at https://www.pwc.lu/en/banking/docs/pwc-banking-in-luxembourg -2019.pdf.

Raizer, T. (2018). Rester compétitif sans faire une course au dumping. (Interview with Pierre Gramegna, Luxembourg's Minister of Finance. Paperjam). Available at https:// paperjam.lu/article/news-rester-competitifs-sans-faire-une-course-au-dumping.

Rana, K.S. (2018). Economic diplomacy: A developing country perspective. In: van Bergeijk, P.A.G. and Moons, S.J.V. (Eds) *Research Handbook on Economic Diplomacy* (CheltenhamEdward Elgar Publishing), pp. Cheltenham 317–325.

Région Hauts-de-France. (2020). *Les Hauts-de-France pionniers d'une économie durable et connectée. Avec REV3 retrouvons-nous pour une nouvelle étape de l'histoire de notre région, construisons ensemble les Hauts-de-France 2030* (Région Hauts-de-France: Lille). Available at https://rev3.fr/brochure-rev3/.

Rifkin, J. (2011). *The Third Industrial Revolution How Lateral Power Is Transforming Energy, the Economy, and the World* (Palgrave Macmillan: London).

Rixen, T. and Viola, L.A. (2016). Historical institutionalism and international relations – Towards explaining change and stability in international institutions. In: T. Rixen, L.A. Viola and M. Zürn (eds.), *Historical Institutionalism and International Relations: Explaining Institutional Development in World Politics* (Oxford University Press: Oxford), pp. 3–29.

Rokkan, S. (1999). State formation, nation-building and mass politics in Europe. In: P. Flora, S. Kuhnle and D. Urwin (eds.), *The Theory of Stein Rokkan* (Oxford University Press: Oxford), pp. 4–15.

Simmons, B. and Martin, L.L. (2002). International organizations and institutions. In: W. Carlsnaes, Th. Risse and B.A. Simmons (eds.), *Handbook of International Relations* (Sage: London), pp. 192–211.

Skocpol, T. (1992). State formation and social policy in the United States. *American Behavioral Scientist* 35(4–5): 559–584.

Smith, H.A. (1999). Caution warranted: Niche diplomacy assessed. *Canadian Foreign Policy Journal* 6(3): 57–72.

SpaceWatch. Global (SWG). (2020). Étienne Schneider, architect of Luxembourg's space sector, so step down in February 2020. Available at https://spacewatch.global/2020/01 /etienne-schneider-architect-of-luxembourgs-space-sector-to-step-down-in-february -2020/ (accessed 22 January 2021).

Stinchcombe, A.L. (1975). Social structure and politics. In: F.I. Greenstein and N.W. Polsby (eds.), *Macropolitical Theory. Handbook of Political Science* (Addisson-Wesley: Reading, MA), Vol. 3, No. 1, pp. 557–622.

Strupczewski, J. (2021). EU eyes another go at more unified European business taxation. *Reuters*. Available at https://www.reuters.com/world/europe/eu-eyes-another-go-more -unified-european-business-taxation-2021-05-17/.

Sustainability Magazine. (2015). *Luxembourg: 1st country to commit. Interview with Etienne Schneider, Vice-Prime Minister / Minister of Economy of Luxembourg*, September 2015 (IMS Luxembourg: Luxembourg). Available at https://www.troisiemerevolutionindu strielle.lu/2015/10/02/3eme-revolution-industrielle-le-luxembourg-sengage/.

The 3rd Industrial Revolution Luxembourg (TIRLUX). (2016). The 3rd industrial revolution strategy study for the grand duchy of Luxembourg. Available at https://www.troisiemere volutionindustrielle.lu/wp-content/uploads/2016/11/TIR-Strategy-Study_Short.pdf.

Thelen, K. (1999). Historical institutionalism in comparative politics. *Annual Review of Political Science* 2(1): 369–404.

Thelen, K. (2002). The explanatory power of historical institutionalism. In: R. Mayntz (ed.), *Akteure-Mechanismen-Modelle. Zur Theoriefähigkeit Makro-Sozialer Analysen* (Campus: Frankfurt), pp. 91–107.

Thirion, E. (2017). *EU Single Market: Boosting Growth and Jobs in the EU. EPRS Briefing European Added Value in Action* (European Parliamentary Research Service). Available at https://www.europarl.europa.eu/RegData/etudes/BRIE/2017/611009/EPRS_BRI %282017%29611009_EN.pdf.

Thorhallsson, B. (2011). Domestic buffer versus external shelter: Viability of small states in the new globalised economy. *European Political Science* 10(3): 324–336.

Thorhallson, B. (2015). *How Do Little Frogs Fly? Small States in the European Union.* Policy Brief 12/2015. (Norwegian Institute of International Affairs). Available at https:// www.researchgate.net/publication/327075090_How_Do_Little_Frogs_Fly_Small _States_in_the_European_Union 12/2015.

Thorhallson, B. (2018). *The Role of Small States in the European Union* (Routledge: Abington).

Torkington, S. (2023). We're on the brink of a 'polycrisis' – How worried should we be?. *World Economic Forum*, 13 January. Available at https://www.weforum.org/agenda /2023/01/polycrisis-global-risks-report-cost-of-living/.

van Bergeijk, P.A.G. and Moons, S. (2009). Economic diplomacy and economic security. In: C.G. Costa (ed.), *New Frontiers for Economic Diplomacy* (Instituto Superior de Ciéncias Sociais e Politicas: Lisbon), pp. 37–54.

van Veestra, M.-L., Yakop, M. and van Bergeijk, P.A.G. (2011). *Economic Diplomacy, the Level of Development and Trade* (Netherlands Institute of International Relations Clingendael: Den Haag).

Veenendaal, W.P. and Corbett, J. (2015). Why small states offer important answers to large questions. *Comparative Political Studies* 48(4): 527–549.

Viola, L.A. (2019). The G20 through the lens of historical institutionalism. In: S. Slaughter (ed.), *The G20 and International Relations Theory* (Edward Elgar Publishing: Cheltenham), pp. 116–135.

Wang, X. (2020). Leadership-building dilemmas in emerging powers' economic diplomacy: Russia's energy diplomacyand China's OBOR. *Asia Europe Journal* 18(1): 117–138. https://doi.org/10.1007/s10308-019-00536-4Beijing 102249.

Wardle, M. and Mainelli, M. (2020). *The Global Financial Centres Index 28* (Long Finance and Financial Centre Futures: London). Available at https://www.longfinance.net/media /documents/GFCI_28_Full_Report_2020.09.25_v1.1.pdf

Wayne, T. (2019). What is economic diplomacy and how does it work?. *The Foreign Service Journal* 1–2: 23–27. Available at https://afsa.org/sites/default/files/fsj-2019-01 -02-january-february.pdf.

Wivel, A. (2016). From small state to smart state: Devising a strategy for influence in the European Union. In: R. Steinmetz and A. Wivel (eds.), *Small States in Europe. Challenges and Opportunities* (Routledge: Abington), pp. 15–29.

Woolcock, S. (2012). *European Union Economic Diplomacy. The Role of the EU in External Economic Relations* (Routledge: Abingdon).

World, Bank (WB). (2021). TC data 360: Luxembourg. Available at https://tcdata360 .worldbank.org/countries/LUX?indicator=41578&countries=CYP,MLT&viz=line _chart&years=2017,2019&country=LUX.

8 Small states, subregional minilateralism and European foreign policy

Marion Foster and Michael Mosser

8.1 Introduction

The European Union has long been regarded as a pluralistic security community, a regional order in which members no longer regard force as a viable mode of interaction. This characterization remains valid but describes only one – internal – dimension of security in EU-Europe. In its external security management, the European Union has long relied on a modern form of great power concert, combined with multilateralism in a format we refer to as 'embedded concert.'[1] With the number of small EU member states steadily increasing, subregional coalitions and minilateralism have developed as a new element of external security management.

This chapter investigates the new security minilateralism among small member states in the context of European foreign and security policy. We define security minilateralism as security cooperation between individual member states within the larger multilateral context of the EU's Common Foreign and Security Policy (CFSP). As Högenauer and Mišík note in the introduction to this volume, there is no unified definition of small states. As a result, they are often defined by what they are not, i.e., neither regional powers nor microstates (Neumann and Gstöhl, 2006). Therefore, what counts as a small EU member state is defined not exclusively by material factors but also by the perception of relative power over policy influence in a given context (Steinmetz and Wivel, 2016).

This chapter addresses the research questions of how subregional coalitions are formed, which benefits member states derive from them and how coalitions evolve over time. We pull together insights from sources focusing on single case studies of subregional coalitions, drawing attention to the fact that subregional coalitions are not isolated *sui generis* cases but part of a process that has been observed in other fields, such as economic and environmental policy. We argue that subregional minilateralism represents a potential way forward for closer integration in EU foreign and security policy, a field where consensus among all member states is difficult to achieve. Minilateral coalitions can be instruments for small states to advocate for their security concerns and thus render EU foreign and security decision-making more pluralistic. At the same time, we recognize the risk that these coalitions may increase perceptions of fragmentation.

To situate subregional analysis in the context of EU foreign and security policy, this chapter begins with a discussion of the EU as both a regional order and

DOI: 10.4324/9781003380641-10

a foreign policy actor. We subsequently examine the role subregional coalitions play as tools of security governance through a review of the extant literature and empirical case studies of security minilateralism within the Nordic-Baltic Six, the Visegrád Group and the Quadro Group. The concluding section summarizes our main findings and points to questions for further research.

8.2 The European Union: Regional security order and foreign policy actor

The analysis of the European Union's role in the world is complicated by its ambiguity as an international actor. It represents, on the one hand, a global power with a population of close to 450 million and a combined GDP of more than €16 trillion (European Union, n.d.). Yet, the EU member states retain national sovereignty over specific policy fields, first and foremost over foreign and defence policy. For these reasons, the EU can be analyzed as both a regional order and a foreign policy actor.

Since its inception, the European Community (EC) has been a subject of study for scholars interested in regionalism. Indeed, many theoretical frameworks of regional integration were developed based on empirical observation of the EC (Söderbaum, 2016), including the concept of the pluralistic security community (Deutsch, 1957; Adler and Barnett, 1998; Job, 1997). The related concept of regional community implies that members not only share values and a preference for cooperative conflict resolution but have also developed a sense of 'cognitive regionalism' (Ayoob, 1999). Tavares (2008) argues that the post-1991 European Union is the sole empirical case of a regional community. He notes that this has implications beyond the question of European regional security because it confers on the EU 'actorness' outside its own region. However, scholars often find it difficult to account for the EU's actorness, due to its unique type of supranational political entity but also to its self-perception as a 'normative power' (Bendiek, 2019).

At the core of this self-perception lies a dual commitment to multilateralism, which refers both to the EU's relations with other actors in the international system and its internal functioning. Externally, multilateralism manifests in a preference for peaceful forms of conflict management, active membership in international organizations and the maintenance of multifaceted relations with many countries and regional organizations. Internally, EU multilateralism rests on a commitment to act on the basis of treaties and to adhere to unanimity in foreign policy decision-making (Bendiek, 2019).

This formal commitment to multilateralism is, however, not always adhered to in practice, thus giving rise to an alternative view, which argues that the transformative power of the EU cannot be understood outside the context of imperial modes of governance. According to this interpretation, the European Union reverses the Westphalian model of the state whose sovereignty is absolute domestically but set within clear territorial boundaries. The EU blurs borders by spreading its norms and standards through the *acquis communautaire* not only to its member states, where the *acquis* overrides national law, but also to its less well-developed neighbours.

In this way, the EU gains a measure of control over in its neighbourhood through processes of association. This makes the EU a 'cosmopolitan empire,' a voluntary alliance held together by a strong centre. As a consequence, EU foreign and security policy cannot rely solely on the multilateralism of the Common Foreign and Security Policy (CFSP) process but requires close interaction between the large member states as well as on 'coalitions of the willing' (Bendiek, 2017).

This perception of a more conditional and limited multilateralism becomes plausible when considering the EU's trajectory since the end of the Cold War. Post-1991, we observe both a broadening and deepening of European integration. The European Community admitted new member states. Simultaneously, additional policy fields gradually shifted from member state competence to supranational competence. In the field of foreign and security policy, this necessitates better coordination within an increasingly diverse regional community, a need recognized in the 1997 Treaty of Amsterdam. In 2007, 'enhanced cooperation' in foreign and security policy was inscribed into the Lisbon Treaty (Fiott et al., 2017).

In the 1990s, Papayoanu (1997) predicted that the post-Cold War regional order of western Europe was most likely to evolve into a blend of concert and collective security arrangement. Close collaboration between the EU's large member states would resemble an oligopolistic collusion between major powers to overcome collective action problems, embedded in the EU's normatively stipulated multilateral framework (Rosecrance and Schott, 1997; Job, 1997). This scholarly notion of 'embedded concert' was borne out by the steps taken towards the establishment of the CFSP. Consensus and compromise between the European great powers, specifically Germany, France and the United Kingdom, underlay integration of the policy field (Fiott et al., 2017). After Brexit, Germany has, at times reluctantly, taken the place of Great Britain as France's partner on the institutionalization of the CFSP.

Spurred by a combination of external and internal pressures, in 2016 Franco-German cooperation injected a sense of dynamism into the CFSP, leading the EU member states to adopt the programmatic notion of a 'Europe of Security' (Puglierin and Franke, 2020; Beckmann and Kempin, 2017; Bendiek, 2017). At the heart of the political initiative for an external defence union was a German-French agreement on Permanent Structured Cooperation (PeSCo). PeSCo provides a framework for enhanced cooperation between those member states willing to take on binding commitments on defence spending (Fiott et al., 2017). It represents a compromise between an ambitious French vision for the development of the EU's foreign and security policy and a German preference for inclusiveness. Its outcome highlights the importance of both cooperation between Paris and Berlin on EU foreign and security policy and the constraints placed on the 'Franco-German engine' by the EU's internal commitment to multilateralism (Blockmans and Crosson, 2019).

Even though PeSCo represented a step forward for policy integration, doubts remain about the increase in coordination and capacity that it will be able to engender. An intriguing study undertaken by Blockmans and Crosson (2019) on the actual projects initiated under PeSCo reveals that cooperation among member states is significantly determined by their geographic, cultural and linguistic proximity. This raises the question of whether patterns of minilateral cooperation among geographically clustered member states are limited to defence industrial cooperation or whether such patterns transfer to the EU's common foreign and security policy more broadly. Are member states particularly inclined to cooperate with regional neighbours? And if so, what benefits do they expect from this cooperation?

8.3 Subregional minilateralism in EU foreign policy-making

Scholars of regionalism in IR have typically treated the European Union as one, coherent type of regional order, in line with the general propensity of research focused on macro regions. Buzan and Wæver's (2003) influential notion of Regional Security Complexes (RSCs), for instance, divided their European regional security complex into an 'EU-Europe' and a 'post-Soviet space,' with Turkey and the non-EU member states of the Balkans sitting uneasily in between. However, this approach has increasingly encountered criticism because it obscures the multifaceted processes of regional cooperation operating simultaneously, at times reinforcing each other and at times competing with each other, within these macro regions as well as across their boundaries.[2]

Söderbaum (2016) proposes instead to treat regionalism – of which the formalized and legalistic regionalism of EU integration is only one example – as a body of ideas, values and policies aimed at creating a region. This allows us to understand regions not as geographical givens but as socially constructed and politically contested concepts. Various approaches, including social constructivism, New Regionalism and post-structuralism, focus attention on identity as a basis for interests, the plurality of regionalisms within one (macro-)region and the discursive practices underlying the politics of defining and redefining regions.

Applying these insights to our notion of EU foreign policy-making as an embedded concert, we recall that the large European powers need to gain the agreement of the continent's smaller state to respond to external challenges and institute foreign policy changes. However, the smaller states are not merely passive recipients of Franco-German compromises on foreign and security policy, and neither do they support or resist the policy proposals put forward by Paris and Berlin as a monolithic bloc.[3] What we observe empirically in EU policy-making is a 'variable geography,' in which smaller states use shifting coalitions to pool power in order to resist and/or influence policy change.

This tendency has been well established in other policy fields. The Benelux Union between Belgium, the Netherlands and Luxembourg was formed even before the establishment of the European Economic Community and continues to cooperate closely on economic, mobility and justice issues (Rūse, 2013). More recently, seven central and central-eastern member states have cooperated in the Salzburg group on internal security and justice affairs. The 'Frugal Four' (Austria, Denmark, the Netherlands and Sweden) opposes distributive EU budget policies and advocates for fiscal conservatism.

Blockmans and Crosson (2019) note that in defence cooperation, coalitions are often clustered in a sense that is broadly speaking geographical. This observation is supported by Rūse's (2013) findings which detect habits of cooperation between neighbouring states in the framework of EU Council negotiation processes. These habits are based on both utilitarian and normative grounds, i.e., they aim to increase voting power and overcome information asymmetries but also follow cultural/identitarian and value-based logics. Territorially constituted coalitions are facilitated by the existence of cooperation networks, institutional frameworks for intergovernmental cooperation and established traditions of consulting each other (Rūse, 2013) but they may also challenge received definitions of regions, as will be demonstrated in our case study on the Nordic-Baltic Six.

Processes of Europeanization (Deas and Lord, 2016; Söderbaum, 2016) and the interplay of domestic coalitions and regional issues (Ayoob, 1999; Solingen, 1997) play important roles in shaping conceptions of shared challenges and common interests. In the case of the Nordic-Baltic Six, for instance, the challenge of mastering EU approximation and policy-making processes within the Union prompted close cooperation between the Baltic and Nordic states. Interestingly, we find subregional security minilateralism in all regions where smaller member states cluster geographically, i.e., central Europe (Visegrád Four), northern Europe (Nordic-Baltic Six) and southern Europe (Quadro Group).

Moreover, this coalition architecture is complex, with overlapping formats that are more or less well institutionalized. For instance, the above-mentioned Salzburg Group has increasingly become involved in migration issues in central Europe and includes the Visegrád Four but also other central, central-eastern and south-eastern member states. The Trimarium, or Three Seas Initiative, on the other hand, gathers countries from Estonia to Bulgaria, roughly on a north-south axis between the Baltic, Black and Mediterranean Seas and has a more explicit geopolitical focus. The Nordic-Baltic Six slots into a complex regional cooperation architecture that includes the Nordic and Baltic Council of Ministers, the Council of Baltic Sea States, the Northern Lights Groups, etc.

What benefits do these coalitions provide for smaller states in particular? Thorhallsson and Steinsson (2018) argue that small states tend to seek political, economic and societal shelter to and mitigate vulnerabilities associated with their size. In the EU context, Janning and Zunneberg (2017) identify three main purposes for member state coalitions within an increasingly heterogenous Union. According to them, coalitions can serve to (1) build consensus; (2) establish majorities of member states in the Council through vote pooling; and (3) enhance cooperation in specific policy fields by facilitating 'core building,' in other words by leading to deeper integration between subsets of member states.

Janning and Zunneberg's study identifies groups of states that are generally regarded as influence and cooperation leaders. The authors also make two observations that are particularly relevant for the purposes of this chapter: first, they note that neighbouring countries often see each other as essential partners, citing specifically the Visegrád Four's cooperation on security and defence. Second, they argue that coalitions, and informal coalitions in particular, can serve an important function for agenda setting.

This second point gains importance in light of Rūse's (2013) observation that policy-making in the EU council is largely based on informal norms such as issue linkages and vote trading, and that there is a tendency towards informal cooperation before formal meetings take place. As such, the 'pre-negotiation stage' is increasingly important for policy outcomes, and member states have discovered that their cooperation is more effective when they can rely on established structures, networks and routines. It is in the pre-negotiation phase that small member states may increase their bargaining power through the information exchange, expertise pooling and rhetorical action provided by coalitions (Rūse, 2013).

Coalitions as tools for agenda setting do not necessarily need extensive bureaucratic organizations. Instead, they often operate on the basis of highly informal routine cooperation and 'unwritten agreement' (Rūse, 2013) and often resemble networks of select participants that facilitate higher levels of openness and cooperative behaviour (Söderbaum, 2016). Moreover, patterns of interactions established at one level – such as between heads of mission in Brussels gathered at the Committee of Permanent Representatives (COREPER) – can spread to other levels, for instance, civil servants in member state capitals' line ministries, or to expert communities. Gradually, therefore, informal coalitions can develop entry points to influence policy at different levels of the EU's policy-making process (Rūse, 2013). To investigate how such coalitions work in practice and how they are evaluated by their members, we now turn to three empirical case studies: the 'Visegrád Group,' 'Nordic-Baltic Six' and the 'Quadro Group.'

8.3.1 Visegrád as a (potential) case of subregional minilateralism

When and how do minilateral coalitions form? And are they merely strategic/instrumental, or is there a deeper ideational reason for their formation? The case of the Visegrád states of Central Europe provides some insights into the potential reasons for coalition formation. In 1991, at a conference in the Hungarian city of Visegrád, the states of Poland, (then) Czechoslovakia and Hungary formed the Visegrád Group (V3).[4] It was premised, in the words of its official statement, on:

1. the desire to eliminate the remnants of the communist bloc in Central Europe;
2. the desire to overcome historic animosities between Central European countries;
3. the belief that through joint efforts it will be easier to achieve the set goals, i.e. to successfully accomplish social transformation and join in the European integration process; and
4. the proximity of ideas of the then ruling political elites. (Visegrad Group, n.d.a)

Visegrad began simply: as an institutionalized coordination mechanism for states in a common geographic region. And despite its official rhetoric, Visegrád has, since the beginning, been more of a concept than a tangible reality. It modelled itself on existing multinational groupings within Europe such as Benelux (Belgium, the Netherlands and Luxembourg) and the Nordic Group (Norway, Sweden and Finland) (Götz and Haggrén, 2009) but this was arguably as much for legitimacy and efficacy as it was for common cultural heritage (Fawn, 2001, 2013). Substantial national differences existed among the members (either V3 or V4), and Czech prime minister and later president Vaclav Klaus has even gone so far as to say that Visegrád was an 'artificial creation of the West.'[5] But Visegrád did, it appears, have some unifying elements around which to rally. One important area which has clear effects on Visegrád is its cohesiveness in the negotiations surrounding accession first to NATO and later the EU.

The Visegrád case gives this chapter's minilateralism model additional nuance, by arguing that minilateral coalitions are most likely to form when a clear target objective such as IO membership, or increased credibility within that IO, is in sight. For Visegrád, the roots of the coalition developed in the early 1990s, when the Visegrád (V4) states collectively began intensive negotiations with NATO on possible accession of its members. On 7 January 1994, the defence ministers from the V4 states met in Warsaw. According to the minutes of the meeting, ministers discussed coordination of applications before the upcoming NATO summit, resolving to obtain NATO's promise to admit them (Visegrad Group, n.d.b). Later that month, the V4 Ministers of Foreign Affairs met with the US president Bill Clinton at a meeting in Prague, where cooperation between the V4 led to a joint communiqué 'expecting a clear signal from NATO of its opening to new members' (Visegrad Group, n.d.b).

As with NATO, so with the EU. There is some evidence in the secondary literature for Visegrád acting collectively to take advantage of existing EU rules in their accession negotiations. Dangerfield (2008: 638) notes: 'It is also widely acknowledged that the collective approach to the EU played an important part in the EU's decision to sign Europe Agreements with the V3 in December 1991, thereby granting them a "privileged" status with the EU.' Fawn (2001: 53) argues similarly, implying the strong connections between the Visegrád states gave them leverage in NATO negotiations:

> By 1991, the three central European states understood that NATO was not offering immediate membership of the alliance. As a result, the three countries avoided establishing formal military structures among themselves that could relieve NATO of a sense of responsibility to the region and their desire for the meaningful security guarantee that only full alliance membership provided.

Moreover, some interesting anecdotal evidence that coordination was occurring comes from diplomats on the ground at the time. In a remarkable memoir-like account of various high-level meetings in the early 1990s surrounding the issues of NATO and EU expansion, Gábor Hárs, the Hungarian Ambassador to Poland from 1995 to 1998, spoke of the vigorous discussions each Visegrád leader had surrounding the accession strategies for NATO and the EU. Hárs seems to indicate that Visegrád cooperation was primarily instrumental and would capitalize on Western European perceptions that the Visegrád countries would naturally have common positions due to their geographic proximity (Hárs, n.d.).

In recent years, thanks to external actions such as the 2015–2016 migration crisis and the 2022 Russian invasion of Ukraine that have directly affected its members, Visegrád has been reinvigorated. There is a Visegrád Battle Group on standby in the EU, which served its first rotation in 2016 (Ministry of Defence and Armed Forces of the Czech Republic, 2016). Visegrád has recently been feted by China, whose foreign minister called the group a 'dynamic force' in the European Union (Reuters, 2018). Visegrád reinvigoration appears to show that, in a time of institutional flux, these minor actors would not just seek to capitalize on existing norms of the organization but also seek to renegotiate their positions within the organization.

Along with the reinvigoration of Visegrád in the operational sphere, scholarship on Visegrád has been re-energized, with works examining the grouping's strong collective stance during the 2015–2016 migration crisis specifically from an identity-centric framework. Braun (2020) looks at Visegrád's collective antipathy towards the EU's Common Asylum Policy and the actions the group has taken since 2015 to shape EU migration policy. Employing textual analysis of statements by Visegrád policy-makers focused on migration as an identity-forming issue, Braun (2020: 936) notes that 'the narrative of the V4 and the migration crisis is contributing to the development of a V4 identity' and posits that this differentiated identity may be instrumental in allowing the V4 to strengthen cooperation on future issues. In the same vein, Vetrovcova (2021) uses the migrant crisis to examine the state of intra-Visegrád coherence and the effects this internal consistency might have on common negotiating positions in the future. Eckert (2021: 147) explores the effects of the migrant crisis on the evolution of the 'inferiority complex' of the Central and Eastern European countries (CEECs) of the EU and posits that a 'change in communication' between Brussels and its member states will be necessary before any future enlargement takes place.

The migrant crisis solidified Visegrád in the minds of its own leaders as well as those in Brussels. But as the migrant crisis of 2015–2016 fades into the background of EU policy-making, Visegrád's continuing internal coherence remains very much in doubt. Moreover, recent political developments in all four countries may put external relationships on the back burner until internal political coalitions can be re-established. But the rules of the EU are not changing, and the norms of the EU remain in many ways at odds with the stated positions of Visegrád leaders from all sides of the political spectrum. This is quite evident in what we are seeing with Visegrád's lack of collective response to the situation in Ukraine.

The Russian invasion of Ukraine in February 2022 has shone a spotlight on the Visegrád states, particularly on Poland and Hungary. Owing to its staunch anti-Russian (and specifically anti-Putin) position that dates to at least 2010 with the Smolensk air disaster, Poland has been emphatic in its support of Ukraine as it struggles to defend itself and potentially expel Russia from its sovereign territory. For its part, Hungary has walked a fine line between pro-Russia sentiments from its leadership and the desire to stand with other European Union member states in solidarity against territorial aggression. Gosling (2022) notes that, with recent pro-Western governments in place in Czechia and Slovakia, Visegrád has essentially already become the 'Visegrád 2+2,' with the group barely hanging together. The Russian invasion has the potential to further isolate Orban's Hungary to the point at which Visegrád becomes either a '3+1' orientation or disintegrates completely.

Insofar as it has a collective identity, Visegrád came together to foment easier accession to NATO and the EU. It may now be seen that collective identity only goes so far. Now deeply embedded within each of these institutions, Visegrád may lose its identity cohesion and may in fact end up disintegrating (Walsch, 2022).

8.3.2 The Nordic-Baltic Six (NB6) as a 'first circle of friends'

The Nordic-Baltic Six (NB6) forms an informal coalition composed of three Scandinavian (Denmark, Sweden and Finland) and three Baltic (Estonia, Latvia and Lithuania) EU member states that is part of a mesh of various cooperation formats established in the Baltic Sea region (Kuusik and Raik, 2018a). Systemic efforts to build up intergovernmental cooperation began among the Nordic countries after the end of World War II. Based on the 'Nordic model' of strong commitment to democracy, pluralism, progressive socio-economic policies and environmentalism, they cooperated regionally and coordinated their actions within the framework of multilateral diplomacy (Rūse, 2013). With the end of the Cold War and the integration of Sweden and Finland into the European Union, the conditions for regional cooperation changed. The EU Council presidencies of Sweden (2001), Denmark (2002) and Finland (2006) provided renewed impetus to strengthen a common Nordic voice in the EU. All three Scandinavian member states also supported EU accession of the Baltic states (Rūse, 2013), and for the Baltic states, inclusion in a Nordic-Baltic framework of cooperation was important for building up a solid position within the European Union (Kuusik and Raik, 2018a).

The NB6 grew out of a Swedish initiative to engage the Baltic states in EU decision-making procedures (Kleinberga, 2019) and transitioned over time into a format of cooperation and coordination based on a more equal partnership (Haukkala et al., 2017). The NB6 has not evolved a formalized agreement or bureaucratic structure. Instead, its members share the administrative burdens of cooperation through a system of 'rotating chairs' and frequently come together in informal settings,. The NB6 operates on various levels of the EU governance process: it includes regular meetings of the member countries' permanent representatives in Brussels as well as of heads of states and ministers of foreign affairs. Consultations are also held on the level of senior civil servants in line ministries and within expert networks, between the countries' EU directors and the advisors to their prime ministers (Kuusik and Raik, 2018b; Rūse, 2014).

Russia's invasion of Ukraine has accelerated processes of convergence within the NB6. Sweden and Finland's application for NATO membership means that, once accession is agreed and completed, all countries in this group will be part of the North Atlantic Alliance. In the wake of the Russian invasion, Denmark also held a referendum to abolish its opt-out from the EU's Common Security and Defense Policy. Danish voters approved of the notion in June 2022. Consequently, Denmark is now able to fully participate in EU defence policy-making (Friis and Schacke-Barfoed, 2022).

This convergence, however, predates the events of February 2022. First, practical cooperation on security had been increasing among the NB6 members over a longer period of time. It manifested in co-location arrangements for diplomatic missions but also in the development of joint military procurement and training formats (e.g. Nordefco) and the establishment of a Nordic Battle Group within the EU (Haukkala et al., 2017). These cooperation gains are not strictly speaking due to the NB6 format, since the co-location of diplomatic representations, for instance, preceded the establishment of the coalition. Nevertheless, interaction effects between these older arrangements and the NB6 format are likely to facilitate both further practical cooperation on the ground and coordination, information sharing and potentially policy alignment within the NB6.

Second, the NB6 shares some overarching security concerns. They are generally supportive of a strong transatlantic security partnership and NATO-EU compatibility in defence and security. This common understanding has contributed to a notable increase in defence cooperation of Finland and Sweden with the United States. It has also facilitated the active participation of the NB6 countries in European joint defence initiatives, such as the UK-led Joint Expeditionary Force or the French-led European Intervention Initiative (Kuusik and Raik, 2018a, 2018b). Other areas in which NB6 countries hold largely similar positions are on questions of EU enlargement, the European Neighborhood Policy and the Eastern Partnership (Haukkala et al., 2017).

Third, the Russian invasion has only accelerated the convergence of policy preferences within the NB6 since the onset of the Ukraine conflict in 2014. In 2016, the NB6 ministers of foreign affairs issued a joint declaration on Crimea, and they often display a common position with regard to the EU's policy vis-à-vis Russia. Moreover, cybersecurity and the countering of hybrid threats feature prominently among security policy priorities for all NB6 countries (Kuusik and Raik, 2018a, 2018b). Where policy preferences converge, coordinated action in the framework of EU Council negotiations becomes more likely and the accompanying potential for influence grows.

Finally, the informal and open character of NB6 cooperation contributes to keeping the coalition stable even if preferences on specific issues diverge. The coalition members work together where they share policy positions, but there is no obligation to agree or even engage with initiatives tabled by the individual countries. The countries' representatives do, however, usually first discuss such initiatives within the NB6 format as a way to consult each other and identify possible red lines (Kuusik and Raik, 2018a, 2018b). This exchange of information and pooling of expertise is a crucial benefit of the coalition for its members: by demonstrating coherence, they can jointly attract potential partners outside the coalition to cooperate on issue areas where they possess competitive advantages (Kuusik and Raik, 2018a; Rūse, 2014; Kleinberga, 2019). In a sense, the NB6 coalition involves little cost and significant benefits for its members, an aspect that is highlighted by the relatively low burden of administrative duties.

Beyond these utilitarian benefits, scholars have also noted that informal cooperation with its relatively high interaction frequency has led to the accumulation of 'social capital' within the NB6 coalition. As Kleinberga (2019: 26) was told in an interview by the Permanent Representative of Latvia in Brussels, for the NB6 members their coalition partners form a 'first circle of friends' to be contacted in case of emergent EU issues. Haukkala et al. (2017: 33) note the emergence of a seemingly natural affinity and 'we-feeling' as the Nordic and Baltic countries engage each other in ongoing conversations. This feeling is shared by other EU member states that often view the NB6 as a (natural) bloc, pointing to the NB6's success in shaping perceptions of regional space:[6] the coalition has eroded the division of the Baltic Sea region into a northern and eastern part. What emerges instead is a Baltic regional identity within the EU, acknowledged within the NB6 and by other EU members and increasingly associated with common positions on regional security. The analysis of the NB6 demonstrates a case in which a minilateral coalition was created to tackle a specific policy challenge – integration of the Baltic states into the EU – but subsequently evolved through largely informal coordination to provide both utilitarian and normative benefits to its members.

8.3.3 *Southern Europe and the Quadro Group: Issue leadership and internal conflict*

The southern EU member states form another area that is often perceived, both inside and outside the region, as a political, cultural and socio-economic entity. This is despite their considerable geographical distance from each other and their varied topographies and identities. This diversity together with questions, such as whether France should be considered a southern European country, show the challenges of identifying consistent and objective criteria in defining region-ness (Pedaliu, 2013). Nevertheless, the idea of a distinct southern European region is closely interlinked with the process of European integration. The role of the European Economic Community (EEC) in southern Europe increased dramatically after Portugal, Greece and Spain all transitioned from authoritarian to democratic rule within a short time span in the mid-1970s. Their accession to EEC membership in 1981 and 1986, respectively, also coincided with a stabilization of the Italian political system (ibid.).

EEC membership institutionalized interaction between these four countries, while at the same time significantly increasing the felt diversity of the European Community in terms of political and economic systems. Greece, Spain and Portugal were perceived, frequently together with Italy, as an entity that had to catch up to a purportedly European standard of democratic governance. As the EEC morphed into the European Union during the 1990s, southern European states became major recipients of structural and cohesion funds (Dobrescu et al., 2017). Further, while Italy and Spain are among the largest EU member states by geographical and population size, their relative weight with regard to political decision-making in the

Union is not on a par with that held formerly by the United Kingdom, which is of comparable size (Conti et al., 2010). Taken together, the southern member states are often perceived as a political and economic periphery, suggesting that what counts as a small state is defined not only in absolute terms (such as territory, population, military strength, etc.) but also in terms of relative power within a given context (Mainwaring, 2014).

In terms of foreign and security policy, migration became a major concern with the EU accession of Malta and the Republic of Cyprus (RoC) in 2004. High levels of instability in the countries of northern Africa and the Middle East shaped perceptions of southern Europe as a migration 'gateway' into the EU. Malta in particular became very proactive in putting the question of immigration and burden sharing on the EU's agenda. In the second half of 2008, the Maltese government turned to Greece, Italy and Cyprus to work out a common position on these issues, resulting in a format of cooperation named the Quadro Group (Dobrescu et al., 2017).

The quartet met on both ministerial and technical levels on several occasions during the winter of 2008–2009 and eventually tabled a paper demanding a reform to the Dublin Regulation, specifically a more equitable allocation of responsibility for the examination of asylum applications in Europe. The countries' rhetorical action surrounding the demand focused on the exceptional burden carried by the Mediterranean states in receiving migrants and administering asylum claims as well as on their security role of 'gatekeepers' to the EU (Dobrescu et al., 2017; Mainwaring, 2014). In contrast to the NB6 coalition, the Quadro Group remained concentrated on a single issue, and interaction was strongest on the level of technical experts (Rūse, 2013).

The evaluation of this coalition's effectiveness is mixed. Rūse (2013) notes that despite their internal coordination in the run-up to the Swedish Council presidency in the first half of 2009, the countries were not able to achieve a bargaining advantage in the context of negotiations over the Stockholm Program, which sought to adopt a political agreement for setting the EU's agenda in the field of Justice and Home Affairs (JHA). The author attributes this failure to the heterogeneity of policy preferences within the Quadro Group.

Notably, while the coalition became active again in 2011 and was even joined by Spain, these differences could not be overcome (Dobrescu et al., 2017): when the European Commission presented a proposal on a new resettlement and European distribution scheme, Spain indicated it would not comply with the plan; Cyprus, Malta and Greece called for solidarity; and Italy threatened a 'Plan B.' Ever since, the Quadro Group has not made any significant policy proposals at the EU level. Recent analyses of the priorities in immigration policy pursued by Italy and Malta, whose cooperation was originally viewed as the driver of the Quadro Group's advocacy activities on the European level, fail to mention the coalition and also point to increasing conflicts between Rome and Valletta over the issue (Schumacher, 2020; Saini Fasanotti, 2021).

Mainwaring (2014), on the other hand, claims that the Quadro Group had some successes. She notes that it managed to shift the debate on burden sharing on migration within the European Union from one primarily centred on financial assistance to one focused on equally distributing refugees over the Union's member states. This perception appears accurate, given that most member states that do not have an external border were not interested in accepting burden sharing on refugees but were forced to at least take a position on the issue and make some concessions following the Quadro Group's advocacy. While the Quadro Group did not manage to insert its policy preferences into the Stockholm Program, there clearly was an expectation from the side of the Swedish Council presidency that the group would press its demand. Said a Swedish official: 'The Quadro group is a typical and visible group in the field of immigration and asylum policies. We expected them to increase their voice during the negotiations' (Rūse, 2013).

In addition, Greece, Malta and Cyprus received significant assistance from the EU to manage migration flows, in terms of financial support but also through the EU's border management agency Frontex and through the decision to headquarter the European Asylum Support Office (EASO) in Valetta (Mainwaring, 2014). While not all of these benefits can be unequivocally attributed to the Quadro Group, it is reasonable to assume that its members derived at least some benefits from the group's successful advocacy.

Nevertheless, the lack of stability and coherence in the Quadro Group calls into questions its effectiveness as a coalition: it may have produced (some) benefits for its members on the individual level, but it has not led to a feeling of community or even cooperation comparable to that present in the NB6. Conversely to the experience of the Nordic-Baltic Six, the Quadro Group remained focused on a specific policy challenge, did not extend significantly beyond formal government-level coordination and seems not to have produced normative benefits of cooperation. This prompts the question of whether single-issue coalitions are less effective in conferring benefits to their members and thus less likely to be sustainable over the medium and long term. Similarly, the nature of the issue at hand, and its repercussions in the domestic political field of individual states, may influence the likelihood of minilateral coalitions to remain cohesive or splinter.[7]

8.4 Conclusion

The goal of this chapter is to examine the role minilateral coalitions play for small states' participation in the 'embedded concert' of EU security governance. In a growing and more heterogenous EU, small member states have learned that they can amplify their voice by leading or joining coalitions. Minilateral coalition building appears to be a trend in many fields of EU policy. In the area of foreign affairs, security and defence, these coalitions are often subregional. Our case studies highlight three examples of such subregional coalitions, namely the Visegrád Four, the Nordic-Baltic Six and the Quadro Group. As these case studies demonstrate, coalitions often remain informal. They may even fall dormant for a while and then get reactivated when specific policy issues return to salience on the EU agenda.

Our analysis indicates that the benefits of coalitions are both utilitarian and normative. Small EU member states profit from exchange of information and pooling of expertise that helps them overcome information asymmetries and increase bargaining power. The Quadro Group, for instance, was successful in keeping the issue of migration front and centre in the EU Council, and its members extracted tangible benefits from cooperation. But the example of the NB6 shows that governments also value the feeling of social trust and community that accumulates within coalitions as a result of frequent interaction over extended periods of time.

Nevertheless, questions about the utility of coalitions remain. The relationship between utilitarian and value benefits, and how these benefit correlate with different types of coalitions, requires further research. We still need to answer the question of whether utilitarian and value benefits reinforce each other, for instance, whether coalition stability leads to a convergence of policy preferences within the coalition over time that can be translated into greater bargaining effectiveness. Conversely, coalitions that generate normative benefits and social capital may remain more stable over time than task-specific coalitions that primarily seek to influence specific policy outcomes.

Another important debate centres around whether coalitions serve as tools for consensus building within the EU or whether coalitions may, to the contrary, lead to fragmentation. The conditions under which coalitions have a reinforcing function for deeper European integration need to be investigated and specified, just as the conditions under which the formation of regional blocs strengthens centrifugal forces that decrease the likelihood of EU-wide compromise. Finally, we also find that small EU member states are not equal in terms of their propensity to lead, join or opt out of coalitions. It remains to identify the factors influencing coalition-seeking or coalition-averse behavior and whether they are rooted in ideational norms, a perception of 'communities of fate' or even party-political affinities.

Notes

1 Rosecrance and Schott (1997) provide an exposition of the concept of concert in the post-Cold War period, while Papayoanu (1997) applies this concept to post–Cold War Europe. Papayoanu notes in his contribution that contemporary western Europe combines features of an international concert with those of a collective security system. Our notion of embedded concert builds on this insight, even though we refer to the system of EU foreign policy governance of one combining features of concert and multilateralism. The term 'embedded' is used here to denote two systems of partially conflicting rationales, as originally developed in Ruggie (1998).

2 For a general critique of such metageographical approaches see Martin W. Lewis and Kären Wigen, *The Myth of Continents: A Critique of Metageography* (Berkely and Los Angeles: University of California Press, 1997).

3 For a useful discussion of the forms of resistance small states apply to respond to great power politics, see Amitav Acharya, 'The Emerging Regional Architecture of World Politics,' *World Politics* 59, no. 4 (2007): 640–642, 646–648.

4 When Czechoslovakia broke up peacefully into the Czech and Slovak Republics in 1993, Visegrád expanded from three to four members (V3 to V4) and has kept its membership at this number since then.

5 Klaus made this remark in a speech in 1992, accusing the West of seeing Central European countries as second class compared to their Western European counterparts (Hagen, 2003).

6 Note that this perception of regional space is historically contingent and contestable: it overcomes the historic division imposed by Cold War bloc confrontation, yet it is at the same time both inclusive and exclusive – for instance, it does not encompass the two other (large) riparian states of the Baltic Sea, Poland and Germany.
7 The authors thank Hillary Briffa for drawing their attention to the potential impacts of the type of issue and threat faced on coalition cohesion.

Bibliography

Acharya, A. (2007). The emerging regional architecture of world politics. *World Politics* 59(4): 629–652.

Adler, E. and Barnett, M. (eds.). (1998). *Security Communities* (Cambridge University Press: Cambridge).

Ayoob, M. (1999). From regional system to regional society: Exploring key variables in the construction of regional order. *Australian Journal of International Affairs* 53(3): 247–260.

Beckmann, R. and Kempin, R. (2017). EU defence policy needs strategy: Time for political examination of the CSDP's reform objectives. *SWP Comments*, September, Berlin.

Bendiek, A. (2017). *A Paradigm Shift in the EU's Common Foreign and Security Policy: From Transformation to Resilience*. SWP Research Report 11 (Stiftung Wissenschaft und Politik: Berlin).

Bendiek, A. (2019). *Democratization First: The Community Method in CFSP as a Precondition for a European Defense Policy* (Institut Français des Rélations Internationales: Paris). Éditoriaux de l'Ifri.

Blockmans, S. and Crosson, D.M. (2019). *Differentiated Integration within PESCO - Clusters and Convergence in EU Defence*. CEPS Research Report 2019(04) (Center for European Policy Studies: Brussels).

Braun, M. (2020). Postfunctionalism, identity and the Visegrad group. *JCMS: Journal of Common Market Studies* 58(4): 925–940.

Buzan, B. and Wæver, O. (2003). *Regions and Powers: The Structure of International Security* (Cambridge University Press: Cambridge, UK).

Conti, N., Cotta, M. and Tavares de Almeida, P. (2010). Southern Europe: A distinctive and more Pro-European region in the EU? *South European Society and Politics* 15(1): 97–118.

Dangerfield, M. (2008). The Visegrád group in the expanded European Union: From preaccession to postaccession cooperation. *East European Politics and Societies: And Cultures* 22(3).

Deas, I. and Lord, A. (2016). From new regionalism to unusual regionalism? the emergence of non-standard regional spaces and lessons for the territorial reorganisation of the state. *Urban Studies* 43(10): 1847–1877.

Deutsch, K.W. (1957). *Political Community and the North American Area: International Organization in the Light of Historical Experience* (Princeton University Press: Princeton, NJ).

Dobrescu, M., Schumacher, T. and Stavridis, S. (2017). Southern Europe: Portugal, Spain, Italy, Malta, Greece, Cyprus. In: A. Hadfield, I. Manners and R.G. Whitman (eds.), *Foreign Policies of EU Member States: Continuity and Europeanisation* (Routledge: London), pp. 83–99.

Eckert, S. (2021). The construction of identity and crisis in the Visegrád-states since the Schengen crisis. *European Policy* 142.

European Union. (n.d.). The economy. Available at https://europa.eu/european-union/about -eu/figures/economy_en (accessed 25 February, 2021).

Fawn, R. (2001). The elusive defined? Visegrád Cooperation as the contemporary contours of central Europe. *Geopolitics*6(1): 47–68.

Fawn, R. (2013). Visegrád: Fit for purpose? *Communist and Post-Communist Studies* 46(3): 339–349.

Fiott, D., Missiroli, A. and Tardy, T. (2017). *Permanent Structured Cooperation: What's in a Name?* Chaillot Paper 142 (European Union Institute for Security Studies: Paris).

Friis, L. and Schacke-Barfoed, I.T. (2022). Denmark's Zeitenwende. *European Council on Foreign Relations*, 7 June 2002. Available at https://ecfr.eu/article/denmarks -zeitenwende/ (accessed 23 February 2023).

Gosling, T. (2022). The war in Ukraine undermines Orban's illiberal project. *Foreign Policy*, 10 May.

Götz, N. and Haggrén, H. (2009). *Regional Cooperation and International Organizations: The Nordic Model in Transnational Alignment* (Routledge: London).

Hagen, J. (2003). Redrawing the imagined map of Europe: The rise and fall of the "center." *Political Geography* 22(5): 489–517.

Hárs, G. (n.d.). Visegrád: A personal memoir of cooperation. Available at http://www .visegradgroup.eu/the-visegrad-book/hars-gabor-visegrad (accessed 20 March 2018).

Haukkala, H., Etzold, T. and Raik, K. (2017). The Northern European member states. In: A. Hadfield, I. Manners and R.G. Whitman (eds.), *Foreign Policies of EU Member States: Continuity and Europeanisation* (Routledge: London), pp. 23–38.

Janning, J. and Zunneberg, C. (2017). *The Invisible Web: From Interaction to Coalition Building in the European Union. ECFR/210* (European Council on Foreign Relations: Berlin).

Job, B.L. (1997). Matters of multilateralism: Implications for regional conflict management. In: D.A. Lake and P.M. Morgan (eds.), *Regional Orders: Building Security in a New World* (Pennsylvania State University Press: University Park, PA), pp. 165–191.

Kleinberga, V. (2019). Bowling together: Nordic Baltic six in the European Union. *Latvijas Intereses Eiropas Savienībā* 2: 17–31.

Kuusik, P. and Raik, K. (2018a). *The Nordic-Baltic Region in the EU: A Loose Club of Friends.* European Policy Analysis 2018:10 (Swedish Institute for European Policy Studies: Stockholm).

Kuusik, P. and Raik, K. (2018b). *The Nordic-Baltic Region in the EU27: Time for New Strategic Cooperation* (International Center for Defence and Security: Tallinn).

Lewis, M.W. and Wigen, K. (1997). *The Myth of Continents: A Critique of Metageography* (University of California Press: Berkely, CA).

Mainwaring, C. (2014). Small states and nonmaterial power: Creating crises and shaping migration policies in Malta, Cyprus, and the European Union. *Journal of Immigrant and Refugee Studies* 12(2): 103–122.

Ministry of Defence and Armed Forces of the Czech Republic. (2016). V4 EU Battlegroup serves its first rotation. Available at http://www.army.cz/en/ministry-of-defence/newsroom /news/v4-eu-battlegroup-serves-its-first-rotation-122886/ (accessed 22 March 2018).

Neumann, I.B. and Gstöhl, S. (2006). Lilliputians in Gulliver's world? In: J. Beyer, I.B. Neumann and S. Gstöhl (eds.), *Small States in International Relations* (University of Washington Press: Seattle), pp. 3–36.

Papayoanu, P.A. (1997). Great powers and regional orders: Possibilities and prospects after the cold war. In: D.A. Lake and P.M. Morgan (eds.), *Regional Orders: Building Security in a New World* (Pennsylvania State University Press: University Park, PA), pp. 125–139.

Pedaliu, E. (2013). The making of Southern Europe: An historical overview. In: E. Karamouzi, E. Pedaliu, E. De Angelis and Z. Koustoumpardi (eds.), *A Strategy for Southern Europe*. Special Report 017 (LSE Ideas: London), pp. 8–14.

Puglierin, J. and Franke, U.E. (2020). *The Big Engine That Might: How France and Germany Can Build a Geopolitical Europe. Policy Brief ECFR/332* (European Council on Foreign Relations: Berlin).

Reuters. (2018). China hosts Visegrad group, calls them 'dynamic force' in EU. Available at https://www.reuters.com/article/us-china-easteurope/china-hosts-visegrad-group-calls -them-dynamic-force-in-eu-idUSKBN1GZ0A9 (accessed 25 March 2018).

Rosecrance, R. and Schott, P. (1997). Concerts and international intervention. In: D.A. Lake and P.M. Morgan (eds.), *Regional Orders: Building Security in a New World* (Pennsylvania State University Press: University Park, PA), pp. 140–163.

Ruggie, J.G. (1998). Embedded liberalism and the postwar economic regimes. In: J.G. Ruggie (ed.), *Constructing the World Polity: Essays on International Institutionalization* (Routledge: London), pp. 62–84.

Rūse, I. (2013). *(Why) Do Neighbours Cooperate? Institutionalised Coalitions and Bargaining Power in EU Council Negotiations* (Budrich University Press: Leverkusen, Germany).

Rūse, I. (2014). Nordic-Baltic interaction in European Union negotiations: Taking advantage of institutionalized cooperation. *Journal of Baltic Studies* 45(2): 229–246.

Saini Fasanotti, F. (2021). Malta under pressure. *GIS Reports*, 28 May 2021. Available at https://www.gisreportsonline.com/malta-under-pressure,politics,3524.html (accessed 6 March 2023).

Schumacher, L.R. (2020). Malta, Italy, and Mediterranean migration: A long history of an ongoing issue. Available at https://www.fpri.org/article/2020/09/malta-italy-and -mediterranean-migration-a-long-history-and-an-ongoing-issue/ (accessed 6 March 2023).

Söderbaum, F. (2016). *Rethinking Regionalism* (Palgrave: London).

Solingen, E. (1997). Economic liberalization, political coalitions, and emerging regional orders. In: D.A. Lake and P.M. Morgan (eds.), *Regional Orders: Building Security in a New World* (Pennsylvania State University Press: University Park, PA), pp. 68–100.

Steinmetz, R. and Wivel, A. (2016). Introduction. In: R. Steinmetz and A. Wivel (eds.), *Small States in Europe: Challenges and Opportunities* (Routledge: London), pp. 3–14.

Tavares, R. (2008). Understanding regional peace and security: A framework for analysis. *Contemporary Politics* 14(2): 107–127.

Thorhallsoon, B. and Steinsson, S. (2018). A theory of shelter. In: B. Thorhallsson (ed.), *Small States and Shelter Theory: Iceland's External Affairs* (Routledge: London), pp. 24–58.

Vetrovcova, M. (2021). The Visegrad countries in the European Union: Understanding the identity-solidarity nexus in the context of migration and EU enlargement. PhD diss.

Visegrad Group. (n.d.a). History of the Visegrád group. Available at http://www .visegradgroup.eu/about/history (accessed 20 March 2018).

Visegrad Group. (n.d.b). Selected events in. 1998 and earlier. Available at: http://www .visegradgroup.eu/calendar/1998-and-before (accessed 20 October 2021).

Walsch, C. (2022). Is the Visegrad group disintegrating? A case study on the diversification of the Visegrad states' EU enlargement policy since 2014. *Eastern Journal of European Studies* 13(SI): 53–72.

9 Small state influence in EU security policy-making

PESCO, Frontex and the integration dilemma

Béranger Dominici, Olivier Lewis and Sebastian Steingass[1]

9.1 Introduction

This contribution explores some of the literature's key propositions on how small member states in the European Union (EU) respond to the trade-off between (formal) autonomy and security cooperation. Since small states often have little influence on the outcome of negotiations over security cooperation, they face take-it-or-leave-it situations, what small state scholars call the 'integration dilemma.' In security and defence matters, member states traditionally dominate policy-making, and their contribution towards the outcome is generally proportional to their relative resources (Pedi, 2021; Wivel et al., 2014). Despite their supposedly limited role, the attention on small states in security cooperation has grown, regularly evidencing that small states are not always impotent (Arter, 2000; Bailes et al., 2016; Jakobsen, 2009; Weiss, 2017). This raises the question as to what extent exerting influence on security policy-making in the EU has become a way of dealing with the integration dilemma.

Regarding small-state security cooperation, we observe significant variations in reactions to the integration dilemma. Compare, for instance, the cases of Luxembourg, Denmark and Iceland; these three states have dealt with the security integration dilemma in very different ways (Thorhallsson and Wivel, 2006: 655). Few small-state scholars have compared variation in terms of cooperation/integration systematically, especially concerning security and defence. Generally, systematic comparisons of small-state responses to security integration are lacking (Haugevik and Rieker, 2017). Most research looks at the role of individual small states or groups of small states and tends to have a success bias, i.e., focussing on instances when these countries exerted influence successfully.

Looking at concrete cases of small-state security cooperation in the EU, we observe that influence does not seem to be the primary path to managing the dilemma. Instead, despite attempts at moving integration in different security-related areas forward, we observe that the EU attenuates the dilemma for small states, not by giving them a stronger role or influence but by allowing them to fit new initiatives into their existing strategies. To illustrate this argument, we focus on two security-related reforms in different policy areas, defence policy and border control, where traditional state competences were at stake. The reforms are the 2017 launch of the Permanent Structured Cooperation (PESCO) and the 2019 reform

DOI: 10.4324/9781003380641-11

of the European Border and Coast Guard Agency (Frontex), respectively. First, based on the literature, we develop propositions on how small EU member states react when faced with initiatives for security cooperation. The integration dilemma in the EU may not be strong, as initiatives tend to safeguard autonomy, but small states will seek to maintain a seat at the table even when their influence is marginal. Second, we briefly outline the case of EU security policy-making and suggest that there is added value in looking at both defence and border security. We then provide some illustrations of how small states deal with the potential trade-offs in the different cases of EU security policy-making. Considering various geographic dimensions and existing security strategies, we draw on the cases of the Baltic states, Luxembourg, Malta, Cyprus and Ireland.

9.2 Security cooperation trade-offs and small states responses

George Liska (1968) described the trade-off regarding autonomy and security cooperation when he argued that 'a free hand might come to mean an empty and unarmed hand,' while Robert Keohane (1969) noted, inversely, that 'the price of alignment is the loss of real independence and effective sovereignty.' According to Laurent Goetschel (1998), in the pursuit of power, state actors might seek influence, but they might also seek to avoid the influence of others (what he called autonomy). He argued that these two policy goals often conflict, especially 'in the realm of international security' (Goetschel, 1998: 19). State actors, especially those of relatively smaller states, face a trade-off. Being able to influence increases the risks of being influenced. Hence, security cooperation comes with loss of autonomy, as small states risk being more influenced than influential.

Small-state scholars have studied this policy trade-off, examining concrete instances of security cooperation and integration and suggesting that smaller states might face an 'integration dilemma,' i.e., having to choose between (formal) national autonomy and integration (Haugevik and Rieker, 2017; Petersen, 1998; Thorhallsson and Wivel, 2006: 651–652). The concept of an integration dilemma is based on the premise that small states have little influence on the collective, even more so in the area of security than in other policy areas (Thorhallsson and Wivel, 2006: 658–659) and thus either accept the influence of others in return for collective protection or bypass this influence (e.g., seeking opt-outs) to protect their autonomy, even despite potentially reduced effectiveness. Yet, cooperation and integration are often a question of degree; the concepts are rarely binary. Compromise and consensus are the norm in international organizations. Formal organizations, such as the EU, supposedly attenuate the dilemma. Small states are powerful when every member has a veto, which in security decision-making (i.e., high politics) is often the case. The formal equivalency of statehood can provide disproportionate power to smaller states. Differentiated integration, aimed at increasing effectiveness, may, however, circumvent veto power, thus adding pressure on small states, sharpening the take-it-or-leave-it dilemma.

How do small EU member states deal with the integration dilemma in this changing institutional context? Much attention in the literature has gone to how small EU member states seek to exert influence in security cooperation (Haugevik and Rieker, 2017; Pedi, 2021; Weiss, 2017), which would constitute a way of dealing with the dilemma. The influence of small states often appears in combination with taking the lead. Arguably, small state studies regularly constitute efforts to show, counterintuitively, that there is academic and practical value in studying smaller, poorer and weaker states. Logically, those studying 'underdogs' tend to study instances where smaller states took the initiative (in the EU, for example, during a rotating presidency) to set the agenda and frame issues. However, in security policy, smaller EU states tend to be excluded from the ad hoc decision-making processes that lead to the establishment of new structures. Security agreements on structures tend to be prearranged by a few large member states. This first-mover advantage implies that late joiners have little hope of making major changes, and small late-joining states even less so. Hence, the limitation of focusing on taking the initiative is its selection bias. Failure and impotence are understudied. This leaves out studying the role of smaller member states to oppose or at least modify larger member states' initiatives.

A key question is how small EU member states react when faced with a new initiative for security cooperation. Gunta Pastore (2013: 68) argues that geography matters because it is a proxy for material interdependencies, such as cross-border movements of goods and people. She suggests that for smaller states limited resources mean limited foreign policy ambitions and proximity taking priority (Pastore, 2013: 69–72). Hence, 'frontline' small states will face a different integration dilemma than those afar, but will also concentrate their attention and capacity to react when faced with a potential trade-off. Linked to such 'geographic' preferences is a certain path dependence, with previous responses to the integration dilemma creating routines and dispositions, as seen, for example, with established traditions of neutrality and strategic shelter (cf. Vaicekauskaitė, 2017). Having such preferences, i.e., being directly 'affected' by proposed security cooperation, seems to constitute a prerequisite for small state participation and, eventually, influence. As small member states have limited resources, they concentrate them where they are most relevant. Simultaneously, such engrained preferences are easily recognized by larger states.

Within EU structures, no matter who launches a legislative or policy proposal, state actors habitually consult and consort. This applies to both larger and smaller member states. Although intrinsic to diplomacy, such instincts are especially important to smaller and weaker states, especially in formal organizations such as the EU. Tom Long (2016: 196–200), for example, argues that 'uniting with other states' is one of the three bases of small-state power – the other being 'gaining concessions from patrons' and controlling scarce resources, such as territories, commodities or a salient skill. For small states in the EU, such partnering may include connecting to large states driving the initiative, building like-minded coalitions (geographic or functional) and/or joining forces with EU institutions, especially the Commission (Björkdahl, 2008: 145–146; Pastore, 2013: 77–79; Thorhallsson and Wivel, 2006: 660). Hence, even as small states may not be part of a coalition that launches a security cooperation initiative, they may form coalitions and partner with other state and/or institutional actors to seek to influence these initiatives.

While rebellions short of formal opting out can come in many forms, including constructive abstentions and public denunciations or provocations, there is a tendency to avoid this unless necessary. Small states in the EU tend to be vigilant of their reputation. Hence, unless national interests are seriously contravened, they try to avoid being seen as troublemakers – reputation is a key currency for small states. Echoing what international relations scholars once called 'the shadow of the future,' a state's reputation and standing seem to affect outcomes: past behaviour, cooperative and compromise-seeking attitudes, apparent expertise, moral authority, and suspected ulterior motives all influence how others interpret proposals and objections, even more so for *smaller* states (Arter, 2000: 691; Björkdahl, 2008; Jakobsen, 2009: 86; Knudsen, 1996: 12–13; Long, 2016: 190, 195, 199; Pastore, 2013: 74; Tow and Parkin, 2007: 324). Due to their vulnerability of being sidelined by larger states, small EU member states seek participation to secure a 'seat at the table' or even develop niche capacities of use to larger states – especially visible in military organizations (see also Rickli, 2008). Hence, small trade-offs (i.e., some limiting of autonomy despite little influence or few benefits) may be accepted to remain 'at the table' and maintain an established reputation, which is often, if not always, considered vital for future cooperation.

Taking these aspects together suggests that, even as the EU seeks to enhance the effectiveness of its security cooperation, the nature of EU policy-making seems to remain generally inclusive (thus avoiding formal opt-outs). Consequently, initiatives for security cooperation may not necessarily constitute stark integration dilemmas as the final agreement may turn out not to contradict existing small states' security policies and strategies. Hence, we expect formal opting out to remain the exception and for autonomy to be favoured over effectiveness and integration. At the same time, we expect that small EU member states try to keep a 'seat at the table' and make concessions, focusing on a few key messages they need to see acknowledged and reflected, usually coordinated with key partners among other member states and EU institutions.

Before looking at concrete instances of small-state responses in EU security policy-making, we briefly define what we mean by small states and security in the EU and how the cases selected can lead to insights regarding the integration dilemma.

9.3 Cases of security cooperation in the EU

The EU became a security organization in fits and starts via ad hoc reactions to crises and in a piecemeal fashion. EU leaders have gradually integrated security structures, often formalizing procedures occurring informally or outside of the EU as an organization. This makes security cooperation in the EU effectively a case of differentiated integration, where small EU member states have potentially faced integration dilemmas (i.e., participation without influence or opt-out without benefit). In this contribution, we focus on examples of enhancing cooperation in defence and border control, namely the launch of PESCO in December 2017 and the reform of the European Border and Coast Guard Agency (traditionally known as Frontex), particularly the creation of a category of operational staff with executive powers, including the use of force and weapons, introduced with the fourth regulation of the agency's activities in November 2019.

When it comes to which states count as small, definitions of smallness vary and continue to be a point of contention. Regarding security, a relational approach (Long, 2017; Thorhallsson and Wivel, 2006) seems appropriate. The smallest EU member states vary slightly depending on the applied measure, e.g., population, gross domestic product, military expenditure, armed forces or number of police officers. Another aspect that characterizes the EU's smallest member states is that they are often outliers (even more so after Brexit and the end of Denmark's Common Security and Defence Policy (CSDP) opt-out), due to their often extreme situations and/or geographies, making systematic comparison difficult. To account for these differences and variations (e.g., military neutrality and geographic location), we draw on the examples of Ireland, Luxembourg, Malta, Cyprus, Estonia and Latvia.

Small-state influence in EU defence policy has mostly received attention due to a preference for neutrality. For decades neutrality has been a key feature of small-state foreign policies. In contrast, for the new frontline member states in the Baltics, strategic shelter in EU and NATO became the dominant strategy. Events, such as the war in Ukraine since 2014, have led many in EU small states to reconsider their foreign policies and security and defence cooperation. The Baltic states have sought to bolster multilateral and bilateral cooperation, especially with NATO and the United States (Vaicekauskaitė, 2017: 14). In contrast, the citizens and leaders of Ireland and Malta seek to maintain a degree of military neutrality. Arguably, these developments give relevance to the advent of PESCO. The activation of 'legally binding' commitments in defence matters is directly relevant to the study of security-autonomy trade-offs and small-state integration dilemmas (Blockmans, 2017; Weiss, 2017).

Comparing defence cooperation and border control cooperation is interesting because the legal foundations and geopolitics are somewhat different, as are the roles of smaller EU member states. After the Lisbon Treaty, defence cooperation in the EU (broadly) maintained its special legal status. In contrast, cooperation in the area of freedom, security and justice (AFSJ), which includes police cooperation and border management, became part of EU competences. Having said that, effective AFSJ opt-outs were preserved, notably, for those countries that are not part of Schengen, such as Ireland and Cyprus. By creating armed EU staff, the 2019 regulation represents a significant change for Frontex, member states and the EU. It represents a (albeit partial and conditional) transfer of traditional functions and symbols of statehood to a supranational polity (Meissner, 2021). By arming EU officials, member states are, *de facto* and *de jure*, reducing their monopolies of the regulation violence, a definition of European statehood.

In this contribution, we look at PESCO and Frontex together to understand how small states perform in different institutional settings regarding security decision-making. Policy-making processes differ in the two cases. While the decision to launch PESCO was intergovernmental, the Frontex reform was the result of an ordinary legislative procedure (i.e., Community method). This has repercussions not just for which actors are involved (e.g., EU institutions as potential allies) but also for the cost of opting out, which may affect the role of small states. Our comparison across different modes of (security) policy-making, i.e., intergovernmental and Community method, suggests that, in the latter case, smaller states with strong (national) preferences, such as frontline states, will also have a stronger reaction to the integration dilemma than in the case of defence, and actively seek to mediate it (and have more channels to do so, i.e., via EU institutions). While the cases do not cover all aspects of security policy-making in the EU, or even in the discussed policy areas, they provide prominent cases of security-related integration dilemmas to illustrate the viability of the literature's propositions.

9.4 How small EU states deal with security/autonomy trade-offs

9.4.1 Defence cooperation: PESCO

When PESCO was launched with a Council decision in December 2017, the result was favourable to many small EU member states but hardly a product of small-state influence. PESCO can be generally considered a 'big state' initiative. When in the summer of 2016 mainly Germany and France decided to push forward with PESCO after it had remained unused for years, small EU states were more reactive than proactive. The process leading to the launch of PESCO was shaped by French, German and Italian non-papers in the autumn of 2016 (Mauro and Santopinto, 2017), with Germany having been particularly active (Fiott et al., 2017: 20). Available evidence suggests that the smallest EU member states played a marginal role in the design of PESCO, especially in the final stages before the formal agreement. Much of the fine-tuning was done by large, committed member states. Given that PESCO was 'watered down' at the start of the drafting process, strong responses to the integration dilemma were not to be expected. Still, some small states, such as Ireland and Malta, provide important illustrations of the integration dilemma. Generally, small member states either opted for participation (at little cost for autonomy), as in the case of Luxembourg, Ireland, Cyprus and the Baltics, or for opting out, as in the case of Malta.

While the Lisbon Treaty wording of PESCO intentionally provided an avenue for differentiated integration (to avoid consensus via the lowest common denominator), this path was not taken. In the wake of Brexit, the desire to legitimize the EU (through inclusion) trumped efforts to increase (effective) defence and military integration between larger states. By the autumn of 2016, PESCO's autonomy-effectiveness trade-off was already addressed. The conclusions of the November 2016 FAC meeting highlighted 'inclusion' in connection to PESCO and added the concept of a 'modular approach' (Council of the European Union, 2016). Via the notion of inclusion and modularity, EU solidarity would be favoured over effectiveness via differentiated integration (Major, 2017). Modularity meant that cooperation would be favoured over integration, attenuating national autonomy loss (Clancy, 2020).

Yet aversion to the loss of state autonomy was not the only issue. Post-Brexit, symbolism mattered more than effectiveness. In its final form, PESCO was not principally a way to reach a strategic end; it was one of several ways to reach a political, symbolic end. Put simply, larger states sought to include smaller states despite their not bringing much value added, and many smaller states made an effort to join an initiative that (due to small national forces and inexistent defence industries) was of little benefit – a major motivation for most was simply to demonstrate solidarity and maintain 'a seat at the table.'

Hence, despite being a large-state initiative, in its final form the PESCO initiative aligned with small-state preferences, especially those of the Baltics and Ireland that favoured inclusivity over exclusivity. In the Baltics, preferences were defined early, and the PESCO initiative, as it practically developed along the more inclusive lines, seemed aligned, despite limitations in participating in Europe's defence industrial base and risks of the US government's discontent. With NATO as the principal security guarantor, it was vital that PESCO would not compete with, let alone challenge, NATO's role, but at best lock in others to complement the capabilities of NATO, especially infrastructure for the deployment of military forces, including NATO forces, and in the field of cybersecurity. Hence, the binding nature of the contributions, which was considered as the way to enhance European defence spending and capabilities, was voiced by Baltic policy-makers at a time when this was lagging behind from the Baltic perspective (Šešelgytė, 2019). From the perspective of the integration dilemma, for the Baltic states, it was relevant not to be excluded from such a security cooperation. At the same time, participation could not come at the cost of effective security cooperation via other, existing formats, especially NATO. Estonia therefore wanted a 'PESCO-light' without any obligation to buy European military equipment (Mauro and Santopinto, 2017: 25–27). Latvia favoured an inclusive approach to PESCO but was also interested in creating 'objectively assessed commitments' (Mauro and Santopinto, 2017: 26). This reaction illustrates an integration dilemma in the case of overlapping – and potentially competing – types of security cooperation, which was mitigated by the fact that the inclusive nature of PESCO had prevailed early in the process.

There is evidence that preferences had not been as clearly defined in other cases. When researchers for the think tank of the European Parliament sent a questionnaire to member states, overall, ten (mostly smaller) member states did not answer the questionnaire, including Ireland, Luxembourg and Malta (Mauro and Santopinto, 2017: 40). Malta's initial silence was not surprising, and it eventually constituted an 'opt-out' case. When it comes to defence and military issues, it is one of the least active neutral EU member states, not even participating in the formation of (unused) EU battlegroups and only occasionally sending personnel on EU CSDP missions. Despite the inclusive approach, by November 2017, the government of Malta had already decided not to participate in PESCO. Unlike in Luxembourg or Ireland, there was no perceived need to demonstrate EU solidarity post-Brexit. At the time, a government spokesperson explained:

> Malta fully understands and supports other EU Member States' motivation and interest to use the Permanent Structured Cooperation (PESCO) as provided under the Treaties. At this stage, Malta will follow the developments

that will take place under the PESCO within its overarching governance structure. (The Malta Independent, 2017)

By December 2017, going against the grain, Malta maintained its somewhat contradictory and confused position at apparently little political cost. While Prime Minister Joseph Muscat suggested that PESCO itself did not pose any apparent legal problems vis-à-vis neutrality, it was better for Malta to wait and see how it would develop (Malta Today, 2017).

While Malta sought a way out of the integration dilemma by opting out, Luxembourg preferred a seat at the table. Even though its preferences were not fully met, PESCO did not pose much of an integration dilemma. As with Cyprus, opportunities for companies in Luxembourg and Ireland were limited and with such small armed forces Luxembourg did not have much military autonomy to lose (Lewis, 2022). Participating in PESCO was seen as symbolically important, possibly bolstering future cooperation in other sectors. For Luxembourg, keeping a seat at the table was an evident motivation, and it sought to be as involved as possible.

The leadership of Luxembourg often narrates the state's history as a founding member of the EU, and its armed forces virtually always operate in cooperation with other EU member states, especially Belgium, France, Germany and the Netherlands (Lewis, 2022). Accordingly, in Luxembourg, former prime minister Jean-Claude Juncker suggested that PESCO was a step towards a European Defence Union and argued that 'Europe cannot and should not outsource our security and defence' (Luxembourg Times, 2017). Despite its small military force and defence industry, Luxembourg's leaders seem to have been able to use their long-standing cooperation with Belgium and the Netherlands to have their voice heard (Chambre des Députés, 2017). Although they welcomed the inclusive and industrial approach, they were interested in including the improvement of the EU's troop deployment times, a position close to the French preference. While PESCO remained far from a European Defence Union, by December 2017, Luxembourg seemed satisfied that it could participate in projects in line with the state's preexisting plans (e.g., military mobility and training).

In contrast to Malta, Cyprus and Ireland took different approaches regarding the PESCO initiative, outlining a different perspective on the integration dilemma it posed. While Cyprus lacked the requisite military capability, it sought to participate in the PESCO process – like Ireland and Malta, Cyprus is not a NATO member (notably due to its conflict with Turkey). With an unresolved conflict on the island, conflictual relations with Turkey and an US arms embargo at the time, the government of Cyprus was happy that the inclusive approach, advocated by Germany, was confirmed in December 2017 (helping to mitigate the effect of arms embargoes). Yet, there is little sign that Cyprus had any role in producing this outcome (Efstathiou, 2019).

Ireland, arguably, is a special case. Its concern for neutrality and less inclination for EU federalism (especially in security and defence matters) meant that it was not clear how preferences would develop and how it would deal with the potential integration dilemma posed by the initiative – the EP think tank report put it erroneously in the category of non-participants (Mauro and Santopinto, 2017: 40). The history and position of Ireland is often narrated in reference to the United Kingdom. It is through this context that Irish understandings of the integration dilemma should be understood:

> As a former colony, with a bitter experience of imperialism and a strong sense of independence, Ireland's pooling of sovereignty with its European partners has most often been presented as a desirable trade-off between legal, formal sovereignty and effective sovereignty. Having a seat at the main table [...] was deemed to be a major advance, one that allowed the state more effectively to pursue its interests. (Tonra, 2019)

Balancing this trade-off is reflected in the Irish reaction. Prime Minster Enda Kenny was already in favour of major initiatives to increase EU-based defence cooperation (Houses of the Oireachtas, 2017b). However, Ireland was among the last countries to agree on its participation. At every step in the policy-making process the government sought to communicate how the initiative fitted into the country's existing security cooperation in relation to neutrality, peacebuilding operations and opportunities for cost reduction – and in no way a step towards a 'European army' (Houses of the Oireachtas, 2017f.).

While the way the Irish government and press were presenting PESCO as related to the UN peacekeeping missions was different from the way it was presented in Brussels and other capitals, PESCO, in the end, turned out to pose less of an integration dilemma (similar as with the Baltic states despite the very different national situations). The extent to which Ireland contributed to this outcome, however, is questionable. As PESCO negotiations advanced, opposition members became increasingly critical. They suggested that Ireland rarely instigates and shapes EU policy and instead is only 'reactive,' determining their position 'post factum' (Houses of the Oireachtas, 2017e). The Irish government was reaching out to key drivers of the initiative to communicate essential aspects. In October 2017, for instance, Prime Minister Leo Varadkar met with French President Emmanuel Macron and discussed PESCO. Faced with an interlocuter known for wanting to increase the EU's ability to conduct 'the most demanding' military operations, the Irish prime minister highlighted that:

> We would like a scenario where all member states are involved but we are clear that there cannot be any impact on our neutrality and there cannot be anything that would contradict the treaties to which we have signed up. (Houses of the Oireachtas, 2017d)

Stressing that PESCO was conducted within the realm of the treaties suggests that it would not interfere with the country's existing balance of security/autonomy trade-offs, which constituted a key condition for Ireland's participation. When adopting the motion to join PESCO just days before the initiative was launched, the government reassured parliament that 'At Ireland's insistence, PESCO's participation criteria expressly stipulate that PESCO will be undertaken in full compliance with the Treaty on European Union and the associated protocols' (Houses of the Oireachtas, 2017a).

Aside from rhetoric, however, it seems that even this relatively large small state only played a minor role in PESCO negotiations. Despite seemingly not providing a significant value added (neither for Ireland nor PESCO), one of the main reasons for joining PESCO, according to the Irish government, was 'to maintain a central influence on the development of CSDP' (Houses of the Oireachtas, 2017c) and hence retain a voice in EU security and defence policy-making. Another reason may have been that Irish support for PESCO was a 'repayment' for EU support for Irish interests in the Brexit negotiations (Houses of the Oireachtas, 2017f.). Brexit, then, might be one factor that helps explain the stark difference between Ireland and Malta regarding both preferences and participation. This suggests that participation was important for Ireland, given the limited costs for autonomy, if only to maintain working relationships in the halls of European power.

9.4.2 Border control cooperation: Frontex reform

When it comes to border control, preferences of 'frontline' states had been reinforced at least since the increase in the arrival of migrants and refugees at the EU's external borders in 2015. Hence, in contrast to PESCO, we expect more clearly defined preferences of the Southern member states. Yet, while this may be considered a necessary condition for modifying an initiative once it is on the table, it may not be sufficient. Available evidence suggests that small EU member states were active in seeking to influence the design of the 2019 Frontex regulation, which created the agency's operational staff with executive powers, arguably an EU initiative with big state backing. Many small frontline member states, in contrast, expressed their reservations regarding the creation of a category of EU staff with executive powers already at the early stages of the proposal's preparation. Instead, they had other views on what would be more relevant.

Though the number of border crossings had dropped significantly, the EU was deeply divided on the migration issue, which was presented as an 'existential challenge' for the Union by France and Germany ('Meseberg Declaration: Renewing Europe's promises of security and prosperity,' 2018) ahead of European elections. In addition to the Schengen zone crisis that materialized by the return of border checks at Schengen states borders, the arrival of a new right-wing government in Italy closing its ports to rescue boats and internal disputes within the German coalition over migration issues in late spring 2018 further increased the pressure to find a quick solution. In this context, while other migration-related reforms (such as the Dublin regulation reform or the creation of the EU asylum agency) remained at a standstill (Angelescu and Trauner, 2018), 'strengthening external border management [appeared as] the lowest common denominator among Member States' (Bossong, 2019: 1), and the Commission's idea of strengthening the capacity of Frontex with its own manpower, i.e., setting up a genuine European border force, received support by France and Germany ('Meseberg Declaration: Renewing Europe's promises of security and prosperity,' 2018).

This reform, which arguably changed the very nature of the agency (Fernández-Rojo, 2021), provoked immediate opposition not only from small frontline states in the South but also from Luxembourg. For the Baltic states, at the time, the focus was much less on the potential function of Frontex than was the case near the Mediterranean Sea (Gustafsson, 2018). Hence, the potential integration dilemma posed by the 2019 reform was, apparently, less relevant. These countries had, however, considered the prospects of other potential migration-related policy reforms. Thus, when on 24 June 2018 the mostly smaller 'frontline' states in the Baltics (and the Visegrad group) boycotted a mini summit called by Commission president Jean-Claude Juncker, backed by Angela Merkel (Le Monde, 2018), the provocation was less aimed at the Frontex reform proposal and more generally at the EU's refugee and migration policy, especially the still prevalent idea of relocation. It is not, then, the prospect of armed EU agents that were most concerning autonomy-wise but rather the idea of conceding additional autonomy in migration policy-making and control. In this sense, the relevant integration dilemma for the Baltic states was more about legal sovereignty than actual border guarding autonomy.

For Ireland, not a Schengen member, the situation regarding the integration dilemma was even clearer, which became evident in a reply by the prime minister:

As Ireland is not part of the Schengen area, this does not impact directly on us. Our position is to support those member states most impacted. It is to be proactive and supportive in the negotiations because there are differing views depending on the member state and its location in the EU in terms of closeness to borders. We need to show solidarity to those member states which are most impacted. We know, particularly in terms of the Brexit negotiations, the member states that are least impacted have shown solidarity towards Ireland. (Houses of the Oireachtas, 2018)

While Ireland did not face an integration dilemma directly, the statement shows an understanding that (small) states, which due to their location are forced into such a dilemma, as Ireland was during the Brexit negotiations, need support to attenuate their dilemma.

Luxembourg voiced explicit criticism of the creation of standing corps and did not see much value added. For example, two months before the Commission's proposal was published, in July 2018, the Minister of Foreign Affairs of Luxembourg, reporting before parliament on an informal JHA meeting in Innsbruck (during which the creation of a standing corps was discussed), did not hide his 'scepticism' about the proposal to increase the agency's operational staff to 10,000 (up from 1,500 under the 2016 regulation), questioning the 'purpose of such an increase' (Chambre des Députés, 2018).

Attention to the reform was, expectedly, higher for the EU member states in the South. The leaders of many 'frontline' states such as Greece, Italy, Malta and Spain were, even more than the other member states, reluctant to delegate more sovereign powers to Frontex and its standing corps (Meissner, 2021; Statewatch, 2019). In Malta, the Minister for Home Affairs and National Security expressed doubts that this institutional innovation could effectively reduce migratory flows in the central Mediterranean (arguably the country's top priority) and called for the extensive use of the possibilities offered by the 2016 regulation then in force (Government of the Republic of Malta, 2018b). At an earlier occasion, the minister expressed fears that the deployment of such a category of personnel could place states in a 'perpetual state of assistance' and could have a 'serious impact on the member state's own resources and sovereignty' (Government of the Republic of Malta, 2018a). Instead, the country's leaders insisted that the reform should focus on enhancing the agency's mandate in the area of return and of cooperation with third countries – chiefly Libya (Government of the Republic of Malta, 2018b).

Early in the negotiation process, Malta joined forces together with other frontline states (Greece, Italy, Spain) that appeared to have pushed, together with France, as soon as early June 2018 to have centres, built on the model of hotspots, established within the EU and in neighbouring third countries, notably to alleviate their responsibility for the reception of migrants and refugees on their seas and shores (Le Monde, 2018; Times of Malta, 2018). The initiative proved initially successful as it was endorsed with explicit reference to Malta's needs during the June 2018 European Council ('Remarks by President Donald Tusk on the European Council meetings of 28–29 June 2018,' 2018), and the idea of setting up such centres on EU soil was included in the Commission's proposal. However, this coalition building proved insufficient as the initiative did not make it into the final regulation.

Although some controversial elements of the proposal did not survive the negotiation phase and other major adjustments were made, the creation of the EBCG standing corps was in the end approved by the member states, albeit in a weaker form than planned. Like the previous reform, the 2019 Frontex reform was adopted relatively quickly (14 months after the Commission published its proposal in September 2018), while other migration-related texts remained in limbo until the end of the legislature. According to Perkowski et al. (2023), although the migratory context was highly different from the one having pushed member states to agree on a text in a record time in 2016, 'the sense of ongoing, protracted crisis' fostered by the agency of the Commission, 'contributed to their willingness to compromise' despite the strong concerns (Perkowski et al., 2023: 120).

The creation of EBCG standing corps, though initially met with reluctance by member states, for instance, expressed in the Luxembourgish scepticism, was adopted, albeit with lowered ambition. The Austrian presidency under chancellor Kurz, who launched the process, appeared committed to reinforcing the 'protection of external borders' and actively facilitated reaching a common position on the standing corps (Statewatch, 2019). While the Commission had proposed to establish a 10,000 officer-strong standing corps as soon as 2020, an idea supported by Germany (Bossong, 2019), following negotiations in the Council, the number was qualified and implementation delayed. The extent of the powers Frontex was to be granted was also changed during the legislative process in order to preserve EU member states' sovereign power, with the Council moving the list of 'tasks requiring executive powers' from the annex (in the Commission proposal) to the main body of the final regulation, reinforcing oversight on their activities, including the country hosting the operation, and specifying the conditions under which they were to carry and use weapons (Statewatch, 2019).

9.5 Conclusions

This contribution looked at two cases that had the potential to confront smaller EU member states with an integration dilemma in security and defence to understand how small states cope with integration dilemmas in these policy areas. Not all small states experienced these dilemmas equally. To understand small state reactions to the integration dilemma, our contribution confirms the relevance of geography. Yet, the simultaneous comparison with 'non-frontline' states highlights the relevance of existing security strategies and previous (and expected future) experiences in EU policy-making. The latter was particularly visible in the case of Ireland.

Both cases, PESCO and the 2019 Frontex reform, were big state-backed initiatives, which meant that small states could, at most, react. Despite the different formal policy-making modes (intergovernmental vs. Community method), in both cases, arguably, outcomes favoured autonomy over effectiveness. However, some independence has been lost for those participating with often little gain for smaller states, which, nevertheless sought to maintain a seat at the table and show their willingness to cooperate. While compromise orientation and accommodation of small states in the AFSJ may be by default and expected (as opt-outs are effectively highly costly), in the case of PESCO such eagerness for inclusiveness was, arguably, by choice, and the comparison suggests that this outcome is somewhat independent of the policy-making mode, which calls for additional, systematic investigation.

Our focus was on the extent to which small EU member states seek to exert influence to affect outcomes that attenuate the dilemma in security policy-making. Small states sought to exert some influence over final outcomes, especially when they had clear preferences, as in the case of the Frontex reform. Coalition building with others member states and, in the case of Frontex, EU institutions took place to upload preferences to initiatives of big member states but did often not prove sufficient in the final decision-making stage. Hence, influence could not alleviate the dilemma. Instead, despite the advent of differentiated integration, the EU seems to attenuate the dilemma for small states not by giving them a stronger role or influence but by allowing them to fit new initiatives into their existing strategies to facilitate the selling of the reforms to national audiences. Even more, when little is at stake for them, in EU security policy-making the weak tend to confront the integration dilemma and suffer (attenuated versions of) what they must.

Note

1 Authors are listed in alphabetical order. The authors would like to thank the editors for their helpful comments on earlier versions of this contribution.

Bibliography

Angelescu, I. and Trauner, F. (2018). *10,000 Border Guards for Frontex: Why the EU Risks Conflated Expectations.* Policy Brief 21 (European Policy Centre: Brussels), September.
Arter, D. (2000). Small state influence within the EU: The case of Finland's 'Northern Dimension Initiative'. *JCMS: Journal of Common Market Studies* 38(5): 677–697.
Bailes, A.J.K., Thayer, B.A. and Thorhallsson, B. (2016). Alliance theory and alliance Shelter: The complexities of small state alliance behaviour. *Third World Thematics: A TWQ Journal* 1(1): 9–26.
Björkdahl, A. (2008). Norm advocacy: A small state strategy to influence the EU. *Journal of European Public Policy* 15(1): 135–154.
Blockmans, S. (2017). The Benelux approach to EU integration and external action. *Global Affairs* 3(3): 223–235.
Bossong, R. (2019). The expansion of Frontex. Symbolic measures and long-term changes in EU border management. *SWP Comment* 47, December, Berlin.
Chambre des Députés. (2017). *Procès-verbal de la réunion du 04 décembre 2017, Commission des Affaires étrangères et européennes, de la Défense, de la Coopération et de l'Immigration*, 18 December (Chambre des Députés: Luxembourg). Available at https://wdocs-pub.chd.lu/docs/exped/0007/012/14120.pdf (accessed 12 May 2023).
Chambre des Députés. (2018). *Procès-verbal de la réunion du 18 juillet 2018, Commission des Affaires étrangères et européennes, de la Défense, de la Coopération et de l'Immigration*, 23 July (Chambre des Députés: Luxembourg). Available at https://wdocs-pub.chd.lu/docs/exped/0012/069/24699.pdf (accessed 12 May 2023).
Clancy, P. (2020). Arise, sleeping beauty: What PESCO means for Ireland. In: F. de Londras and S. Ní Mhaolealaidh (eds.), *The Irish Yearbook of International Law* (Hart Publishing: Oxford), pp. 79–98.
Council of the European Union. (2016). Council conclusions on implementing the EU global strategy in the area of security and defence. *Council Conclusions* 14149/16 (14 November), Brussels.
Efstathiou, Y.-S. (2019). *PeSCo: The Cyprus Perspective.* Policy Paper 35 (The French Institute for International and Strategic Affairs (Iris): Paris), February.
Fernández-Rojo, D. (2021). *EU Migration Agencies: The Operation and Cooperation of Frontex, EASO and Europol* (Edward Elgar: Cheltenham).
Fiott, D., Missiroli, A., and Tardy, T. (2017). *Permanent Structured Cooperation: What's in a Name?* Chaillot Paper No. 142 (EU Institute for Security Studies: Paris), November.
Goetschel, L. (1998). The foreign and security policy interests of small states in today's Europe. In: L. Goetschel (ed.), *Small States Inside and Outside the European Union: Interests and Policies* (Springer: Boston, MA), pp. 13–31.
Government of the Republic of Malta. (2018a). Press release by the ministry for Home Affairs and National Security: Minister Michael Farrugia attends the Home Affairs Council meeting in Luxembourg, PR182203, 12 October. Available at https://www.gov.mt/en/Government/DOI/Press%20Releases/Pages/2018/October/12/pr182203.aspx (accessed 11 May 2023).
Government of the Republic of Malta. (2018b). Press release by the ministry for Home Affairs and National Security: Minister Michael Farrugia participates in the Home Affairs Council meeting, PR182658, 7 December. Available at https://www.gov.mt/en/Government/DOI/Press%20Releases/Pages/2018/December/07/pr182658.aspx (accessed 13 May 2023).
Gustafsson, Å. (2018). The Baltic Sea Region Border Control Cooperation (BSRBCC) and border management in the Baltic Sea region: A case study. *Marine Policy* 98: 309–316.
Haugevik, K. and Rieker, P. (2017). Autonomy or integration? Small-state responses to a changing European security landscape. *Global Affairs* 3(3): 211–221.
Houses of the Oireachtas. (2017a). Dáil Éireann debate - Thursday, 7 December 2017. Available at https://www.oireachtas.ie/en/debates/debate/dail/2017-12-07/38/ (accessed 12 May 2023).

Houses of the Oireachtas. (2017b). Dáil Éireann debate - Tuesday, 21 March 2017. Available at https://www.oireachtas.ie/en/debates/debate/dail/2017-03-21/12/ (accessed 11 May 2023).

Houses of the Oireachtas. (2017c). Dáil Éireann debate - Wednesday, 22 November 2017. Available at https://www.oireachtas.ie/en/debates/question/2017-11-22/246/ (accessed 12 May 2023).

Houses of the Oireachtas. (2017d). Dáil Éireann debate - Wednesday, 25 October 2017. Available at https://www.oireachtas.ie/en/debates/debate/dail/2017-10-25/10/ (accessed 11 May 2023).

Houses of the Oireachtas. (2017e). Dáil Éireann debate - Wednesday, 28 June 2017. Available at https://www.oireachtas.ie/en/debates/debate/dail/2017-06-28/11/ (accessed 12 May 2023).

Houses of the Oireachtas. (2017f). Select Committee on Foreign Affairs and Trade, and Defence Debate - Wednesday, 6 December. Available at https://www.oireachtas.ie/en /debates/debate/select_committee_on_foreign_affairs_and_trade_and_defence/2017-12 -06/2/ (accessed 11 May 2023).

Houses of the Oireachtas. (2018). Dáil Éireann debate - Wednesday, 24 October 2018. Available at https://www.oireachtas.ie/en/debates/debate/dail/2018-10-24/21/ (accessed 13 May 2023).

Jakobsen, P.V. (2009). Small states, big influence: The overlooked Nordic influence on the civilian ESDP. *JCMS: Journal of Common Market Studies* 47(1): 81–102.

Keohane, R.O. (1969). Lilliputians dilemmas: Small states in international politics. *International Organization* 23(2): 291–310.

Knudsen, O.F. (1996). Analysing small-state security: The role of external factors. In: W.C. Bauwens Armand and O.F. Knudsen (eds.), *Small States and the Security Challenge in the New Europe* (Brasseys: London), pp. 3–20.

Le Monde. (2018). Crise des migrants: à Bruxelles, un mini-sommet pour apaiser le débat, 25 June. Available at https://www.lemonde.fr/europe/article/2018/06/25/migration-un -mini-sommet-pour-depassionner-un-debat-qui-frise-l-hysterie_5320638_3214.html (accessed 12 May 2023).

Lewis, O. (2022). *Security Cooperation between Western States: Openness, Security and Autonomy* (Routledge: London).

Liska, G. (1968). *Alliances and the Third World* (Johns Hopkins University Press: Baltimore, MD).

Long, T. (2016). Small States, Great Power? Gaining Influence Through Intrinsic, Derivative, and Collective Power. *International Studies Review* 19(2): 185–205.

Long, T. (2017). Its not the size, its the relationship: From small states to asymmetry. *International Politics* 54(2): 144–160.

Luxembourg Times. (2017). First steps towards European Defence Union, 11 December. Available at https://www.luxtimes.lu/en/european-union/first-steps-towards-european -defence-union-602d3c02de135b923636e871 (accessed 12 May 2023).

Major, C. (2017). *Credible EU Defense Means Rethinking Sovereignty* (Carnegie Europe: Brussels), 15 June.

Malta Today. (2017). Malta to wait and see before deciding on PESCO defence pact, Muscat says. *Malta Today,* 15 December. Available at https://www.maltatoday.com.mt /news/europe/83085/malta_to_wait_and_see_before_deciding_on_pesco_defence_pact _muscat_says#.ZFzWdhHP25c (accessed 11 May 2023).

Mauro, F. and Santopinto, F. (2017). *Permanent Structured Cooperation: National Perspectives and State of Play.* Study PE, 603.842 (European Parliament. Directorate-General for External Policies of the Union: Brussels), July. Available at https://data .europa.eu/doi/10.2861/773220.

Meissner, V. (2021). The European Border and Coast Guard Agency Frontex After the Migration Crisis: Towards a 'Superagency'? In: J. Pollak and P. Slominski (eds.), *The Role of EU Agencies in the Eurozone and Migration Crisis: Impact and Future Challenges* (Springer: Cham), pp. 151–174.

Meseberg declaration: Renewing Europe's Promises of Security and Prosperity. (2018). 19 June. Available at https://www.diplomatie.gouv.fr/en/country-files/germany/events/article/europe-franco-german-declaration-19-06-18 (accessed 13 May 2023).

Pastore, G. (2013). Small new member states in the EU foreign policy: Toward 'small state smart strategy?' *Baltic Journal of Political Science* 2 (2): 67–84.

Pedi, R. (2021). Small EU member states and the European security and defence integration. In: G. Voskopoulos (ed.), *European Union Security and Defence: Policies, Operations and Transatlantic Challenges* (Springer: Cham), pp. 55–73.

Perkowski, N., Stierl, M. and Burridge, A. (2023). The evolution of EUropean border governance through crisis: Frontex and the interplay of protracted and acute crisis narratives. *Environment and Planning. Part D,: Society and Space* 41(1): 110–129.

Petersen, N. (1998). National strategies in the integration dilemma: An adaptation approach. *JCMS: Journal of Common Market Studies* 36(1): 33–54.

Remarks by President Donald Tusk on the European Council meetings of 28–29 June 2018. (2018). 29 June. Available at https://www.consilium.europa.eu/en/press/press-releases/2018/06/29/remarks-by-president-donald-tusk-on-the-european-council-meeting-of-28-june-2018/ (accessed 13 May 2023).

Rickli, J.-M. (2008). European small states military policies after the Cold War: from territorial to niche strategies. *Cambridge Review of International Affairs* 21(3): 307–325.

Šešelgytė, M. (2019). Baltic concerns and moderate engagement. *L'Europe en Formation* 389(2): 177–193.

Statewatch. (2019). EU: Frontex proposal: Presidency attempts to accommodate Member States concerns over standing corps and executive powers, 23 January. Available at https://www.statewatch.org/news/2019/january/eu-frontex-proposal-presidency-attempts-to-accommodate-member-states-concerns-over-standing-corps-and-executive-powers/ (accessed 11 May 2023).

The Malta Independent. (2017). Government waiting to assess implementation of EU Army pact before signing on, 19 November. Available at https://www.independent.com.mt/articles/2017-11-19/local-news/Government-waiting-to-assess-implementation-of-EU-Army-pact-before-signing-on-6736181621 (accessed 11 May 2023).

Thorhallsson, B. and Wivel, A. (2006). Small states in the European Union: What do we know and what would we like to know? *Cambridge Review of International Affairs* 19(4): 651–668.

Times of Malta. (2018). Migration: A good basis to build on, 1 July. Available at https://timesofmalta.com/articles/view/migration-a-good-basis-to-build-on.683201 (accessed 11 May 2023).

Tonra, B. (2019). *Ireland and the European Union, Oxford Research Encyclopedia of Politics* (Oxford University Press: Oxford), 23 December. Available at https://oxfordre.com/politics/view/10.1093/acrefore/9780190228637.001.0001/acrefore-9780190228637-e-505.

Tow, W.T. and Parkin, R. (2007). Small state security postures: Material compensation and normative leadership in Denmark and New Zealand. *Contemporary Security Policy* 28(2): 308–329.

Vaicekauskaitė, Ž.M. (2017). Security strategies of small states in a changing world. *Journal on Baltic Security* 3(2): 7–15.

Weiss, T. (2017). *Promoting National Priorities in EU Foreign Policy: The Czech Republics Foreign Policy in the EU* (Routledge: London).

Wivel, A., Bailes, A., and Archer, C. (2014). Setting the scene: Small states and international security. In: C. Archer, A. Bailes and A. Wivel (eds.), *Small States and International Security: Europe and Beyond* (Routledge: London), pp. 3–25.

10 Challenges and opportunities: Estonia's role in shaping EU cybersecurity policy

Xinchuchu Gao

10.1 Introduction

It is often stated that small member states have played only a marginal role in shaping the European Union's security and defence policy (ESDP), particularly with regard to conventional security issues (Wivel, 2005). This is due to the fact that, possessing limited or no military capabilities, small member states are more vulnerable than larger member states when it comes to addressing traditional security challenges, such as warlike threats and internal conflicts. Consequently, small member states do not have much choice other than to accept the leadership of large member states in ESDP (Bartmann, 2002). However, the modern concept of security has evolved to encompass much more than military threats. Since the 1990s, non-traditional security threats, such as cyber threats, illegal migration and transnational crimes, have gained significance globally. The increasing importance of non-traditional security issues has reshaped the role of small states in ESDP. It is mainly because in non-traditional security realms, intangible assets such as expertise and knowledge are being employed more often than conventional military resources to tackle security-related challenges. As a result, small member states have an opportunity to wield more influence by leveraging these non-military resources, thereby enhancing their role in the overall EU security landscape.

In line with the overarching theme of the edited volume, which focuses on examining institutional and policy dynamics of small member states in the EU, this chapter investigates the involvement of Estonia, a representative example of a small EU member state, within the realm of the EU's cybersecurity policy, an increasingly important domain of non-traditional security. This chapter contributes to a deeper understanding of small states' role in ESDP. Moreover, it takes a step towards mitigating the overwhelming focus on the military dimension in ESDP literature.

The chapter answers the following questions: at what juncture did Estonia opt to proactively participate in the decision-making process to maximize its impacts in the domain of EU cybersecurity? What strategies did Estonia adopt to overcome the challenges posed by its relatively small size and limited resources, allowing it to leverage more influence? To answer these questions, the chapter draws on insights from the concepts of critical juncture and policy entrepreneurship. By

DOI: 10.4324/9781003380641-12

adopting the concept of critical juncture, this chapter considers the importance of timing when understanding small states' foreign policy strategies. It is argued that the timing that Estonia chose to proactively participate in the EU's cybersecurity policy-making could be attributed to a window of opportunity provided by a critical juncture, namely the cyberattack against Estonia in 2007.

Furthermore, this chapter adopts the term 'policy entrepreneurship' to account for Estonia's strategies to enhance its influence on the EU's cybersecurity policy. The chapter argues that in response to the cyberattack in 2007, Estonia has utilized its forerunner reputation, coalition-building capability as well as financial and human resources to leverage its influence on this policy domain.

The chapter is structured as follows. Section 1 reviews the existing literature concerning the impact of small member states on ESDP. This section highlights the challenges that small member states face in exerting influence on other member states in the realm of security and defence. The section then discusses how the increasing significance of non-traditional security issues in the EU has presented opportunities for small member states to avoid marginalization in this domain. Section 2 develops a theoretical framework by drawing on insights from the concepts of critical juncture and policy entrepreneurship. In Section 3, small states' participation in ESDP will be illustrated by an empirical case, namely Estonia's participation in the making of EU's cybersecurity policy. Section 4 sums up the key findings of the analysis presented in the previous sections.

10.2 Foreign policy choices of small member states and their influence in the EU

Due to their relative weakness in terms of size, population and resources, small states are usually in an asymmetrical power relationship in international society, merely acting as observers or minor players at best (Maass, 2016). Therefore, small states tend to seek influence over international events through membership of international institutions and organizations. The idea is that small states in general have a stronger preference for international cooperation because international institutions and organizations provide platforms for conflict resolution and present opportunities for small states' voices to be heard. Nevertheless, inside international institutions and organizations, small states are still in an asymmetrical power relationship. In return for the security and benefits provided by international institutions, small states have to adhere to the institutional rules set by big powers. Small states therefore expand their influence in international affairs through participating in international institutions and organizations, even though participation typically reduces their autonomy (Goetschel, 1998). This presents a security dilemma for small states, namely the balancing act between influence and autonomy (Rickli, 2008).

In the context of the EU, this security dilemma is also evident. On one hand, EU membership protects small member states from regional and global threats and enables them to leverage more influence on the international stage (Wivel, 2005). On the other hand, when the European integration becomes more binding and encompasses a broader range of issues, small states are left limited options for opting out, potentially leading them to compromise their autonomy (Petersen, 1998). Nevertheless, in the face of such a security dilemma, small EU member states have been surprisingly successful in safeguarding their interests.Extensive research focused on small states reveals that they can effectively shape the policy-making process in the European Union by employing strategies such as cooperative actions, persuasive advocacy, coalition building, skilful utilization of their EU presidency and bolstering their domestic capacity for engagement (see, e.g., Wivel, 2005; Björkdahl, 2008; Jakobsen, 2009; Nasra, 2011; Svetličič and Cerjak, 2015; Panke and Gurol, 2018).

However, when it comes to EU security policy, the role of small member states has often been overlooked in the ESDP literature. The reason is twofold. Firstly, small states are generally considered as military weak due to their relatively small populations and economies and less investment on research and development of military technology (Thorhallsson and Steinsson, 2017). Due to their limited or no military capacity, small member states find themselves more exposed than larger states to traditional security challenges, such as warlike threats and internal conflicts. Consequently, small member states tend to accept the leadership of large member states in this domain, in return for military support from larger member states. A second point closely linked to the first is that traditional security identity of small states is rooted in principles such as 'conflict resolution, peaceful coexistence and a just world order' (Wivel, 2005). The official discourse of small states' security policy usually carries a non-military tone. In other words, small states tend to avoid participating in wars or supporting other parties militarily. This stance is a manifestation of their intent not to present any military threats, thereby minimizing their risk of being involved in the conflict. Instead, small states have historically contributed to the de-escalation and prevention of conflicts. This approach to security is also evident in small member states within the EU. Consequently, it is not surprising that these small member states tend not to proactively participate in the military aspects of the ESDP since such engagement would diverge from their established identity as generally neutral actors.

Nevertheless, the evolution of the non-military dimension within the framework of the ESDP has presented small states with opportunities to exert their influence on the ESDP without deviating from their established stance as neutral security actors. In recent times, the EU has placed a significant focus on non-traditional security issues when developing its security policy. For instance, the 2003 European Security Strategy (ESS) identified three non-traditional security challenges (terrorism, organized crime and state failure) but only two traditional challenges (regional conflicts and the proliferation of WMD) as the main security challenges (Council of the European Union, 2003). Similarly, in the Global Strategy, out of five external action priorities, the EU identified three non-traditional security concerns: counterterrorism, cybersecurity and energy security (EEAS, 2016). The growing importance of non-traditional security matters has profoundly impacted the participation of small member states in the domain of the ESDP. From one perspective, despite limited or absence of military resources, small member states possess non-military assets, such as expertise and knowledge, which are frequently used to address these emerging non-traditional security issues. This empowerment enhances small states' presence in non-traditional security realms. Moreover, the non-military nature of these non-traditional security matters means that small states' participation in these domains does not undermine the conventional security identity of small member states, still positioning them as 'neutral and semi-neutral small powers' within the EU context (Wivel, 2005).

Scholars have examined the influence of small states on the European non-traditional security agenda. Examples include the research on Sweden's promotion of conflict prevention (Björkdahl, 2008), and the analysis of the Nordic countries' influence on civilian ESDP (Jakobsen, 2009). Furthermore, adopting a two-level analysis approach (international and. domestic corresponding to system and state), Crandall takes Estonia's reaction to soft security threats, including cyber-security, energy security and national identity security, as a case study and argues that Estonia's efforts to address these security threats have been synchronized at both the international and domestic levels (Crandall, 2014). Among these studies, Jakobsen (2009) has given the most comprehensive overview of factors contributing to small states' influence on EU foreign policy. Jakobsen challenged the view that European security and defence policy is primarily determined by the great powers, such as the United Kingdom, France and Germany. He argues that the Nordic countries have played a major role in the development of the EU's civilian ESDP by leveraging their reputation as forerunners, providing convincing arguments, building coalitions and committing resources to supporting EU initiatives (ibid.).

When examining the influence of small states on the EU's security policy, arguments that presume the role of small states as norm entrepreneurs have been widely raised by scholars. Ingebritsen (2002) looks at how Scandinavian states have acted as norm entrepreneurs in areas such as environmental politics, conflict resolution and developmental aid. Similarly, Björkdahl (2008) studies the process of Swedish promotion of conflict prevention and examines its norm-building efforts such as, framing, agenda setting, diplomatic tactics and the power of the presidency. Goetschel (2011) examines how and why small European neutral states act as successful norm entrepreneurs and argues that neutrality is traditionally used as a foreign policy tool for small states to justify their foreign policies. Crandall and Allan's work evaluates how successful Estonia has been to use norm-building efforts as a method of managing their national security (Crandall and Allan, 2015). In a similar vein, Adamson and Homburger (2019) analyze how the Netherlands and Estonia have acted as norm entrepreneurs in cyberspace.

However, despite their insights into the engagement of small states within the EU's decision-making process, existing studies have primarily focused on entrepreneurship efforts of small member states to exert influence, often overlooking the crucial factor of timing in their efforts. In other words, existing literature does not explain explicitly at what juncture small member states choose to strategically participate in the decision-making process in the EU to leverage their influence. This work contends that the element of timing is of significant importance. To effectively function as policy entrepreneurs and maximize their impacts within the

EU, small member states must carefully choose the appropriate timing. Their participation in the EU's policy-making therefore cannot be understood in isolation; it necessitates a broader temporal perspective.

To address this aspect, the following section draws insights from critical junctures and develops an analytical framework that considers the importance of timing of small states' foreign policy choices. Additionally, the section will present potential strategies that small states might employ to take advantage of a critical juncture, thereby leveraging more influence. This discussion will be informed by insights derived from the literature on policy entrepreneurship.

10.3 A framework for studying small states' strategic participation within the EU

According to Capoccia and Kelemen (2007), a critical juncture is defined as relatively short periods of time when, due to external events, the path of institutional evolution is interrupted. In such periods, exogenous shocks break the bonds of institutional constraint and subsequently institutional change occurs. Employing the concepts of critical junctures, 'institutional change is episodic and dramatic rather than continuous and incremental' and external shocks are important in order to relax constraints on institutional change (Krasner, 1984). To be identified as a critical juncture, an event must have an impact on future events (Capoccia, 2016). In the context of foreign policy, examples of critical junctures include sudden changes in the geopolitical landscape, the emerging security threats or shifts in public opinion.

A critical juncture can present a unique opportunity for small states to leverage influence within international politics. During the juncture, the established power structures, institutional framework and norms can be temporarily interrupted, For small states, which are usually featured with structural disadvantages in terms of size, population and resources, these disruptions create openings for them to navigate the changing landscape and find avenues to exert influence in ways that might not have been feasible during more stable times. By capitalizing these critical moments, small states can strategically position themselves to engage with larger power on a more level playing field. Therefore, the concept critical juncture helps to explain the timing that small states choose to challenge the status quo, redefine their roles and potentially contribute to shaping new norms, policies and institutions in international politics.

Nevertheless, a critical juncture does not automatically lead to an increase in the influence of small states. it necessitates the proactive involvement of small states that can identify and exploit the opportunities provided by a critical juncture. As Hacker argues (2005), due to institutional constraints, external pressures do not automatically lead to institutional change. This means that external pressures must be interpreted and framed in order to be translated into changes. In other words, purposeful actors, often referred to as policy entrepreneurs, help to overcome institutional constraints and translate external pressures into strategic actions and subsequent institutional changes. Consequently, to answer the question of the mechanisms through which small states leverage critical junctures and contribute to shaping new policies, institutions and norms within the EU, it is essential to analyze actions and strategies of these small states as policy entrepreneurs.

To understand strategies adopted by small states acting as policy entrepreneurs, this work builds upon the works of Arter (2000), Honkanen (2002), Wallace (2005) and Jakobsen (2009) and argues that to exert influence on the EU's policy-making, small member states must, at a minimum, have the following capabilities. First, they need to establish a forerunner reputation. As Wallace (2005) argues, 'influence through example' is an important asset in EU negotiations. By putting an issue on the agenda and introducing relevant knowledge, a policy entrepreneur establishes a reputation as a forerunner and a thought leader. This can enhance their credibility, and as a result, their proposals are most likely to be taken seriously (Kingdon, 1984). Given the limited resources possessed by small member states, it is beneficial to invest their energies in a few issues (Björkdahl, 2008). As Grøn and Wivel (2011) point out, small states' goals and means must be highly focused. Therefore, EU small states frequently use their forerunner reputations in specific policy domains to exert more influence. For instance, Maes and Verdun (2005) argue that Belgium and the Netherlands have played pivotal roles in the creation of the European Monetary Union, mostly because of their established reputations gained through their early economic cooperation and creative proposals. Similarly, according to Nasra (2011), Belgium's influence on EU foreign policy towards the Democratic Republic of the Congo (DRC) has benefited from its good reputation resulting from the development of its effective national policies towards the DRC. Furthermore, Jakobsen (2009) identifies multiple sources of forerunner reputations, including expertise and knowledge.

Second, small states must have the coalition-building capability, which is particularly important for small states. This is mainly because small states are generally considered as neutral, therefore it is easier for them to identify the common interest and mobilize possible support (Björkdahl, 2008). In other words, 'small states use their lack of power to gain influence over selected issues' (Grøn and Wivel, 2011). Diplomatic tactics, such as bilateral constatation, help small states to identify like-minded supporters and potential opposition. Meanwhile, frequently held meetings at different levels within the EU Commission, the Council Secretariat and the European Council have served as platforms for small states to build coalitions (ibid.). In particular, the rotating presidency often presents opportunities for small states to set the agenda (Björkdahl, 2008; Panke and Gurol, 2018). As previously mentioned, the limited resources available to small states necessitate them to concentrate on a smaller number of key issues. Through the Council Presidency, these small states possess a formal position of authority, which enables them to chair the Council meetings and ensures that their prioritized issues are on top of a wide range of concerns (Panke and Gurol, 2018).

Third, small states need resources to exert influence. Implementing proposals and initiatives typically requires a wide range of resources, including military, financial and human resources (Jakobsen, 2009). While small states may lack traditional sources of power, such as robust military or economic instruments, they can leverage other types of resources, such as respected leader and experts, to make a significant impact on the policy-making process (Ibid.).

10.4 Estonia's role in shaping the EU's cybersecurity policy

Cyber policy was developed in Estonia and at the EU level in a closely aligned manner. Following its gaining of independence in 1991, Estonia made tremendous efforts to reshape its economic structure away from the Soviet model towards digitalization. As a consequence, Estonia emerged as one of the most digitally connected nations within the EU in the 1990s, characterized by its reliance on digital infrastructures and the adoption of regulatory and policy solutions to its digital economy. At the EU level, the cyber policy of the EU began to emerge from the mid-1990s, mostly driven by interest in tackling computer-related crime. From the late 1990s to the mid-2000s, a series of EU-level initiatives were released, reflecting the increasing concern about the new challenges in cyberspace (Kasper and Vernygora, 2021). Examples include the eEurope 2002 – Information Society for All – Action Plan, which aims to ensure a socially inclusive information society (Commission of the European Communities, 2000), and the Communication on Improving the Security of Information Infrastructures and Combating Computer-Related Crime (Commission of the European Communities, 2001).

Although cyber policy was evolving in both Estonia and at the EU level in a closely aligned manner, there was a notable limitation in Estonia's involvement in the process of shaping cyber policies within the EU. It is the cyberattack that targeted Estonia in 2007 that marked a turning point in Estonia's participation in the EU's cyber policy. The following paragraphs analyze how the cyberattack in 2007 served as a critical juncture, allowing Estonia to contribute to the EU's cybersecurity policies via various strategies, including its forerunner reputation, coalition-building capability and financial and human resources.

10.4.1 The cyberattack against Estonia in 2007 as a critical juncture

The cyberattack in 2007, commonly known as the 'Bronze Solider' incident, makes Estonia the first country to fall victim to nationwide internet attacks. It happened in the wake of domestic unrest following the relocation of a Soviet war monument. The cyberattack targeted government websites, banks and news agencies, aiming to create chaos and panic in Estonia (Tiirma-Klaar, 2008). It remains unclear whether the attack was carried out by the Russian government or supported by Russia because Moscow's lack of interest in cooperating with Estonian investigators lagged the investigation. During the attack, 58 Estonian websites were offline, including those of the government, banks and newspapers (E-estonia, 2017). Estonian information security experts from the public and private sectors responded to the attacks rapidly and professionally. The public noticed a few disruption in online services but did not panic.

The cyberattack in 2007 presented a unique opportunity for Estonia to leverage more influence within the realm of cyber. It was mainly because during this juncture, the established understanding of violence and force was challenged, thereby allowing Estonia to challenge the status quo and contribute to new norms, policies and institutions in this policy domain. As Buchan points out, the 2007 cyberattack made Estonia the first country subject to a new form of cyber violence (Buchan, 2012). This incident caused no physical damage or injury to human beings and was merely disruptive, which challenged 'an ontologically constrained conceptualisation of violence' (Haataja, 2017: 162). Conventionally, without physical damage, cyberattacks cannot be recognized as violence but only be considered as 'a potential breach of the non-intervention principle" (ibid., 170). For instance, despite its ambiguous definition of the notion of 'force' under Article 2(4) of the UN Charter, the prevailing view of violence under the UN framework requires some form of material damage (Maogoto, 2015: 64; Haataja, 2017). A similar definition of violence with a focus on physical damage is also adopted by NATO. Article 5 of NATO, which is designed to provide protection to its member states under attacks. Nevertheless, the Article could only be triggered if a cyberattack results in a major loss of life equivalent to traditional military action (McGuinness, 2017). Therefore, prior to the cyberattack against Estonia, the prevailing view was that only cyberattacks with material effects such as damage to physical objects or injury to human beings were considered as unlawful use of force. Estonia grabbed the 2007 cyberattack as an opportunity, raising a debate regarding the understanding of cyberattack and contributing to the development of policies and institutions addressing cyber threats. Taking advantage of this critical juncture, Estonia exerted influence on the EU's cybersecurity policies via various strategies, including its forerunner reputation, coalition-building capability and financial and human resources.

10.5 The forerunner reputation

Using the cyberattack of 2007 as an opportunity, Estonia has built its forerunner reputation in governing cyberspace and proactively set cybersecurity on the EU's agenda. In its 2008 Cybersecurity Strategy, Estonia stated that 'ensuring cyber security and combating cybercrime concerns all EU member states' (Estonian Ministry of Defence, 2008: 23). To promote best practices in the field of cybersecurity at the EU level, Estonia stressed the need to enhance cooperation with other member states in the investigation of cyberattacks and to promote international projects in line with the Commission's policies on cybersecurity (ibid.). In a 2012 meeting with Cecilia Malstrom, the European Commissioner for Home Affairs, Estonian president Toomas Ilves stressed the need to boost cyber defence capabilities and develop a common cyber strategy (Office of the President of the Republic of Estonia, 2012). He assured that Estonia would offer its support to both the European Commission and other member states (ibid.).

In addition to its persistent activism to promote the cybersecurity issue in the EU, Estonia has also utilized other organizational platforms, such as North Atlantic Treaty Organisation (NATO) and the United Nations (UN), to stress the importance of cybersecurity. Immediately after the cyberattack, Estonia raised the question of NATO's role for its member states, therefore calling for a common

NATO policy to address cyber threats. Since this attack was seen as the first case of cyberwarfare and was referred to as a 'wholly new type of social and economic disturbance' (Kello, 2013), it was not clear how NATO should respond to cyberattacks against its member states. Estonia defense minister Jaak Aavikso said that 'at present, NATO does not define cyber-attacks as a clear military action. This means that the provisions of Article V . . . will not automatically be extended to the attacked country' (Gold, 2019). Furthermore, Estonia was an initiator of the NATO Cooperative Cyber Defence Centre of Excellence (CCDCOE) in Tallin. Despite recognizing the need for a cybersecurity centre as early as in 2004, NATO did not establish its centre until 2008, shortly after the 2007 cyberattack. The NATO CCDCOE resulted in the publication of the Tallinn Manual on the International Law Applicable to Cyber Warfare, which is a non-binding, academic study on how international law applies to cyber conflicts and cyberwarfare. It is considered as the most authoritative and comprehensive of its kind and is continuously developed by the CCDCOE with input from nearly 50 states.

Within the UN framework, Estonia has also positioned itself as a key player in shaping policies governing cyberspace. In September 2007, in an address to the United Nations (UN) General Assembly, Estonia urged the UN member states to step up their efforts to defeat cybercrime (United Nations, 2007). In particular, Estonia's experience during the 2007 cyberattacks contributes to the revival of the UN Group of Governmental Experts (GGE) within the First Committee of the General Assembly of the United Nations (UNGA) as well as its involvement in UN deliberation such as the UN GGE process (Adamson and Homburger, 2019: 231).

Through its advocacy of cybersecurity and promotion of cyber norms in the EU, NATO and the UN, Estonia has established its reputation as a forerunner in governing cyberspace. This reputation has been instrumental in Estonia's efforts to play a significant role in shaping EU cybersecurity policies. Jean-Claude Juncker stated that the EU depends on Estonia's cybersecurity know-how (Stupp, 2017). A significant indicator of EU's dependence on Estonia's expertise and knowledge is the emphasis on resilience in the EU's cybersecurity strategy, reflecting Estonia's long-standing commitment to this principle. For instance, Estonian 2007 CERT crisis response guidelines stated that 'if something goes down and it is not really vital, let it be down until there is enough free time to bring it back up' (Tuohy, 2012). The EU's latest cybersecurity strategy emphasizes the need to enhance Europe's collective resilience against cyber threats and ensure that all citizens and businesses can benefit from trustworthy and reliable digital tools and services (European Commission, 2022).

10.5.1 The coalition-building capability

Estonia's ability to exert greater influence on the EU's cybersecurity policy is notably demonstrated through its skilful coalition-building capability. A key avenue for this influence was Estonia's rotation into the position of the European Union presidency from 1 July to 31 December 2017. This role enabled Estonia to allocate substantial resources to the realm of cybersecurity policy and to serve as an impartial intermediary in discussions (Tallberg, 2004). During its tenure, Estonia's foremost agenda was the advancement of a digital Europe and the facilitation of unhindered data movement. Officially, the presidency's program emphasized harnessing the advantages of ongoing technological advancements, which were affecting citizens, businesses and governmental operations. Estonia's presidency particularly concentrated on the following focal points (Estonian Presidency of the Council of the European Union, 2017):

1. Free flow of data: recognizing its role in nurturing a digital society, Estonia championed the importance of free data movement as an essential component.
2. Robust Internet connectivity: the presidency aimed to foster high-speed, top-quality, and widely accessible internet connectivity.
3. E-commerce and E-service Development: Estonia aimed to advance the expansion of e-commerce and digital services, aligning with its commitment to digital innovation.
4. Trust and security: Acknowledging the significance of trust and security, Estonia emphasized these aspects in the digital landscape.

In parallel to its policy initiatives, the Estonian presidency orchestrated a series of cybersecurity-focused events. These included the Digital Single Market Conference centred on data mobility, a Conference on the Evolution of Data Protection and an EU Cybersecurity Conference. It is noteworthy that Estonia's dedicated efforts to confront cybersecurity challenges during its presidency garnered widespread recognition, earning it the designation of 'the digital Presidency,' testament to its discerning focus and commendable leadership role (Microsoft, 2017). Through these concerted efforts, Estonia solidified its influence over the EU's cybersecurity policy trajectory and substantiated its capacity to drive transformative change on the international stage.

10.5.2 *Financial and personnel resources*

After the cyberattack in 2007, Estonia devoted many resources to putting cybersecurity on the agenda and keeping it there. Its commitments and contributions can be classified into the following categories. Firstly, Estonia has invested substantial funds in cybersecurity. For instance, it worked closely with the EU to establish the European IT Agency in Estonia (Kangsepp, 2012). Initially, Estonia competed with France to host this new agency. Estonia explicitly expressed its eagerness to host the agency, with Interior Minister Marko Pomerants stating that 'this IT agency is meant for us as a state. We have the right environment for it, because it's our everyday life – paying bills, using bank accounts – we do it all online' (Pop, 2010). The Estonian government has also set aside around €17 million for the new agency's headquarters and support team (ibid.). In December 2012, the European IT Agency opened its doors in Tallinn, Estonia. Since then,

Estonia has been responsible for the operational management of large-scale databases through this agency. Since the IT Agency has been called the biggest information technological challenge of the whole EU, any country that hosts the agency is regarded as a high-level provider of cybersecurity services and IT solutions all over Europe (Estonian World, 2013). By hosting such an important agency, Estonia solidifies its image as an information technology leader in the EU (ibid).

Secondly, Estonia has devoted significant personnel resources to the field of EU cybersecurity policy. For instance, Andrus Ansip, an Estonian politician who was in charge of Digital Single Market from 2014 until July 2019, played a significant role in advocating for cybersecurity norms at the EU level. In a speech given by Ansip at the Digital Day 2019 in early April 2019, he called for 'stronger cybersecurity' and 'better protection against online threats' (European Commission, 2019). He further stressed that an internal market law was needed to address the challenge of cybersecurity threats. Observers point out that partly due to Ansip's influence, Estonia has been a driving force behind the EU's cybersecurity policies (Roeder, 2019). Another example is Tunne Kelam, an Estonian member of the European Parliament. He produced a report on cybersecurity that was approved by the European Parliament. This report calls for the development of a comprehensive cybersecurity strategy at the EU level and urges member states to complete their national cybersecurity and defence strategies (Aasmae, 2013). More recently, Juhan Lepassaar was elected as the new executive director of the European Union Agency for Cybersecurity. It is believed that the appointment is great recognition both for Lepassaar and for Estonia (BNS/TBT Staff, 2019).

Apart from Estonian politicians' active engagement in the area of EU cybersecurity policy, Estonia has been a leading force within the EU on cyber diplomacy and cyber sanctions by providing experts. Since early 2018, Estonian experts (along with partner institutions from the United Kingdom and the Netherlands) have been assigned by the EU to support the cyber development of four countries in Africa and Asia – Mauritius, Sri Lanka, Ghana and Botswana. The Cyber Resilience for Development (Cyber4Dev) project ran until June 2021. In addition, Estonia hosts a wide range of events and exercises aimed at bolstering EU member states' cyber defence positions. One telling example is EU CYBERID, a cyber exercise testing the EU's ability to respond to a potential attack by hackers. Minister of Defence of Estonia, Jüri Luik, stressed that the training exercise would bring to the forefront the limits of the EU and NATO when responding to cyberattacks (AFP, 2017). Through creating cybersecurity-related platforms and hosting cyber exercises, Estonia offers important services to the EU and the EU has come to rely more on Estonia for its expertise and resources in the field of cybersecurity.

10.6 Conclusion

It is often stated that small member states have played only a marginal role in shaping the European Union's security and defence policy (ESDP), particularly with regard to conventional security issues. However, the growing significance of non-traditional security issues has notably influenced the role of small states in the EU's security and defence policy. In these domains, immaterial resources like expertise and knowledge are being employed more often than military resources to tackle security challenges. This situation has generated an additional opportunity for small states to exert greater influence. However, existing studies have mostly focused on small EU member states' entrepreneurship efforts to exert influence while overlooking the timing that small states make these efforts. In other words, existing literature does not explain explicitly when small EU member states choose to strategically participate in the decision-making process in the EU to enhance their influence.

Using Estonia's significant role in the development of EU cybersecurity strategy as a case study, this chapter argues that non-traditional security issues allow small states to avoid marginalization in the process of EU policy-making. This chapter made a twofold argument. First, this chapter highlights the importance of timing when understanding small states' foreign policy strategies. Estonia has taken advantage of 2007 cybersecurity attack as a window of opportunity to play a leading role in the EU's cybersecurity policy. Secondly, this chapter points to the importance of small states' strategic participation in EU's security policy-making to avoid marginalization. Estonia has leveraged its experience gained from the 2007 cyberattack to build a reputation as a forerunner in the field of cybersecurity policy. Another Estonia's key strengths has been its ability to build coalitions with other EU member states, particularly through its role as the rotating presidency of the European Union. During its presidency, Estonia invested significant resources in cybersecurity policy and acted as a honest broker in setting the EU's cybersecurity agenda. This allowed Estonia to prioritize issues that it deemed important and to push for the development of a digital Europe that promotes the free movement of data. In addition, Estonia has made substantial financial and personnel resources to exert more influence on the EU's cybersecurity policy.

In conclusion, this chapter illuminates Estonia's noteworthy journey in steering the EU's cybersecurity strategy, accentuating the transformative potential of non-traditional security issues for small states. Through calculated timing, strategic engagement, coalition building and resource commitment, Estonia serves as a prime example showing how small states can assert their influence and avoid marginalization within the EU policy-making.

Bibliography

Aasmae, K. (2013). The poster child for cybersecurity right: How Estonia learnt from under attack. ZDNET. Available at https://www.zdnet.com/article/the-poster-child-for-cybersecurity-done-right-how-estonia-learnt-from-being-under-attack/ (accessed 1 April 2023).

Adamson, L. and Homburger, Z. (2019). Let them roar: Small states as cyber norm entrepreneurs. *European Foreign Affairs Review* 24(2): 217–234.

AFP. (2017). EU defence minsters put to test in mock cyberattack. *The Citizen*. Available at https://www.citizen.co.za/news/eu-defence-hacking/ (accessed 1 April 2022).

Arter, D. (2000). Small state influence within the EU: The case of Finland's 'Northern dimension initiative'. *Journal of Common Market Studies* 38(5): 677–697.

Bartmann, B. (2002). Meeting the needs of microstate security. *The Round Table* 265(91): 361–374.

Björkdahl, A. (2008). Norm advocacy: A small state strategy to influence the EU. *Journal of European Public Policy* 15(1): 135–154.

BNS/TBT Staff. (2019). Estonia: Juhan Lepassaar elected executive director of EU Agency for Cybersecurity. *The Baltic Times*. Available at https://www.baltictimes.com/estonia_ _juhan_lepassaar_elected_executive_director_of_eu_agency_for_cybersecurity/ (accessed 2 May 2021).

Buchan, R. (2012). 'Cyber attacks: Unlawful uses of force or prohibited interventions?' 17. *Journal of Conflict and Security Law* 211: 221.

Capoccia, G. (2016). Critical junctures. In: Fioretos, O., T.G. Falleti, and A. Sheingate (eds.), *The Oxford Handbook of Historical Institutionalism* (Oxford University Press: Oxford), pp. 89–106.

Capoccia, G. and Kelemen, R.D. (2007). The study of critical junctures: Theory, narrative, and counterfactuals in historical institutionalism. *World Politics* 59(03): 348.

Commission of the European Communities. (2000). eEurope 2002: An information society for all: Draft action plan prepared by the European Commission for the European Council in Feira. COM (2000) 333 final.

Commission of The European Communities. (2001). Communication from the commission to the council, the European Parliament, the economic and social committee and the committee of the regions: Creating a safer information society by improving the security of information infrastructures and combating computer-related crime. COM (2000) 890 final.

Council of the European Union. (2003). *European Security Strategy: A Secure Europe in A Better World* (Council of the European Union: Brussels).

Crandall, M. (2014). Soft security threats and small states: The case of Estonia. *Defence Studies* 14(1): 30–55.

Crandall, M. and Allan, C. (2015). Small states and big ideas: Estonia's battle for cybersecurity norms. *Contemporary Security Policy* 36(2): 346–336.

E-estonia. (2017). How estonia became a global heavyweight in cyber security. Available at https://e-estonia.com/how-estonia-became-a-global-heavyweight-in-cyber-security/.

EEAS. (2016). *A Global Strategy for the European Union's Foreign and Security Policy* (European External Action Service: Brussels). Available at: https://www.eeas.europa.eu /sites/default/files/eugs_review_web_0.pdf.

Estonian Ministry of Defence. (2008). *Cyber Security Strategy* (Estonian Ministry of Defence: Tallinn).

Estonian Presidency of the Council of the European Union. (2017). The European Committee of the regions and the Estonian presidency of the council of the European Union. Available at https://cor.europa.eu/en/engage/brochures/Documents/The%20European %20Committee%20of%20the%20Regions%20and%20the%20Estonian%20Presidency %20of%20the%20Council%20of%20the%20European%20Union/3210_Broch_ET %20Presdcy_EN_web.pdf.

Estonian World. (2013). EU's it agency sets up in Estonia, Estonian world. Available at https://estonianworld.com/technology/eus-it-agency-sets-up-in-estonia/ (accessed 2 May 2021).

European Commission. (2019). Opening speech by Vice-President Andrus Ansip at the digital day 2019. Available at https://ec.europa.eu/commission/presscorner/detail/en/ SPEECH_19_2068 (accessed 5 May 2021).

European Commission. (2022). Proposal for a Regulation of the European Parliament and of the council on horizontal cybersecurity requirements for products with digital elements and amending. Regulation (EU) 2019/1020. COM (2022) 454 final.

Goetschel, L. (1998). The foreign and security policy interests of small states in today's Europe. In: L. Goetschel (ed.), *Small States Inside and Outside the European Union* (Kluwer: Dordrecht): 13-31.

Goetschel, L. (2011). Neutrals as brokers of peace building ideas? *Cooperation and Conflict* 46(3): 312–333.

Gold, J. (2019). How Estonia uses cybersecurity to strengthen its Position in NATO, RKK ICDS. Available at https://icds.ee/en/how-estonia-uses-cybersecurity-to-strengthen-its-position-in-nato/ (accessed 6 May 2022).

Grøn, C.H. and Wivel, A. (2011). Maximizing influence in the European Union after the Lisbon Treaty: From small state policy to smart state strategy. *Journal of European Integration* 33(5): 523–539.

Haataja, S. (2017). The 2007 cyber attacks against Estonia and international law on the use of force: An informational approach. *Law, Innovation and Technology* 9(2): 159–189, 162.

Hacker, J.S. (2005). US welfare state retrenchment. In: W. Streeck and K.A. Thelen (eds.), *Beyond Continuity: Institutional Change in Advanced Political Economies* (Oxford University Press: Oxford): 40–82.

Honkanen, K. (2002). *The Influence of Small States on NATO Decision-Making: The Membership Experience of Denmark, Norway, Hungary and the Czech Republic* (FOI-Swedish Defence Research Agency: Stockholm).

Ingebritsen, C. (2002). Norm entrepreneurs: Scandinavia's role in world politics. *Cooperation and Conflict* 37(1): 11–33.

Jakobsen, P.V. (2009). Small states, big influence: The overlooked Nordic influence on the civilian ESDP. *Journal of Common Market Studies* 47(1): 81–102.

Kangsepp, L. (2012). Estonia to host EU's IT agency. *Wall Street Journal*, 29 Nov.2012. Available at http://blogs.wsj.com/emergingeurope/2012/11/29/estonia-to-host-eus-it-agency/ (accessed 2 May 2021).

Kasper, A. and Vernygora, V. (2021). The EU's cybersecurity: A strategic narrative of a cyber power or a confusing policy for a local common market? *Deusto Journal of European Studies* 65: 29-71.

Kello, L. (2013). The meaning of the cyber revolution: Perils to theory and statecraft. *International Security* 38(2): 7–40.

Kingdon, J.W. (1984). *Agendas, Alternatives, and Public Policies* (Little Brown: Boston, MA).

Krasner, S. (1984). Approaches to the state: Alternative conceptions and historical dynamics. *Comparative Politics* 16(2): 223–246, 234.

Maass, M. (2016). Small enough to fail: The structural irrelevance of the small state as cause of its elimination and proliferation since Westphalia. *Cambridge Review of International Affairs* 29(4): 1303–1323.

Maes, I. and Verdun, A. (2005). Small states and the creation of EMU: Belgium and the Netherlands, pace-setters and Gate-Keepers. *Journal of Common Market Studies* 43(2): 393–412.

Maogoto, J.N. (2015). *Technology and the Law on the Use of Force* (Routledge: London).

McGuinness, D. (2017). How a cyber attack transformed Estonia. *BBC NEWS*. Available at https://www.bbc.co.uk/news/39655415.

Microsoft. (2017). From submarines to cyber: Estonia's innovation journey. Microsoft corporate blogs. Available at https://blogs.microsoft.com/eupolicy/2017/11/29/submarines-cyber-estonias-innovation-journey/ (accessed 11 May 2022).

Nasra, S. (2011). Governance in EU foreign policy: Exploring small state influence. *Journal of European Public Policy* 18(2): 164–180.

Office of the President of the Republic of Estonia. (2012). President Ilves: European Union needs a common cyber policy. Available at https://vp2006-2016.president.ee/en/media/press-releases/7238-president-ilves-european-union-needs-a-common-cyber-policy/index.html (accessed 2 May 2022).

Panke, D. and Gurol, J. (2018). Small states as agenda-setters: The council presidencies of Malta and Estonia. *Journal of Common Market Studies* 56(S1): 142.

Petersen, N. (1998). National strategies in the integration dilemma: An adaptation approach. *Journal of Common Market Studies* 36(1): 33–54.

Pop, V. (2010). Estonia looking for 'peaceful' solution with France on IT agency. *EUobserver*. Available at https://euobserver.com/justice/30994 (accessed 1 May 2021).

Rickli, J. (2008). European small states'. military policies after the Cold War: from territorial to niche strategies. *Cambridge Review of International Affairs* 21(3): 310.

Roeder, F. (2019). How Estonia's cyber security strategy can help the EU cope with China, Estonian World. Available at https://estonianworld.com/opinion/how-estonias-cyber -security-strategy-can-help-the-eu-cope-with-china/ (accessed 1 May 2021).

Stupp, C. (2017). Juncker 'depends' on Estonia's cybersecurity know-ho. EURACTIV. Available at https://www.euractiv.com/section/digital/news/juncker-depends-on -estonias-cybersecurity-know-how-during-eu-presidency/ (accessed 1 May 2021).

Svetličič, M. and Cerjak, K. (2015). Small countries' EU Council Presidency and the realisation of their national interests: The case of Slovenia. *Croatian International Relations Review* 21(74): 5–39.

Tallberg, J. (2004). The power of the presidency: Brokerage, efficiency and distribution in EU negotiations. *Journal of Common Market Studies* 44(5): 999–1022.

Thorhallsson, B. and Steinsson, S. (2017). Small state foreign policy. In: W.R. Thompson et al. (eds.), *Oxford Research Encyclopedia of Politics* (Oxford University Press: Oxford), pp. 1–15.

Tiirma-Klaar, H. (2008). Emerging cyber security agenda: Threats, challenges and responses. In: A. Kasekamp (ed.), *The Estonian Foreign Policy Yearbook 2008* (The Estonian Foreign Policy Institute: Estonia), pp. 153–158.

Tuohy, E. (2012). Toward an EU cybersecurity strategy: The role of Estonia. RKK CDS. Available at http://pdc.ceu.hu/archive/00006852/ (accessed 6 June 2022).

United Nations. (2007). Estonia urges UN Member States to cooperate against cyber crimes. Available at https://news.un.org/en/story/2007/09/232832 (accessed 7 September 2023).

Wallace, H. (2005). Power and influence: Assessing Member States' roles in EU governance and negotiation. In: S. Bulmer and C. Lequesne (eds.), *Member States and the European Union* (Oxford University Press: Oxford), pp. 25–44.

Wivel, A. (2005). The security challenge of Small EU Member States: Interests, identity and the development of the EU as a security actor. *Journal of Common Market Studies* 43(2): 393–412.

11 Conclusion

Size is not everything

Anna-Lena Högenauer and Matúš Mišík

11.1 Introduction

The European Union has been experiencing a series of crises with the COVID-19 pandemic (Beaussier and Cabane, 2020) and the Russian invasion of Ukraine being the last two (Mišík, 2022). The crises have succeeded so closely one after another that the whole period since 2008 was coined as a polycrisis (Zeitlin et al., 2019). Whether these crises originated outside the EU's borders (e.g. the economic or refugee crises) or within the Union (Brexit), they required an EU response that was complicated by the emergence of dividing lines between member countries that supported different approaches. Finding a common solution at the EU level (ideally in the form of a consensus) became a complex endeavour (Schimmelfennig, 2022). While there have been differences between member states in many areas – including economic (economic crisis: northern vs. southern) and geographical (refugee crisis: centre vs. southern periphery) – the emphasis was placed on the role of the biggest member states. For example, while the economic crisis impacted all member states, it was the largest countries that were considered to be the key stakeholders in solving the crisis (Fontan and Saurugger, 2019); while the refugee crisis put extra pressure on the countries at the south of the EU (including small members), it was the German decision not to enforce some of the provisions of the so-called Dublin Regulation that received most attention (Sanchez Salgado, 2022). While Brexit significantly impacted the dynamics between large and small member states by decreasing the former group, the discussions within the EU were centred around its impact on the biggest EU countries. Similarly, the Russian invasion of Ukraine presented a significant turning point for most – Hungary being the major exemption (Lamour, n.d.) – member states; several small EU members became leaders in per capita military and other support of Ukraine. Yet, it was the positions of the biggest countries that were considered to be crucial (Bosse, 2022). Smaller countries were usually only considered if they were 'problematic' or 'extreme' cases in the context of these crises.

However, following Brexit and the loss of one of the biggest member states (Brusenbauch Meislova, 2019), the relations between large and small EU members have changed as the share of small members has increased and so has their aggregated relative size. This does not mean that small states always manage to find a common ground and are able to push their positions vis-à-vis the big member states;

DOI: 10.4324/9781003380641-13

however, the recent developments in connection to adaptation of the EU's sanctions against Russia are showing the strength of a single EU member, independent of its size (i.e. Hungary; Kopper et al., 2023). Therefore, this edited volume studied the small states of the European Union and the challenges and opportunities that membership in the Union presents to them. While the first section of the book examined the strategies that small states employ to succeed in the current institutional settings and in the EU's decision-making process, the second section studied the impact of small states on various common EU policies. Individual contributions focused on policies that are connected to foreign and security policies of the EU – a domain traditionally considered to be dominated by larger states in which small members experience especially a large number of challenges.

11.2 Small states in the EU's institutions: How to compensate for numbers

The first section of the book studied the strategies of small states with regard to key EU institutions, what obstacles they identified and how they tried to overcome them in their quest for influence. The aim was to complement the existing literature, which focuses predominantly on the Council of the European Union and the European Council. In light of the key role of the European Commission and the European Parliament in the policy-making process, and in particular in the areas at the heart of European integration, namely economic and regulatory policies, it is time for a broader perspective. The existing literature has mainly focused on the lower weight of small states in the Council of the European Union, the lesser credibility of the threat of using a veto and the small size of national administrations that limit expertise. However, it has also identified coalition building, prioritization and the adoption of the role of mediator as strategies to gain influence (Thorhallsson and Wivel, 2006; Panke, 2010). The aim of this section was to discuss to what extent these strategies work across the institutions.

In the second chapter, Hamřík looked at the European Commission, which plays a key role in initiating and monitoring EU policies. In the European Commission size matters somewhat less than in the European Parliament or the European Council: while the nationalities of civil servants do roughly reflect the population size of the individual member states, the Commission is well balanced at the highest level: it currently comprises one Commissioner from every member state. However, this does not mean that every state has equal access to influential portfolios. Högenauer studies small states in the European Parliament, the institution where smallness matters the most due to the degressively proportional representation of member states. Grumbinaite, Etzold and Boykanova study the Council of the European Union and intergovernmental relations in their respective chapters, i.e., an institution where majorities are defined both by the number of states and the percentage of population they represent.

Taken together, these chapters allow us to draw a certain number of conclusions about the strategies of small states and their perception of the challenges that affect the different institutions. In the case of the Commission, Hamřík argues that the main challenge was first to ward off attempts to reduce the number of Commissioners to the point where not every member state would have a Commissioner in every Commission (i.e. a rotating Commission). The majority of small states opposed this move on grounds that it would undermine the legitimacy of the European Commission and the credibility of the claim that it represents the general interest of the European Union (cf. also Magnette and Nicolaïdis, 2003; Böttner, 2018). While Commissioners have to swear an oath not to take instructions from governments (and other actors) and to act in the general interest, equal representation is seen as a way to ensure that the Commission is aware of the differential impact of policies on states. Also, for small states, this allows the Commission to counterbalance the Council of the European Union, where large states are perceived as dominant (Wivel, 2010). A second challenge was to ward off the redesign of the Commission into one where only some Commissioners would have voting powers. While the current Commission de facto operates with vice presidents who coordinate other Commissioners, every Commissioner retains their voting rights. Thus, small states have been successful in defending the principle of equal representation.

Size is a far more obvious challenge in the European Parliament, where the smallest member states each hold fewer than 1 per cent of the seats. While this is not unfair, as they also represent only 0.1–0.2 per cent of the population, it is an obvious challenge when it comes to the representation of country-specific interests. Also, while the Members of the European Parliament (MEPs) have organized themselves into party groups rather than national groups, to this date European elections are still broken down into state-sized elections. The MEPs themselves also express this sentiment in research interviews – that they represent not only the European citizens but also – and especially – their constituency (i.e. country). In addition, to the low weight of these MEPs in plenary votes, it is more difficult for small states to cover all parliamentary committees – and impossible for the smallest states. If we add to this the fact MEPs normally divide into national delegations within party groups – i.e. Luxembourgish MEPs in the EPP, Luxembourgish MEPs in the Greens, etc. – there are often just one to two MEPs and a correspondingly low number of assistants looking at EU policies from this national and party perspective. Interestingly, despite these challenges, there is virtually no literature on small states in the EP.

In the context of the Council, Grumbinaite finds that the small size of national administrations is indeed the biggest challenge for the successful organization of the rotating Council Presidency. Some of the smaller and less affluent member states struggle with the burden of having to coordinate all Council meetings at all levels with their limited staff. Etzold acknowledges the limited individual weight of small states in EU decision-making and looks at coalitions as a way to overcome this challenge. Staying in the context of the Council and European Council, Stefanova examines the Central and Eastern European member states that may feel isolated due to different policy preferences and their size. She also explores the use of the veto by small states as a means to force through their preferences. Going beyond the argument in the literature that a veto threat from small states is less credible, she argues that it could be seen as paradoxical, as – according to shelter theory – small states depend on integration for economic and security benefits.

In terms of strategies for overcoming the challenge of size, small states have used slightly different strategies depending on the institution in question. In the context of the European Commission, for example, Hamřík finds that the main difference in nomination strategies between small and large states is that small states tend to nominate considerably more women than large states – they are in fact twice as likely to propose a female Commissioner. It may not be immediately apparent why this might be a strategic move. However, we would argue that when you consider that the Commission was traditionally almost exclusively composed of men, that the European Parliament then put increasing pressure on the member states to nominate women and on the Commission president to ensure that they are not relegated to the least influential portfolios, small states can be said to have supplied a 'rare commodity.' By nominating a woman to the still male-dominated Commission, they increased their chances for a good portfolio compared to a male small state candidate. One only needs to remember the Juncker and Von der Leyen Commissions, where the Commission presidents called on member states to please nominate more women.

Hamřík also found that expertise played less of a role: as all member states traditionally nominate influential figures – usually prime ministers or ministers but at least parliamentarians – there is little room for small states to nominate even more prestigious figures. However, he finds that small states are somewhat more likely to renominate their Commissioners for a second term so that their Commissioners have a greater chance to accumulate experience within the Commission.

In the case of the European Parliament, Högenauer found that the main strategy of MEPs from the two smallest member states – Luxembourg and Malta – was to compensate for size to spread out and cover as much terrain as possible. Thus, each MEP is usually a member and substitute member in several committees, and the aim is to focus on the most important issues in each committee rather than all the issues in one committee. MEPs also often play a very active role in committees where they are only substitute members, e.g., as rapporteurs. At any rate, due to the small number of MEPs, they are under pressure to be able to cover all major issues for the media and in meetings with national stakeholders and the general public. Small-state MEPs are thus pushed towards a less specialized approach. Coalition building was seen as possible but tricky, as other national delegations often had to pursue their own ambitions in terms of posts and even the MEPs from the same country but different parties were divided by government-opposition dynamics.

In the context of the Council Presidency, Grumbinaite found that cooperation was indeed among the strategies that small states used to compensate for limited resources. They benefitted both from the Troika format and from support from the EU institutions with the organization of meetings. Etzold argues that coalitions with like-minded countries are an important instrument for small- and medium-sized European Union member states in order to increase their political weight in EU policy-making in the European Council and Council. Using Korteweg's (2018) distinction of three types of coalitions within the EU: lead groups, ad hoc coalitions and alliances, Etzold comes to the conclusions that the Nordic and Baltic states do not, in fact, prefer alliances, despite the fact that institutionalized alliances are praised as the highest form of coalition. Instead, these governments prefer flexible, issue-specific intergovernmental coalitions that are often established ad hoc and that can include other like-minded countries outside their geographical area. Thus, despite the existence of institutionalized groupings like the Benelux, the Nordic Council or the V4, Etzold comes to the conclusion that pragmatic cooperation plays a bigger role in day-to-day policy-making. Stefanova also examines the use of coalitions in conjunction with the use of vetoes in her chapter. However, she questions their effectiveness in the case of certain Central and Eastern European member states.

On the whole, in terms of influence, Hamřík argues that the role of Commission president is reserved almost exclusively to large states. The sole – but notable – exception is the three Luxembourgish presidents. Luxembourg may have benefited in that regard from the fact that it is a founding state and that it is culturally close to both Germany and France, as well as to the Benelux, which may make it a convenient compromise (cf. Harmsen and Högenauer, 2021). However, the representation of small and large states is nowadays balanced at the level of vice presidents, which suggests that small states are by no means marginalized inside the Commission.

In the case of the European Parliament, Högenauer found that the pressure on small-state MEPs to cover several committees may have beneficial side effects in terms of compensating for the disadvantage of the small size of their groups: MEPs from Malta and Luxembourg are disproportionately powerful according to rankings by Eumatrix (2023). One explanation could be the fact that MEPs from these two countries bring a high level of political experience or practical experience with EU affairs to the EP, but it is likely that their presence in several committees also helps them to build a base of supporters within the institution.

In the context of the Council, Grumbinaite deemed the Council Presidencies of small states as successful as those of large states. However, she also concluded that small states focusing on a limited number of key priorities were more likely to be successful than those trying to pursue a wide range of issues. Etzold also came to the conclusion that alliances of small states can be successful, especially when they are flexible and issue oriented and when small states can ally with a larger state. More institutionalized forms of cooperation, by contrast, are seen more as a means to exchange information and build networks than as a tool to increase policy influence. Stefanova's study of the use of vetoes by Hungary, the Czech Republic, Slovakia and Bulgaria in conjunction with coalitions comes to a more sceptical conclusion. She finds that in the three cases that she studied (the Multiannual Financial Framework, the accession of North Macedonia and the distribution of migrants), the vetoes failed to secure the interests of the member states that used them. The other member states usually found ways to resolve the vetoes with minor compromises and beyond that started to express a preference for majority voting over consensual decision-making wherever possible. Thus, the vetoes had the counterproductive effect of reducing the opportunities to use vetoes in the long term. In addition, the coalitions of blocking states tended to be fragile and to break apart relatively quickly. Thus, she confirms Etzold's finding that institutionalized alliances are not effective in everyday policy-making: she shows that the specific preferences of the V4 diverge considerably in practice, despite being generally perceived as Eurosceptic, and this meant that the willingness of governments to support a blocking strategy that held minor benefits for them was limited.

11.3 Small states and their ability to shape EU policies

The second section of the book investigated member states in connection to various EU policies – two connected to security and two linked to foreign policy. This section aimed at extending our knowledge about the role small member states play during the development of common EU policies. These chapters, however, focused on two main policy areas in which small EU member countries experience numerous challenges and are traditionally dominated by large members. The introduction identified two main research questions connected to this section: How do small members influence individual policies? How does the EU respond (or fail to respond) to the needs of small states? Here we first sketch the overall conclusions of individual chapters in this section and then offer answers to these two research questions.

In the first chapter of the section (seventh chapter in the book) Kavvadia studies with the help of historical institutionalism small states' economic diplomacy in the case of Luxembourg. She argues that one of the main reasons behind Luxembourg's wealth has been its ability to develop a successful economic model supported by economic diplomacy that has been promoting its political and economic priorities within the EU. In the eight chapter of the book, Foster and Mosser examined subregional multilateralism in connection to EU foreign policy and the place of small states in it. They argued that big member states were in the past in charge of the external dimension of EU's security policy which they managed within a multilateral framework. Contrary to this, the authors studied the involvement of small EU members in EU foreign policy via participation in 'minilateral' coalitions. They argued that 'minilateralism' helps small member states of the EU to overcome information asymmetries and increase their bargaining power within EU's decision-making process.

In the nint chapter Dominici, Lewis and Steingass explored small member states' integration dilemma that concerns a trade-off between autonomy (independence) and security cooperation. Cooperation has the potential to significantly improve their security, however, international cooperation (like membership in an international organization) tends to be dominated by big countries with more resources and thus comes at the expense of their autonomy. The authors argued that EU membership attenuates this integration dilemma for small states by enabling them to introduce new initiatives into their existing strategies that help them to persuade the domestic audience about the necessity of these initiatives. However, not all small members experience this dilemma in the same way with geography playing an important role – the ones on the periphery (i.e. on the external borders of the EU) perceive this dilemma much more intensively. The chapter explored these issues on the case of the PESCO initiative and Frontex cooperation within the EU. In the last chapter of this volume, Gao examined the impact of small states on the development of EU cybersecurity policy on the case of Estonia. This chapter argued – in line with argumentation presented in the previous contribution – that small states play only a marginal role in EU security and defence policy; however, the situation is different in non-traditional security areas, for example, in cybersecurity. Here expertise and knowledge are more important than traditional military resources (like the size of military) that are directly linked to size and physical capacities of a state. The chapter examined how Estonia, a small EU member state, has shaped EU cybersecurity policy. It claimed that the 2007 cyberattack on Estonia was a critical juncture that caused the country to focus on this issue. The expertise and knowledge gained in cybersecurity following this event enabled Estonia to actively pursue and shape this topic at the EU level.

Individual chapters contributed to the answer of the first research question asking how small members influence individual policies. Kavvadia (Chapter 7) argued that Luxembourg has changed its economic model and thus also objectives of its economic diplomacy three times following critical junctures that caused changes in global megatrends. While during the first phase coal and steel – the top priorities at the then ECSC level – were also country's priorities, during the second phase Luxembourg changed its priorities and started to focus on financial sector to align its own priorities at home to the development within the EU. During the third – current – phase Luxembourg has shifted its priorities towards knowledge-based economy (i.e. quaternary economic sector) to be able to influence the latest development within the EU and lead the changes in digitalization and innovation sector. Such ability of the country to change its priorities and build on the previous results enabled Luxembourg to increase its influence within the EU over time. Foster and Mosser (Chapter 8) claimed that small members learned to amplify their voice by joining (or leading) minilateral coalitions. These coalitions are usually informal and they help their members to accumulate social capital and develop reciprocal trust within the group. Minilateral groups can be inactive for a while and be waken up when needed by its members. However, the authors claimed that further research is needed in order to learn whether such coalitions lead to consensus building within decision-making process.

Dominici et al. in the ninth chapter argued in a rather opposite way when they claimed that small member states were in a different position when PESCO and the 2019 Frontex reform were discussed within the EU. These two security initiatives were backed by the big states and therefore small EU members did not have a lot of room for influencing the preparatory process and could – at best – react to the development shaped by big states. Small member states therefore gained only a little in the process, although they still showed the willingness to stay at the table. However, the EU still helped small members to attenuate integration dilemma but not by giving them a stronger role in the decision-making process but by helping them to sell reforms at the EU level to the national audience. While traditional security is, indeed, domain of the big EU member states, Gao argued in the last chapter, small states can have an important say in non-traditional security areas, like cybersecurity. This is caused by the fact that military capabilities, directly connected to the size of a country, are not that important in this area where expertise and knowledge – achievable almost independently of size – are much more important. Therefore, Estonia, which built these capabilities following the 2007 cyberattack, was able to shape EU cybersecurity strategy. The chapter argued that the timing was of an essence in this process – Estonia managed to utilize the window of opportunity that the cyberattack presented for the country to play a leading role in EU cybersecurity policy. The experience and expertise gained helped the country to gain a reputation as a forerunner that was utilized during the Estonian presidency of the Council of the EU to build coalitions and act as an honest broker in this area.

When it comes to the second research question of the second section of the book, individual chapters also offered positions on how the EU responds (or fails to respond) to the needs of small states. The overall answer is that small member states are rather active members and they are trying to actively shape the EU and its policies (see the previous discussion on the first research question of this section) so that their national priorities are as close to EU rules as possible and are not waiting for the EU to respond (or not) to their needs. Kavvadia (Chapter 7) claimed that Luxembourg underwent a learning process during which it changed its approach from catching up with other member states in the steel (and coal) sector to a leader in digitalization and innovation sector. The country thus did not rely on EU's help but developed own set of tools – especially economic diplomacy that helped it to shape EU and its policies according to its own preferences. Similarly, Foster and Mosser argued that small states were actively joining minilateral coalitions that helped them to influence the EU and its policies. For example, the Quadro Group (southern members of the EU) managed to keep the migration as the top issue within the Council and its members gained from this cooperation.

In the very last chapter Gao argued that small members can be active and successful member states also in security area; however, they have to focus on non-traditional security issues like cybersecurity. Here small states can utilize tools offered by the EU and its institutions (e.g. rotating presidency of the Council of the EU) to pursue their own goals and preferences at the EU level. However, not all chapters concluded that small EU members are able to be active policy shapers. Dominici et al. argued that when it comes to security policy-making, small states were not able to influence the decision-making process; on contrary, they changed their domestic policy to make it more in line with the EU level. Dominated by big members, security policy update (in form of PESCO and the 2019 Frontex) did not follow needs of small member states, especially those at the external borders of the EU.

11.4 Conclusion

To conclude, small states face different challenges in different institutions. They are relatively well represented in the European Commission and have been reasonably successful in obtaining relevant positions. They are in a weaker position in the Council, where they risk being outvoted and where vetoes annoy other states more than they hinder policy-making. And they are in a difficult position in the European Parliament, where the limited number of MEPs does not allow small states to cover every policy area, but at the same time there is of course pressure to cover more than a handful of issues. In addition, the obtention of certain posts de facto requires MEPs to have the backing of a large national delegation, and small state MEPs would thus need to convince MEPs from other countries to back them rather than their own nationals.

The strategies thus also diverge across institutions, and the conclusions from the literature on the Council do not fit all institutions: prioritization of specific goals is seen to work well for Council Presidencies. Coalition building with other member states can be a very effective tool to increase the political weight of a state, but it only works if the state can find like-minded countries. It works less well when countries try to form static blocks (like the V4) and fail to consider the issue-specific interests of their partners.

In the context of the European Parliament, by contrast, coalition building with other groups is complicated by the ambitions of the members of those groups, and coalition building with MEPs from one's own country but a different party group is hampered by government-opposition dynamics. Thus, it can be useful and successful, but it is difficult to achieve. In addition, prioritization on key issues does not work, as that would result in the coverage of a very narrow range of issues. Instead, small-state MEPs are active in a large number of committees and thus less specialized. However, maybe as a result of this, they are deemed relatively influential within the EP. Having very experienced MEPs also helps them to navigate the complex distribution of posts and tasks.

Finally, while the Commission is a relatively well-balanced institution – at least as far as the College of Commissioners is concerned – getting the most prestigious job of Commission president is virtually impossible for all small states that are not Luxembourg. All other jobs are distributed more evenly. The use of experience/prestige of candidates is difficult as a strategy, as all states tend to send very senior politicians to the Commission. However, small states may have found a niche by proposing more female candidates at a time when they are needed to gender balance the Commission.

The chapters on the EU's foreign and security policies confirm these findings: small states can have influence in EU policy-making and can create situations where their needs are met. They are most likely to succeed when they build foreign policy coalitions, when they anticipate major economic developments and when they manage to acquire a high level of expertise in a policy area. However, the case studies also show that there is a risk of small states becoming policy-takers in cases where they cannot provide leadership in terms of ideas and expertise and/or fail to build political weight through significant coalitions.

Bibliography

Beaussier, A.-L. and Cabane, L. (2020). Strengthening the EUs response capacity to health emergencies: Insights from EU crisis management mechanisms. *European Journal of Risk Regulation* 11(4): 808–820. https://doi.org/10.1017/err.2020.80.

Bosse, G. (2022). Values, rights, and changing interests: The EUs response to the war against Ukraine and the responsibility to protect Europeans. *Contemporary Security Policy* 43(3): 531–546. https://doi.org/10.1080/13523260.2022.2099713.

Böttner, R. (2018). The size and structure of the European commission: Legal issues surrounding project teams and a (future) reduced college. *European Constitutional Law Review* 14(1): 37–61.

Brusenbauch Meislova, M. (2019). Brexit means brexit—or does it? The legacy of Theresa mays discursive treatment of brexit. *Political Quarterly* 90(4): 681–689. https://doi.org/ https. https://doi.org/10.1111/1467-923X.12767.

Eumatrix. (2023). Available at https://eumatrix.eu/en/blog/mep-influence-index-2023-top -100-most-politically-influential-meps (accessed 18 August 2023).

Fontan, C. and Saurugger, S. (2019). Between a Rock and a hard place: Preference formation in France during the Eurozone crisis. *Political Studies Review* 18(4): 507–524. https://doi .org/10.1177/1478929919868600.

Harmsen, R. and Högenauer, A.L. (2021). Luxembourg and the European Union. In: Finn Laursen (ed.)*Encyclopedia of European Union Politics* (Oxford University Press: Oxford).

Kopper, A., Szalai, A. and Góra, M. (2023). Populist foreign policy in central and Eastern Europe: Poland, Hungary and the shock of the Ukraine crisis. In: P. Giurlando and D.F. Wajner (eds.), *Populist Foreign Policy: Regional Perspectives of Populism in the International Scene* (Springer International Publishing: Cham), pp. 89–116. https://doi .org/10.1007/978-3-031-22773-8_4.

Korteweg, R. (2018). Why a new Hanseatic League will not be enough. *Clingendael Spectator*, 9 July 2018.

Lamour, C. (n.d.). Orbán placed in Europe: Ukraine, Russia and the radical-right populist Heartland. *Geopolitics*: 1–27. https://doi.org/10.1080/14650045.2023.2241825.

Magnette, P. and Nicolaïdis, K. (2003). Large and small member states in the European Union: Reinventing the balance. *Notre Europe: Research and European Issues* 25. Available at: https://institutdelors.eu/wp-content/uploads/2018/01/etud25-en.pdf.

Mišík, M. (2022). The EU needs to improve its external energy security. *Energy Policy* 165: 112930. https://doi.org/10.1016/j.enpol.2022.112930.

Panke, D. (2010). *Small States in the European Union. Coping with Structural Disadvantages* (Ashgate: Farnham).

Sanchez Salgado, R.M. (2022). Emotions in the European Unions decision-making: the reform of the Dublin System in the context of the refugee crisis. *Innovation the European Journal of Social Science Research* 35(1): 14–38. https://doi.org/10.1080/13511610 .2021.1968355.

Schimmelfennig, F. (2022). *Differentiated Integration Has Been of Limited Use in the EUs Polycrisis*. Policy Briefs, 2022/31 (European University Institute: Florence).

Thorhallsson, B. and Wivel, A. (2006). Small states in the European Union: What do we know and what would we like to know ? *Cambridge Review of International Affairs* 19(4): 651–668.

Wivel, A. (2010). From small state to smart state: Devising a strategy for influence in the European Union. In: R. Steinmetz and A. Wivel (eds.), *Small States in Europe: Challenges and Opportunities* (Ashgate Publishing Limited: Farnham), pp. 15–29.

Zeitlin, J., Nicoli, F. and Laffan, B. (2019). Introduction: The European Union beyond the polycrisis? Integration and politicization in an age of shifting cleavages. *Journal of European Public Policy* 26(7): 963–976. https://doi.org/10.1080/13501763.2019 .1619803.

Index

Note: Page numbers in *italics* indicate figures, **bold** indicate tables in the text.

Aaviksso, J. 167
Adamson, L. 162
administrative capacity 53–54, 57–59, 67; defining *59*; development of 61; limited 22; RCI and SI components of 66
adversarial coalitions 90–91; in 2015 EU asylum crisis 95–97; application of 95; failure of 97; formation of 92
Allan, C. 162
Amsterdam Treaty 128
Ansip, A. 169
area of freedom, security and justice (AFSJ) 147, 155
Arter, D. 3, 164
Austria 26, 79, 81–82; finance ministers from 82; presidency 154

Bailes, A. 39, 87
Baldacchino, G. 3
Balkans 85, *93*, 97, 129
Baltic countries 144, 148, 177; Baltic Sea Council 56; coalition building 71–72, 74–76, 78–83; integration dilemma for 149, 153; new frontline member states in 147, 153; Nordic-Baltic cooperation 72; Nordic-Baltic Eight 71, 78; Nordic-Baltic Six 71, 78–80, 83, 127, 130, 131, 134–139; PESCO initiative in 149; *see also* Estonia; Latvia; Lithuania
Baltic Sea 56, 79, 134, 136
bargaining power 91, 139; in decision-making 90, 95, 179; increasing through information exchange 131; institutionalism and 90; intergovernmentalism and 90; theories of 90

Belgium 2, 110, 129, 132, 150; in creation of European Monetary Union 164; in deploying shaping strategies 7, 39; foreign policy, influence on 164; forerunner reputation of 164; Luxembourg cooperation with 150
Belgium–Luxembourg Economic Union (BLEU) 110
Benelux Union Treaty 110, 129, 132, 178
Bengtsson, R. 8
Björkdahl, A. 4, 7, 8, 38, 39, 162
Blockmans, S. 4, 128, 130
Bohle, D. 87, 92
border control cooperation 143, 146, 152–155; defence cooperation vs. 147; *see also* European Border and Coast Guard Agency (Frontex)
Botswana 169
Braun, M. 133
'Bronze Solider' incident *see* cyberattack of 2007 (Estonia)
Buchan, R. 166
Budgetary Instrument for Convergence and Competitiveness (BICC) 80
Bulgaria 6, 130; in coalition building in EU policy-making 79; in deploying shaping strategies 7, 39; in European Commission 24, 28, 32; Multi-Annual Financial Framework and 86; Negotiating Framework and 85, 97–99; nomination strategies of 27; non-voting members in 27; policy preferences of *93*; Schengen membership of 91; shaping strategies use of 7; veto power in European Union 85, 97–99, 178; Vice-Presidents, appointment of 32
Buzan, B. 129

Capoccia, G. 163
Central and Eastern Europe (CEE) 6, 96,
176, 178; coalition building capabilities
of member states in 92–93; decision-
making process 86, 97; inferiority
complex of 133; national preferences
of 91; permanent coalition, capacity to
act as 92; policy preferences in 92–95;
sustainable adversarial coalition to form
in 95, 97; as veto players 91–92; veto
power in European Union 85–99
China 3, 106, 133
Clinton, B. 132
coalition building 67, 68, 71–72, 76, 79, 81,
88, 154, 160–161, 164, 167–168, 170,
175; advanced forms of 75; capabilities
of member states in Central and Eastern
Europe 92–93; capability of small states
164, 166; culture and identity based
74; in EU decision-making 72, 96;
among EU member states in decision-
making 72–73, 96; ideological affinity
based 74; institutionalized patterns 74;
interest based 74; with MEPs 177, 182;
minilateral 138; with other states 40,
155, 182; relevance of small states in
EEC *94*; territorially constituted 74; as
ways to mitigate smallness 47
coalitions 87, 135, 138–139, 145, 152;
ad hoc 73–75, 79, 80, 82–83, 86,
88–89, 92, 177, 178; alliances 73,
177; architecture 130; CEE-based 96;
cross-party 48; defence cooperation in
130; domestic 130; formal 72; informal
72, 75, 79, 131, 134; institutionalized
73–75, 77–79, 82–83; internal political
133; intra-EU 75; lead groups 73,
177; minilateral 126, 131–132, 136,
138, 179–181; NB6 135–137; with
other states 47, 71; shifting 90, 129;
subregional 126–127; territorial 74, 130;
as tools for agenda setting 131; types of
73; of willing 128; *see also* adversarial
coalitions; coalition building
cognitive regionalism 127
collective power 87
College 19–23, 182; Barroso I 23, 24, **25**,
28, *29*, 30, *30*, *32*; Barroso II 23, 24, **25**,
28, *29*, 30, *30*, *32*, 34; Juncker 23–24,
25, *28*, *29*, *30*, 30–32, *32*, 34, 153, 167,
177; Prodi 24, 25, **25**, *28*, *29*, 30, *30*,
32; representation of women at level
of *28*; Santer 24, **25**, *28*, *29*, *30*, *32*;

von der Leyen 24, **25**, 27, *28*, *29*, *30*, 31,
32, 34, 177
Collier, D. 108
Committee of Permanent Representatives
(COREPER) 78, 131
Common Foreign and Security Policy
(CFSP) 26, 39, 126, 128, 129, 137
Common Security and Defence Policy
(CSDP) 75, 147, 149
Convention on the Future of Europe 21
Cooperative Cyber Defence Centre of
Excellence (CCDCOE) 167
Cortell, A. P. 107
Council General Secretariat (CGS) 57
Council of the Baltic Sea States (CBSS)
79, 130
Council Presidency 8, 39, 164, 177–178,
182; administrative challenge of 54–56;
Denmark in 134, 164; Finland 164;
France 98; impact of 54, 58–59, 61,
64–**65**, 66–67; inducing learning, role
in 7; in international cooperation 56;
political achievements of 57; preparation
and conduct of 61; rotating 53–55,
57–58, 68, 164, 170, 176; Sweden 134,
137–138
counterterrorism 161
Court of Justice of the EU (CJEU) 95, 96
COVID-19 crisis 1, 8, 80, 96, 174;
multilateralism and global economy
during 3; Recovery Funds 81
Crandall, M. 162
critical juncture 159–160, 166, 180;
cyberattack against Estonia in 2007
as *see* cyberattack of 2007 (Estonia);
for Czech Republic 54; defined 163;
examples of 163; identification of 106–
107; Luxembourg 107–109, 111–113,
115, 117–119
Croatia 24, 32, 79
Crosson, D. M. 128, 130
Csehi, R. 91
Cyber Resilience for Development
(Cyber4Dev) project 169
cyber threats 159; collective resilience
against 167; NATO policy to address
167; policies and institutions addressing
166–167
cyberattack of 2007 (Estonia) 160,
165–170, 180–181
cybersecurity policy 161, 179–181;
allocating resources to realm of 167–
168; cyberattack of 2007 160, 165–170,

180–181; personnel resources, devoting 169–170; trajectory 168
cyberwarfare 167
Cyprus 24, 37, 48, 144, 147–148; administrations of presidency 55; approaches regarding PESCO initiative 150; in deploying shaping strategies 7, 39; EU accession of, migration and 137–138; in nomination of Commissioners in 29; PESCO initiative and 147, 148, 150; veto power in EU politics 91
Czech Republic 54, 80, 178; Council Conclusions and 85, 97; critical juncture for 54; dissenting votes of 95; finance ministers from 82; Multiannual Financial Framework and 96; policy intentions of 93; Presidencies of 7; *see also* Visegrád Group

Dangerfield, M. 132
decision-making process 3, 37, 136, 175–176, 181; active and effective in vocalizing preferences in 76; ad hoc 145; bargaining power in 90, 95, 179; broader coalition-building processes in 96; capacity of small states to influence 91; CEE and ad hoc coalitions in 86, 97; challenge of size and influence in 71–72, 86; challenge of steering 53; coalition building in 72–73, 96; collegial nature of 22; consensus-based 99, 178, 180; consequentiality and cost-benefit consideration in 58; EC's capacity to move forward 26; Estonia, role in 159, 162, 170; foreign policy 126–127; implementing hard interests in 82; institutionalized coalition suitable for influencing 77–78; marginalization of veto power in 97–98; national influence in 77; navigating 6–8; Nordic-Baltic cooperation 79, 83; procedure in Council 88; security 144; strategies in 99; structural disadvantages in 6–7; Swedish initiative to engage Baltic states in 134; terms of visibility in 99; values, norms and policy principles of 85; veto rights to block 90
defence cooperation 143, 146, 148; border control cooperation vs. 147; coalitions in 130; EU-based 151; of Finland and Sweden with United States 135; *see also* Permanent Structured Cooperation (PESCO)

Democratic Republic of the Congo (DRC) 164
Denmark 24, 71, 75, 129, 143; administrations of presidency 55; Council Presidency 134, 164; in deploying shaping strategies 7, 39; in European Parliament 40; finance ministers from 82; in nomination of Commissioners in 29; representation of small states by Commissioners from 32; security integration dilemma 143; veto right 81; in wake of Russian invasion 134–135
derivative power 87, 98
Digital Economy and Society Index 112
Digital Single Market Conference 168
digitalization 79, 112, 180–181; digital cooperation 78; in Estonia 165, 167–169; Europe 170; global competitiveness through 117; Luxembourg 118, 119
domestic buffers 87
Draft Treaty 21
Dublin Regulation 137, 152, 174

EBCG standing corps 154
Eckert, S. 133
Economic and Monetary Union (EMU) 75, 91
Elgström, O. 72
'empty chair crisis' of 1965 89
energy security 79, 161, 162
equality principle 21, 55, 80
Estonia 7, 75, 180–181; coalition building of 160, 167–168, 170; in deploying shaping strategies 7, 39; digitalization in 165, 167–169; e-commerce and e-service development in 168; European IT Agency in 168–169; in EU's cybersecurity policy *see* cybersecurity policy; EU's dependence on 167; financial and personnel resources in 168–169; forerunner reputation of 160, 162, 166–167, 170, 181; free flow of data in 168; influence on non-traditional security 162; influence on security policy 162, 165–166; internet connectivity in 168; in nomination of Commissioners in 29; North Atlantic Treaty Organisation and 166–167; PESCO-light and 149; Presidencies 8; trust and security in 168
EU Coalition Explorer (EUCE) 92, 93
EU CYBERID cyber exercise testing 169
EU treaty reform 88, 90

Eumatrix 178
European Asylum Support Office
    (EASO) 138
European Border and Coast Guard Agency
    (Frontex) 144, 147–148, 155, 179–180;
    as border control cooperation 138,
    152–155; design of regulation 152
European Coal and Steel Community
    (ECSC) 2, 110
European Commission (EC) 5, 7, 37,
    38, 55–56, 96, 127, 128, 164, 166,
    175–177, 181; accession negotiations,
    launching 97; College as member
    states 21–23; composition of 2; EU
    citizens' perceptions of 21; as guardian
    of regional interest 91; infringement
    procedure, launching 95; leadership
    positions, small states' representatives
    in 31–34; national interests within 22;
    nomination strategies of 25, 27–31;
    OECD framework approach adopted
    by 116–117; perceived as the EU's
    institution 22; political leadership
    within 23–24; proposals 81, 86, 137;
    reforming 20–21; size of 19; and
    small EU member states 20–24; small
    states' perspective 22, 26; suspending
    payments for Hungary 97
European Council 3, 7, 21, 38, 78, 80,
    86, 130, 135, 154, 164, 175, 176;
    conclusions on opening of accession
    negotiations 97; on Foreign Relations
    EU Coalition Explorer 76; as key
    foreign and security policy actors 39;
    permanent president of 55; presidency
    see Council Presidency; quotas for
    relocation of refugees, approving 95;
    voting in 1, 2, 5–6, 19
European Council on Foreign Relations EU
    Coalition Explorer of 2020 76
European Economic Area (EEA) 75
European Economic Community (EEC)
    2, 129; membership 136; relevance of
    small states in *94*; in southern Europe
    136
European Free Trade Area (EFTA) 75
European Investment Bank (EIB) 111
European Monetary Union 164
European Parliament (EP) 5, 22, 25,
    28, 50–51, 149, 175–178, 181–182;
    challenge in 176; Council of EU
    in trialogues with 55; Denmark in
    40; dynamics in 39; effectiveness

of lobbying 40; elections to 37–38;
    Estonia as member of 169; Finland
    in 40; impact of empowerment of 39;
    Lisbon Treaty and 61; Luxembourgish
    in 40–42; majority voting 6, 19; Malta
    in 37–39, 41–49, **43**, 51; number of
    representatives in 19; plenary votes in
    37; policies 41–46; questionnaire 149;
    securing positions of power in 46–47;
    strategies for coping 47–49; Sweden in
    40; *see also* Members of the European
    Parliament (MEPs)
European Security Strategy (ESS) 161
European Social Fund (ESF) 61
European Union's security and defence
    policy (ESDP) 39, 127, 135, 143, 147,
    152, 159–162, 169–170, 180
Eurozone: budget 80; crisis 1–2;
    development of 77; Finland as member
    of 75; members and non-members 80;
    members vs. outsiders 82; reforms
    80–81
ever-evolving economic model
    111–118, *113*

Fawn, R. 132
Finland 75, 77; Council Presidency 164;
    defence cooperation of 135; in European
    Parliament 40; finance ministers from
    82; integration into European Union
    134; in nomination of Commissioners
    in 29
Fioretos, O. 107
foreign direct investment (FDI) 110
foreign policy 89, 92, 105, 179, 182; actor
    127; ambitions of France 5; Belgium's
    influence on 164; decision-making 127;
    Franco-German compromises on 129;
    governance 139; limited ambitions
    145; of Luxembourg 106; migration, in
    terms of 137; objectives membership
    as 75; preferences *93*; small states'
    choices 163; small states' influence on
    162; small states' strategies 160, 170;
    subregional minilateralism in 129;
    tool 162
forerunner reputation 165; of Belgium
    164; of Estonia 160, 162, 166–167,
    170, 181; multiple sources of 164;
    of Netherlands 164
France 2, 110, 128, 136, 154, 162;
    Council Presidency 98; Estonia vs.
    168; EU Presidency 97–98; foreign

policy ambitions of 5; -led European
Intervention Initiative 135; PESCO
initiative and 148
Frugal Four 71–72, 74, 81–82, 129; *see
also* Austria; Denmark; Netherlands;
Sweden

Galušková, J. 54
Gergelova, Š. 54
Germany 2, 5, 6, 79, 110, 128, 162, 174;
Council negotiations 96; PESCO
initiative and 148, 150; supported by
other member states 96
Ghana 169
Global Strategy 161
Goetschel, L. 144, 162
Gosling, T. 134
Greece 2, 7, 153; in deploying shaping
strategies 7, 39; migration flows
136–138; veto over Macedonia's EU
accession negotiations 91, 97
Grimaud, M. J. 3
Grøn, C. H. 164
Gurol, J. 8, 39
Hacker, J. S. 163

Haughton, T. 7, 38
Haukkala, H. 136
Henökl, T. 82
historical institutionalism (HI) 58, 106–108,
113, 117–119, 179
Homburger, Z. 162
Honkanen, K. 164
Hoscheit, J.-M. 54
Hungary 79, 134; dissenting votes of
95; EU structural funds to 96, 97, 99;
Multiannual Financial Framework and
85, 86, 96, 99, 178; policy intentions
of 93, *93*; refugee crisis 2; relocation
of refugees 99; Russian invasion of
Ukraine and 133–134, 174; veto right
85, 99; *see also* Visegrád Group

Iceland 3, 71, 75–77, 79; security
integration dilemma 143
Ikenberry, G. J. 107
Ingebritsen, C. 162
institutional embeddedness 87
institutionalism 90; historical 58, 106–108,
117–118, 179; neoliberal 87; rational
choice 58, **64**; sociological 58, **64**
integration dilemma 143–146, 148–151,
153, 155, 179, 180

Intergovernmental Conference 20, 21
intergovernmentalism 90, 99; premises
of 96
International Law Applicable to Cyber
Warfare 167
IO membership 132
Ireland 21, 147; in deploying shaping
strategies 7, 39; European Parliament'
questionnaire to 149; for Eurozone crisis
2; FRONTEX reform and 153; NB6
plus 80; PESCO initiative and 148–152;
Presidency **57**, 59, **60**, **62**, **64**
Italy 2, 136–137, 153; for Eurozone crisis 2

Jacoby, W. 87, 92
Jakobsen, P. V. 4, 39, 162, 164
Janning, J. 72, 130
Jensen, M. D. 54–55

Kaniok, P. 54, 91
Katzenstein, P. 87
Kelam, T. 169
Kelemen, R. D. 163
Kenny, E. 151
Keohane, R. 87, 144
Kirchner, E. J. 56
Klaus, V. 132
Kleinberga, V. 136
Klemencic, M. 72, 74
Korteweg, R. 73, 80, 177
Kuusik, P. 72

Latvia 75; finance ministers from 82;
in nomination of Commissioners in
29; Presidency **57**, 59, **60**, **62**, **64**,
66; representation of small states by
Commissioners from 32
Lepassaar, J. 169
liberal intergovernmental approach 3, 99n1
liberal theory 87
Lisbon Treaty 2, 5, 21, 55, 88, 147;
European Parliament and 61; option of
leaving EU 91
Liska, G. 144
Lithuania 6, 75; in nomination of
Commissioners in 29; Presidency **57**,
59, **60**, **62**, **64**, 66
Long, T. 4, 87, 89, 145
Luik, J. 169
Luxembourg 105–107, 110, **114**, 129, 153;
banking secrecy 116–117; cooperation
with Belgium 150; critical juncture
107–109, 111–113, **115**, 117–119; in

deploying shaping strategies 7, 39; digitalization 118, 119; in European Parliament 40; European Parliament's questionnaire to 149; foreign policy of 106; FRONTEX reform and 153, 154; honest broker, role of 7; Industry 4.0 112, 117; members of the European Parliament 40–51, 176, 177; PESCO initiative and 148–150; Presidency **57**, 59, **60**, **63**, **64**; scepticism 153, 154; security integration dilemma 143

Maass, M. 4
Macedonia 85, 86, 98–99, 178; EU accession negotiations 91, 97; NATO membership 97; Prespa Agreement, signing 97
MacMullen, A. 22
Macron, E. 80, 151
Maes, I. 164
Mainwaring, C. 137–138
Malstrom, C. 166
Malta 2, 152, 153; in deploying shaping strategies 7, 39; EU accession of, migration and 137–138; in European Parliament 37–39, 41–49, **43**, 51, 149; members of the European Parliament 40–43, 45–51, 177; Minister for Home Affairs and National Security 154; in nomination of Commissioners in 29; Presidency 8, **57**, 59, **60**, **63**, **65**, 66
Mauritius 169
Members of the European Parliament (MEPs) 37–40, 178, 181–182; challenge for 45; coalition building with 177, 182; from coalition parties 45; cross-party coalitions of 48; effect of state size on 40–50; from governing parties 45; Luxembourgish 40–51, 176, 177; Maltese 40–43, 45–51, 177; official CVs of 41; opposition 41
Merger Treaty 111
migrants/migration 26, 114, 117, 152, 159; 2015–2016 migration crisis 95, 133; burden sharing on 137–138; EU migration policy 133; Mediterranean states in receiving 137; in Nordic countries 77; policy 137, 153; policy areas spanning 98; Quadro Group 137–139, 181; reception of 154; related reforms 152–153; Salzburg Group in 130; Southern Europe 136–137; in terms of foreign and security policy 137; *see also* refugees

minilateral coalitions 126, 131–132, 136, 138, 179–181
minilateralism 179; security *see* security minilateralism; subregional in 126, 129, 131–134
Moravcsik, A. 3
Multiannual Financial Framework (MFF) 2021–2027 56, 81, 85, 86, 95–96, 178
multilateralism 87, 126–128, 179
Munck, G. 108
Muscat, J. 150

Nasra, S. 2, 164
national identity security 162
NATO membership 132, 134
Nedergaard, P. 54–55
Negotiating Framework 85, 97–99
neoliberal institutionalism 87
Netherlands 2, 81, 110, 129; in creation of European Monetary Union 164; finance ministers from 82; forerunner reputation of 164; influence on security policy 162; NB6 plus 80; Presidency **57**, 59, **60**, **63**, **65**; veto power 91
neutrality 150, 162; legal problems 150; military 147; security cooperation in relation to 151
New Hanseatic League 71, 72, 74, 80–81
non-traditional security 170, 180, 181; agenda 162; challenges 161; concerns 161; Estonia's influence on 162; Nordic countries influence on 162; Sweden's influence on 162; threats 159; *see also* *specific securities*
Nordic Council (NC) 76–77
Nordic Council of Ministers (NCM) 76–77
Nordic states 6, 177, 178; coalition building 71–72, 74–79, 81–83; on European Security and Defense Policy 39, 162; influence on non-traditional security 162; migrants/migration in 77; Nordic-Baltic cooperation 72, 74; Nordic-Baltic Eight 71, 78; Nordic-Baltic Six 71, 78–80, 83, 127, 130–132, 134–139; *see also specific states*
North Atlantic Treaty Organisation (NATO) 56, 150; accession strategies for 133–134; Cooperative Cyber Defence Centre of Excellence 167; Estonia and 166–167; EU compatibility 135; Finland's application for membership 134; limits of 169; Macedonia's membership 97; as principal security guarantor 149;

strategic shelter in 147; Sweden's application for membership 134; Visegrád and 132–134
Nuallain, C. O. 54

OECD framework approach 56, 116–117

Panke, D. 5, 7, 8, 38–40, 42, 58, 72, 74, 86–89
Papayoanu, P. A. 128, 139
particular-intrinsic power 87
Pastore, G. 145
Perkowski, N. 154
Permanent Representation (PermRep) 47
Permanent Structured Cooperation (PESCO) 143, 146–147; advent of 147; autonomy-effectiveness trade-offs 148; Cyprus and 147, 148, 150; defence cooperation 148–152; France and 148; German-French agreement on 128; Germany and 148, 150; Ireland and 148–152; Luxembourg and 148–150; NATO in 149
Peterson, S. 107
Poland 79; administrations of presidency 55; for climate policy issues 2; as largest state 2; Russian invasion of Ukraine and 133; *see also* Visegrád Group
policy entrepreneurship 159, 160, 163–164
polycrisis 1, 105, 174
Pomerants, M. 168
Portugal 136
Prespa Agreement 97
Proksch, S. 38

Quadro Group 127, 130–131; migrants/migration 137–139, 181; Southern Europe and 136–138

Raik, K. 72
rational choice institutionalism (RCI) 58, 66–67
refugees 1–2, 8, **57**, 152–154, 174; burden sharing on 137–138; relocation of 86, 95; *see also* migrants/migration
Regional Security Complexes (RSCs) 129
regionalism 127, 129
Romania 2, 79
Rosecrance, R. 139
Ruggie, J. G. 139
rule-of-law principles 79, 85, 93, 96
Rūse, I. 72–74, 79, 130, 131, 137
Russia: cyberattack by 165; invasion of Ukraine 1, 3, 6, 8, 133–134, 174–175

Salzburg Group 129–130
Sarapuu, K. 95
Schengen Area 89, 147, 153; crisis 152; membership of Bulgaria 91
Schneider, E. 117, 118
Schoeller, M. 91
Schöller, M. G. 80
Schott, P. 139
Schulz, D. F. 82
security cooperation 143, 146–148, 179; initiative 145–146; proposed 145; in relation to neutrality 151; trade-off 144–146; types of 149
security minilateralism 127; defined 126; subregional 130
security policy 126–129, 143–146, 179, 181; dilemma in 155; Estonia's influence on 162, 165–166; migration, in terms of 137; modes of 148; Netherlands's influence on 162; non-traditional security issues when developing 161; official discourse of small states' 161; priorities for all NB6 countries 135; Scandinavia's influence on 162; Sweden's influence on 162; *see also* cybersecurity policy
shelter 105; external 3; function 4; political, economic and societal 130; preferences 91; seeking behaviour 91, 98, 130; strategic 95, 145, 147; theory 3, 85–86, 88–89, 95, 97–98, 176
Slapin, J. 38, 90, 96, 99
Slovakia 80, 178; Council Conclusions and 85, 97; dissenting votes of 95; finance ministers from 82; Multiannual Financial Framework and 96; policy intentions of 93, *93*; Presidency **57**, 59, **60, 63, 65**, 66; representation of small states by Commissioners from 32; *see also* Visegrád Group
Slovenia 7, 24, 32, 79
smallness 87, 91, 106, 110–111, 119, 175; advantages of 49–50; coalition building as ways to mitigate 47; creating challenge 46; defining 4–5, 147; effects of 39; in EU context 4–6; impact of 46; in-depth study due to 106; perception of 4; strategic participation of small states 163–164, 170; strategies for coping with effects of 47–49; way to overcome 47; ways to compensate for 6–8; *see also specific states*
sociological institutionalism (SI) 58, 61, 66, 67

Söderbaum, F. 129
Spain 136–137, 153, 154
Sri Lanka 169
Steinsson, S. 130
Stockholm Program 137–138
subregional minilateralism 126, 129,
    131–134
Sweden 75, 77; Council Presidency 134,
    137–138; defence cooperation of 135;
    in European Parliament 40; finance
    ministers from 82; influence on non-
    traditional security 162; influence on
    security policy 162; integration into
    European Union 134

Tavares, R. 127
Thorhallsson, B. 3, 7, 38, 39, 72, 87–89,
    91, 130
Three Seas Initiative 130
trade-offs: between (formal) autonomy
    and security cooperation 143–146, 179;
    PESCO's autonomy-effectiveness 148;
    policy 144; security-autonomy 147, 148,
    151; between veto rights and exit threats
    90, 97
Treaty of Nice 20–21, 88
Trimarium 130
Turkey 91, 129, 150

United Kingdom (UK) 71, 128, 137, 162;
    Joint Expeditionary Force 135; pre-
    Brexit 2
United Nations (UN) 56; advocacy of
    cybersecurity and promotion of cyber
    norms in 167; peacekeeping missions
    151; UN framework 166–167

United States (US) 106, 132, 135, 147, 149;
    agreement on global minimum corporate
    tax 117; defence cooperation of Finland
    and Sweden with 135

Varadkar, L. 151
Verdun, A. 164
veto power 37, 89, 90; bargaining position
    to maintain 91; in budget negotiations
    81; Bulgaria 85, 97–99, 178; Central
    and Eastern Europe 85–86; Cyprus 91;
    and exit threats, trade-off between 90;
    Greece 91, 97; Hungary 85; Multiannual
    Financial Framework 56, 81, 85, 86,
    95–96, 178; Negotiating Framework 85,
    97–99; Netherlands 91
Vetrovcova, M. 133
Visegrád Group 56, 92, 127, 130–131, 138;
    as case of subregional minilateralism
    131–134; collective antipathy 133;
    cooperation on security and defence
    130; leaders 132–133; migrant crisis
    solidified 133; reinvigoration 133;
    Visegrád 2+2 134; *see also* Czech
    Republic; Hungary; Poland; Slovakia
vulnerability: of being sidelined by larger
    states 146; perceptions of 6

Wæver, O. 129
Wallace, H. 164
Werner, P. 111
Westphalian model 127
Wivel, A. 3, 7, 38, 39, 72, 88, 91, 164

Zollverein membership 109–110
Zunneberg, C. 72, 130